THE
ILLEGIBLE MAN

THE

ILLEGIBLE MAN

Disability and Masculinity

in Twentieth-Century

America

WILL KANYUSIK

INDIANA UNIVERSITY PRESS

This book is a publication of

Indiana University Press
Office of Scholarly Publishing
Herman B Wells Library 350
1320 East 10th Street
Bloomington, Indiana 47405 USA

iupress.org

© 2025 by William B. Kanyusik

Manufactured in the United States of America

First Printing 2025

Cataloging information is available from the Library of Congress.

ISBN 978-0-253-07178-1 (hardcover)
ISBN 978-0-253-07179-8 (paperback)
ISBN 978-0-253-07180-4 (ebook)

FOR MY MOM AND DAD.

CONTENTS

ACKNOWLEDGMENTS

THE CREATION OF THIS BOOK was made possible by the continual support I received from colleagues, mentors, teachers, family, and friends over many years.

I remain grateful to the intellectual mentors who provided crucial guidance as I formulated the ideas that eventually became this book. Siobhan Craig encouraged me to pursue doctoral study, and her support contributed immensely to my intellectual development. Her own work on masculinity in post–World War II European cinema significantly influenced my inquiry into disability and the masculine subject in the postwar United States. She has been a tireless advocate for me and my work, and for this I thank her greatly. Paula Rabinowitz's scholarship has long provided an important model for my own work, and her feedback on my writing proved crucial to the development of this project and my scholarly career as a whole. Maria Damon also greatly inspired the direction of my work. It was her mentoring that pointed me toward an interest in disability and masculinity. Michelle Wright's enthusiasm was a continual source of support during the early stages of this project, and her guidance facilitated important breakthroughs in my writing and in the rigor of my intellectual pursuits. My thanks go to Edward Griffin and David Treuer, whose influence led me to develop and hone my interest in American literature and culture. Jack Zipes has also had a profound influence on my development as a scholar through the breadth and depth of his scholarly expertise. His feedback was invaluable in shaping the direction of this project, and—like the other individuals noted above—he has been an important mentor and supporter of my work.

Colleagues at various institutions provided immeasurable support as I completed this project. Kate McCarthy-Gilmore has been an immensely important mentor to me from early on at Loras College, and her feedback on an early draft of this book's final section helped greatly to clarify its argument and relationship to the rest of this book. Emily DiFilippo's insightful feedback on this project as a whole, and specifically on the book's introduction, helped me refine the book's overall argument. Additionally, her expertise in both disability studies and gender studies was crucial in pointing me in the direction of a number of important voices that needed to be included in this project.

David Cochran, Andrew Auge, and Kevin Koch offered me very helpful guidance as I navigated the publication of this work, and I am grateful for their support. John Pauley and Jayne Marek each read early drafts of this book's introduction, and Jayne in particular offered insightful guidance when I began seeking a publisher. Sara Jo Cohen offered incredibly generous feedback on an early draft of my book manuscript, and her advice helped shape the ultimate form of this project. Ryan Cox and Amanda Cox read drafts of chapters, rationales, and booklists, providing feedback during my writing process. Kristin Anderson-Bricker has been a great supporter of my intellectual work. Teaching with her helped me hone the rigor of my ideas, and she was a great source of encouragement as I pursued this book project. My thanks also go to Eric Brownell, Adam Lindberg, Molly Kelley Gage, Lisa Trochmann, Lelaine Bonine, Wes Burdine, Andrew Marzoni, Robb St. Lawrence, Joe Hughes, and John Kochanczyk for insights they shared with me about my project.

Loras College has been incredibly supportive of my scholarly work. I would like to thank the college and the Loras College Faculty Development Committee for supporting my research. My sabbatical in spring 2024 allowed me to complete the final revisions to this book, and I was fortunate to receive funding from the college to present various parts of this project at national and international conferences. I was also fortunate to receive a faculty travel grant from Simpson College that allowed me to present my work abroad while teaching at Simpson as a visiting assistant professor.

An article-length version of my third chapter entitled "The Problem of Recognition: The Disabled Male Veteran and Masculinity as Spectacle in William Wyler's *The Best Years of Our Lives*" was published in volume 6, issue 2 of the *Journal of Literary and Cultural Disability Studies*. I would like to thank Ria Cheyne, guest editor of this issue, and David Bolt, editor of the journal, for their feedback on my article prior to its publication. My third chapter was the first part of this project I drafted, and Ria and David both provided editorial assistance that contributed greatly to the development of this work. A portion of this book's first chapter titled "The Subject of Disability in *The Sun Also Rises* and *The Sound and the Fury*" first appeared as a chapter in the anthology *Disability, Avoidance, and the Academy: Challenging Resistance*, edited by Dr. Bolt and Claire Penketh and published by Routledge Press in 2016. I would like to thank David and Claire for their editorial guidance on this section of this work. I thank my editor at Indiana University Press, Allison Chaplin, for recognizing potential in this book and for her guidance and incredible work in bringing it to publication.

I want to thank my family for their love and support. My mother and father, Janice and Bob Kanyusik, I thank for their innumerable contributions to my intellectual and personal development and for reading and providing feedback on equally innumerable drafts of this project. My brother, Jake Kanyusik, I thank for his constant encouragement, his good humor, and his remarkable kindness.

THE
ILLEGIBLE MAN

INTRODUCTION

In a new introduction written for the 2005 edition of his autobiography, *Born on the Fourth of July*, Ron Kovic contemplates his disability and its connection to his feelings about the Vietnam War forty years after he enlisted in the Marine Corps at the age of eighteen. In one of the more striking moments in this addition to the memoir, which was originally published in 1976, the author reflects on his reaction to photographs taken of him prior to his enlistment and on his subsequent injury in combat, an event that shattered his spinal cord and left him paralyzed from the waist down. The author writes that he was surprised by the realization that he had kept these black-and-white photos, which he has—somewhat inexplicably—now held on to for most of his life. Kovic refers to the experience of seeing these pictures as "a deeply disturbing dream that I have been trying to repress." He writes, "I remember seeing those photographs after I came home from Vietnam and each time having terrible nightmares that shook me badly. I couldn't look at them, could not face that young man I had been before the war and my injury. I would always promise myself never to look at them again. My trauma was still very deep, and that beautiful boy, that body, had been destroyed, defiled, and savaged. My wounding in Vietnam both physically and emotionally haunted me, pursued me, and threatened to overwhelm me."[1] Viewing photographs of his uninjured body intensifies Kovic's sense of difference from his former embodiment, highlighting his body's deviation, postinjury, from culturally presumed norms of able-bodiedness. The author's discussion of these preinjury images of himself (and our vicarious experience of

1

those images mediated via his first-person language) has the effect of heightening in the mind of the reader the abject nature of the author's disabled body, referenced as "destroyed" and "defiled"—at once irrevocably altered and utterly desecrated by an injury viewed solely in tragic terms.

This book takes as its subject the many figures like Kovic who populate postwar landscapes of the United States, particularly in the latter half of the twentieth century. *Born on the Fourth of July*, Kovic's account of his transformation from a naive young recruit to one of the most well-known and outspoken voices in the American antiwar movement following his injury and mistreatment by Veterans Administration doctors during rehabilitation after the war, focuses in particular on the role these experiences played in the author's political awakening. Yet Kovic remains deeply troubled by his disabling injury and its implications. The author views his disability as a fall from all he understands his former embodiment to signify, his bodily state symbolically linked to the United States' fall from innocence represented by the country's involvement in Vietnam. In the opening paragraph of his reflection, Kovic writes, "There are times in the lives of both individuals and nations when we cross thresholds where there is no going back, no return to the innocence we once knew; the change is utter and irreconcilable. We often sense these moments."[2] Kovic's words evoke the finality of his injury and what it represents. It remains—for him—unassimilable, the source of an essential difference from other men and of a deep sense of unease he feels constantly yet struggles to name precisely.

Kovic uses the occasion of his autobiography's republication in the mid-2000s to reflect on the unlearned lessons of Vietnam forty years later, with the United States mired in ongoing violent conflicts overseas in the years following September 11, 2001. The author's disabled body becomes for him a metaphor for the American body politic and the nation itself. In the equation established in his opening paragraphs, the author's body and the United States are alike in that both exist in an idealized past state and a fallen present state. Kovic sees his disabled body as a marker of irreconcilable difference from his former nondisabled status; this bifurcated sense of self, mapped onto the national landscape, plays out in the memoir as a personal and political wound he seeks to heal by telling his life's narrative through writing and public appearances. Kovic's words present a subject position divided by his injury, defined equally by what he now is (disabled) and what he can no longer be (innocent, whole, uninjured). While historical traumas such as war challenge the legibility of even normative masculinities, this book argues that representations of wartime disability—which stage a sudden loss of masculinity in a subject that once epitomized maleness through physicality—uniquely demonstrate the instability of all masculinities.

Environmental historian William Cronon identifies a deep connection between the imagined nature of the North American landscape and the cultural narratives of American (masculine) identity echoed in Kovic's equation linking a defiled body and a fallen nation. The critic notes in Henry David Thoreau's work in particular "a romantic's lament for the pristine world of an earlier and lost time. The myth of a fallen humanity in a fallen world is never far beneath the surface in Thoreau's writing," Cronon notes, "and nowhere is this more visible than in his descriptions of past landscapes."[3] The landscape of North America looms large throughout American literature, often serving as a forum for mastery of both self and other for the American masculine subject. William Bradford foregrounds the hostile landscape of the North American continent in his account of the founding of the Plymouth Colony. The American wilderness serves in Nathaniel Hawthorne's "Young Goodman Brown" as the setting for the protagonist's life-defining encounter with humankind's capacity for evil and self-deception, a dense forest in which Goodman Brown imagines "a devilish Indian behind every tree."[4] Wilderness imagery serves a similar function in Hemingway's short stories from *In Our Time*, bringing the young Nick Adams into vicarious contact with the reality of death for the first time in "Indian Camp" and providing an arena for the adult Adams to process a deeply hidden wartime trauma in the second half of "The Big Two-Hearted River."

One of the more extreme examples of this trope can be found in James Dickey's 1993 literary bestseller *To the White Sea*, a novel in which a sociopathic American tail gunner who survives the downing of his B-29 during the firebombing of Tokyo near the close of World War II makes his way across the Japanese landscape. He lives off the land using skills learned from his father on the Brooks Range in Alaska during childhood in order to survive and evade capture until he is finally caught and killed by the Japanese. Dickey's first-person narrator rationalizes the series of murders he commits over the course of the narrative as a necessary part of survival in hostile foreign territory, but he reveals to the reader in passing that he once killed a young woman with whom he was romantically involved prior to his enlistment in the military—a college student visiting the Brooks Range who Dickey implies has been the narrator's sole sexual partner.[5] Throughout *To the White Sea*, the narrator's mind continually revisits memories of the vast winter landscape of Alaska, to which he feels intimately connected, while he obsesses over a ruthlessly pragmatic belief system based on his understanding of the relationship between predator and prey developed from his father's hunting lessons. Yet the mythic American landscape has long existed in tension with fraught notions of American progress. Reflecting on the ecological changes already wrought by humans on the American landscape by 1855, Thoreau writes, "I cannot but feel that I live in a tamed, and, as it were, emasculated country."[6] Perhaps one reason disability so disrupts normative understandings of American masculinity is the belief that disability is irreconcilable with the notions of rugged masculine sufficiency that underpin many canonical narratives of American identity.

Narratives of American masculine sufficiency stress the importance of self-reliance predicated on the domination of a physical landscape, imagined as vast and hostile, that functions as a forum for self-actualization—often at the expense of a racialized other. In his *Studies in Classic American Literature*, D. H. Lawrence argues that American subjectivity is split between two tendencies. The first is an impulse of relentless self-perfection Benjamin Franklin inherited from Puritanism (focused in his case on material prosperity rather than spiritual purity). The second is a romanticized view of America eliding a "fundamental tension that becomes definitive of American culture: wanting to be both 'savage' and 'American,' wanting that is, to be both primitive and modern, instinctual and rational, native and European." Lawrence sees this second tendency exemplified in figures like J. Hector St. John de Crèvecœur and in James Fenimore Cooper's *Leatherstocking Tales* by the character Natty Bumppo, a figure whose discipline of ruthless violence and self-imposed chasteness prefigures Dickey's protagonist in *To the White Sea*.[7] A sense of control and autonomy in one's own life often rests on the narratives of self one has access to in a given culture, and narratives of disability have been routinely used in the United States to exclude those deemed unfit for American citizenship from conceptions of personhood that constitute American national identity. In *Extraordinary Bodies: Figuring Physical Disability in American Culture and Literature*, Rosemarie Garland-Thomson argues for "the disabled figure's crucial role in establishing the boundaries of the normate American self." Garland-Thomson writes:

> Freighted with anxieties about loss of control and autonomy that the American ideal repudiates, "the disabled" become a threatening presence, seemingly compromised by the particularities and limitations of their own bodies. Shaped by a narrative of somatic inadequacy and represented as a spectacle of erratic singularity, the disabled figure delineates the corresponding abstract cultural figure of the self-governing, standardized individual emerging from a society informed by consumerism and

mechanization. Cast as one of society's ultimate "not me" figures, the disabled other absorbs disavowed elements of the cultural self, becoming an icon of all human vulnerability and enabling the "American Ideal" to appear as master of both destiny and self.[8]

Garland-Thomson argues that disability functions as the subordinate term against which the liberal democratic subject comes to be defined in Emersonian thought in particular, noting Emerson's repeated use of the invalid figure as a point of contrast to the virtues of American self-reliance championed throughout his writings. In "Self-Reliance," Garland-Thomson notes, Emerson contrasts the figure of American masculinity with "minors," "invalids," and "cowards fleeing before a revolution."[9] In this equation, ability becomes synonymous with both adult male status and moral fortitude: a masculine citizen subject constituted in opposition to physical and emotional weakness. Emerson makes a similar reference to disability in his essay "Fate," "disparaging conservatives by characterizing them as 'effeminated by nature, born halt and blind' and able 'only, like invalids, [to] act on the defensive.'" Thomson argues that not only is Emerson's conception of the liberal individual "a neo-Platonic disembodied form" constituted against a "denigrated, oppositional femininity" (as she notes other scholars have argued), but also "Emerson's invocation of 'invalids' as a related category of otherness . . . mutually constitutes the liberal self." In Emerson's formulation contrasting representations of bodily vulnerability with a self-possessed subject defined through individual mastery, "the invalid body is impotence made manifest."[10] Particularly notable in this formulation is the extent to which disability, though defined primarily via its effects on self-sufficiency, carries with it meanings that are clearly gendered and stigmatize the subject in ways that exceed simple notions of self-reliance.

Disability, and the stigma attached to it, has been and continues to be used to define and exclude marginalized groups from full American citizenship. Those who opposed legal rights and social equality for women cited the female gender's "supposed physical, intellectual, and psychological flaws, deficits, and derivations from the male norm" as justification for subjugation. Slavery and continued racism against the Black population of the United States has been similarly justified by linking disability and Blackness. Moreover, disability functioned as a key category for immigration officials to deny individuals entry into United States well into the twentieth century.[11] In instances when disability functions as a term used to deny a status to a particular group, individuals thus labeled have a stake in distancing themselves from the stigma attached to disability. "Rather than challenging the basic assumptions behind the hierarchy," those who see their rights as citizens called into question through associations with disability "instead [at times] work to remove themselves from the negatively marked categories—that is, to disassociate themselves from those people who 'really are' disabled—knowing such categorization invites discrimination."[12] Sami Schalk has recently added nuance to this perspective with her book *Black Disability Politics*, noting that it has become commonplace in disability studies to uncritically accept the narrative that Black communities at times distance themselves from disability to avoid the associations identified above.[13] Nevertheless, while specific meanings attached to disability change over time and according to context, disability has and continues to function in American society as a central determining factor demarcating the citizen as a subject and as a primary marker by which the essentially permeable boundaries of American masculine identity are policed for exclusionary purposes.

The primary concern of this study is the increasingly illegible nature of the masculine subject as hegemonically constructed in twentieth-century American culture, a historically specific crisis of definition rooted in deeper understandings of more broadly constructed American identity. Over the course of the twentieth century in particular, disability and masculinity became increasingly interconnected as sites on which national identity was contested. The crisis of masculinity this book describes, though rooted in the events of World War I, did not reach full fruition until after World War II, approximately thirty years later, in an attempted codification of discourse surrounding masculinity and the able body that in many ways still resonates today. *The Illegible Man* argues that World War II functions, for the United States, as a key historical moment in the emergence of modern understandings of disability, a moment when an increased quantity of discourse surrounding disability paradoxically contributed to greater incoherence about the definition and cultural meanings of disability and masculinity in America.

World War II gave the United States, through its ascendance as a world power, the opportunity to reinstantiate many cultural myths that had previously been destabilized, first by World War I and the cultural instability of 1920s and then by the socioeconomic instability of the 1930s. But the surface normalcy afforded by the tidy cultural narratives that emerged at the end of World War II obscured an undercurrent of often-violent anxiety surrounding masculinity and sexual identification that came to define America's relationship to both its own citizens and the broader world as the Cold War emerged. Ultimately, the end of World War II saw the rise, in America in particular, of an increasingly invasive culture of scrutiny, expressed in social policies both indirectly and directly related to public concerns about returning veterans and in texts produced by the American culture industry. Modernist narratives of the early twentieth century seek to account for the damage done to human bodies by modern warfare via tropes evoking the limits of representability—depicting the horrors of war as "unspeakable" and "beyond words" through narrative strategies of elision.[14] Late twentieth-century narratives of bodily damage, in contrast, foreground and display bodies directly, framing physical and psychic damage as an obstacle to legibility for the masculine subject. Where modernism reacts to World War I by declaring that violence and its effects cannot be represented—only evoked as unrepresentable—World War II–era texts exhibit a compulsion to examine, surveil, and document nonnormative male bodies rendered illegible not only by violence but also by fields of knowledge developed in response to violence and its effects.

In particular, this book examines how a sudden onset of disability impacts the sense of self of people whose identity was, at least in part, predicated on the possession of an "able" body, an experience that makes particularly visible the structures enabling our shared notions of heteronormative masculinity. Rather than viewing disability as a trope—a predominant tendency in much disability studies scholarship—this book understands disability as a unique subject position: partially embodied and partially formed within a matrix of cultural forces. *The Illegible Man* traces the relationship between disability as understood in American culture and the forces that narrowly define the American masculine subject as hegemonically constructed. It argues that postwar American masculinity has existed in crisis since at least the mid-twentieth century and that it cannot be properly understood without examining the haunting presence of disability in narratives drawn from American literature, culture, and history.

Disability History in the United States

The fraught dynamics presented by the interaction of disability and masculinity have been present in American culture, in some ways, since long before the historical period on which this book primarily focuses. The American Enlightenment of the eighteenth century was particularly important for the development of American attitudes toward disability; this period emphasized the rights of individual citizens based on ability to make sound decisions.[15] Enlightenment rationality produced in the culture a refusal to assume that inequalities between groups and individuals were natural and a corresponding compulsion to "produce a rational explanation" for the discriminatory treatment directed at minority groups and others subject to political and social stigma.[16] Though the basic association of disability with inability to govern oneself has remained fairly consistent throughout American history, the particular cultural valences of disability in the United States have developed and changed in relation to historical context.

Contrasting the experiences of disabled veterans of the Revolutionary and Civil wars helps elucidate this point. In the post–Revolutionary War period, disability did not necessarily serve to exclude men from a place in the social fabric of the newly formed United States or prevent them from functioning as the head of the normatively gendered American household. Significant numbers of men who became disabled while fighting the British found gainful employment after the war's end.[17] In fact, at that historical moment, social and economic conditions were such that disabled and nondisabled veterans tended to find similar work in similar numbers; these rates of poverty and employment remained consistent as late as 1820.[18] Because there was no stark difference between the perceived value of a disabled veteran's life and that of an able-bodied man of a similar background, the stigma attached to disability was much less pronounced than one might expect, particularly in comparison to the experiences of veterans of more recent conflicts. Discussing the postwar experiences of Ebenezer Brown, a Revolutionary War veteran who received a disabling shoulder wound during combat, Kim E. Nielsen explains, "The fact that Brown, our disabled veteran with a shoulder injury, had married and raised two children was unremarkable—which in itself is remarkable. Today people with disabilities have lower marital and family rates than those without disabilities. Disabled Revolutionary War veterans labored, married, had children, and had households typical in size and structures, at rates nearly identical to their nondisabled counterparts." Immediately following the colonial period, Nielsen notes, the socioeconomic conditions of the emerging nation's still-developing market economy were such that adjusting to a new disability did not necessarily preclude reintegrating into the social fabric via useful labor. This analysis, however, does not fully account for certain differences between the postwar experience of the disabled Revolutionary War soldier and his modern counterparts. Nielsen argues that the Civil War, unlike the American Revolution, "forced a rethinking of disability in the United States," even though wounded soldiers of both wars faced similarly low survival rates. Disability remained relatively stigma-free in the immediate post–Civil War period, with certain exceptions. One particular Civil War veteran, Charles

Johnson, "whose wartime injuries," Nielsen notes, "left him sexually 'played out,' led Invalid Corps troops in major combat with Confederate forces in June of 1864."[19] In this instance, further acts of violence following his injury remasculinized the soldier despite his disability. Deprived of sexual potency, Johnson retained normative masculine status because his shrapnel wounds did not prevent him from rejoining combat. In fact, the injury served as a marker of masculine heroism: when asked by his superior if a regiment of disabled soldiers would prove courageous fighters, Johnson is said to have replied, "My men are cripples, and they can't run."[20]

While disability continued to be defined as the "incapacity to perform manual labor" following the Civil War, disabled veterans faced an increasingly complicated negotiation of social forces when adapting to a life newly inflected by physical difference, and the meaning of disability began to shift as "the public seemed to have an expanding curiosity about deviant bodies."[21] Visible physical disabilities incurred during wartime were considered a mark of valor for the soldier whose body displayed them, but only if the injury could be interpreted as evidence of an unambiguously heroic act; moreover, men unable to perform physical labor due to a disability began to view themselves as deficient in their masculinity. Subject to greater legal and medical regulation during this time, disability status began to take on increasingly racialized and class-based connotations.[22] As America became urbanized and industrialized, the ugly laws of the early 1900s attempted to restrict public visibility of disabled people, and noticable physical impairments became one marker of deviance used to restrict immigration through entry points like Ellis Island. Immigration agents at Ellis Island in particular "prided themselves on their ability to make 'snapshot diagnoses'" of people seeking entrance to the country and marked suspect immigrants with a chalked letter, "usually on their back."[23] Much like the chalk letter used to mark the child murderer in Fritz Lang's 1931 film *M*, a letter administered by an immigration official specified a literal designation that carried with it a host of supplemental associations of deviance understood to be threatening to the national character.[24]

Following World War I, as in other eras, disability primarily designated a reduction of one's material self-sufficiency. Lawmakers regulating disability benefits for veterans defined disability as an impairment of bodily or mental capacity that limits an individual's ability to labor and earn a living. The criteria used to evaluate service-related disabilities during this time, however, "applied not only medical criteria but cultural and racial values" in diagnosing potentially disabling conditions.[25] As such, efforts to define disability in purely material terms nonetheless inflected the term with surplus meanings. After World War I, efforts by military medicine to parse legitimate claims for service-related disabilities from illegitimate claims depended on increasingly subjective criteria for defining an individual as disabled. Theoretically, disability was still defined in direct relation to a reduction in earning capacity as established by the War Risk Insurance Act of 1917 and administered by the Bureau of War Risk Insurance and later the US Veteran's Bureau.[26] In practice, however, implementation of this formula was highly subjective. Its details were largely kept secret not only to prevent political pressure from members of Congress aligned with veterans' organizations like the newly formed American Legion from influencing disability ratings but also to create an impression of scientific objectivity through the mystique surrounding the process due to the limited public information available regarding it.[27] Even the standards for evaluating an injury as disabling were highly subjective, as "bureau officials espoused a concept of disability officially based on medical science but that in fact blended clinical evidence with normative judgments of private morality, idealization of the work ethic, and racial stereotypes in an uneasy and often contradictory combination."[28] Whereas earlier in American history, a deviation from normative embodiment counted as disabling primarily according to the extent of the deviation's effect on a person's earning capacity and self-sufficiency, the specific medical model of understanding disability that gained traction following World War I—though it claimed to be objective—helped to load the designation of disability with a host of additional meanings, usually with negative connotations for a disabled individual's personal character. While it would be an oversimplification to argue that disability identity was not stigmatized until the post–World War I period, the increased need to account for disability following that conflict greatly influenced subsequent understanding of disability in the United States. As Maren Tova Linett notes in her work on disability in modernist texts, "eugenics was at its peak in the years between the two world wars, and far from being a fringe movement, it was mainstream science. Now that human populations had become objects of scientific study, 'defects' in individuals became 'defects' in the body politic."[29]

Although treatment of physical disability had in many ways become much less punitive by the end of World War II in the mid-1940s, disability itself was still highly stigmatized even as it grew to be more accepted in American society in general. As disabled individuals became more visible within society, disability itself was subjected to greater scrutiny by social apparatuses that evolved over the course of the twentieth century (in many cases directly from the military's own power mechanisms), which often attempted to connect bodily deviations from assumed norms to the essential nature of disabled subjects themselves. Some mechanisms were officially instituted as early as World War I, while others developed and proliferated before, during, and after World War II. David Serlin notes, for example, that as early as 1917, the army began to use increasingly invasive physical examinations for recruits and draftees, including "institutionalized examinations for 'patulous anus,' during which a gloved physician tested a male recruit's sphincter muscle to see if it had lost proper resistance due to unnatural activities." Physicians looking to screen and exclude men deemed unfit for service instituted practices that "marked a huge methodological shift from the ways that recruitment manuals and inspection officers had assumed that visible ablebodiedness—that is, what could be measured with the naked eye—was a prerequisite for serving in the military." Serlin argues that the application of an "anthropological approach to the study of soldiers to determine their fitness based on racial hierarchies" developed in the 1920s in collaboration with the War Department by Charles B. Davenport and Albert G. Love (who had been proponents of the eugenics movement in the United States) came to greatly inform the process used by doctors to select recruits as the country mobilized for entry into World War II. At this same time, Serlin notes, William Sheldon developed the concept of the *somatotype*, which divides the normative range of body types along a spectrum of body weight using the designations ectomorph, mesomorph, and endomorph, categories that came to be implicitly gendered.[30]

By the 1940s, the figure of the masculine mesomorph—characterized by broad shoulders and a lean but muscular physique—presented an idealized form of masculinity in American popular culture and the medical establishment. In contrast, the endomorph body type became associated with "soft rounded hips, fleshy buttocks, gynecomastia (breast tissue deposits), and gestures that might be considered as 'girlish.'"[31] This linking of a specific body type to heteronormative masculinity reinforced the notion that one's body could be read like a text—that physical difference embodied a fundamental deviance from society that was essential to a person. Yet the conflation of features of physical embodiment (rounded hips and fleshy buttocks) with a person's mannerisms (gestures that might be considered "girlish") in the description of the endomorph demonstrates the extent to which such classifications remain subjective. As Serlin notes, images of idealized masculine bodies populated the American imagination and circulated throughout the culture through film, on television, and in print ads, often with the explicit purpose of creating a specific image of militarized, able-bodied heteronormative masculinity during the period of the war.[32] This proliferation of images and discourse, however, failed to cohere into the stable picture of American masculinity the emerging military-industrial complex sought to produce and culminated instead in the development by the middle of the century of "two competing though overlapping ideologies" through which to define normative masculinity. Serlin argues that "military culture affirmed the military male body as mesomorphic, competent, virile, and heterosexual" and created an atmosphere of hostility toward the endomorph in reaction to fears that the military had become feminized. Alternately, "a second and competing military ideology affirmed the disfigured male amputee as mesomorphic, competent, virile, and heterosexual." Narratives depicting soldiers who regained their masculine status through rehabilitative medicine saturated postwar American culture, and these narratives almost always had an ideological component.[33] The explicit goal of rehabilitation for physically disabled veterans of World War II, as depicted in War Department documentaries and Hollywood films made during and after the war dealing with homecomings of disabled servicemen, was a reclamation of normative masculine status along with a rehabilitation of mind and/or body.

Although World War I can be seen as the origin of a paradigm shift in thinking about presumed links between deviance and nonnormative embodiment, we do not see the full consequences of this initial shift until later, in the context of World War II. The preoccupation in postwar American culture with the disabled male body and the corresponding reification of militarized and idealized masculine bodies can, in many ways, be tied to two related factors: the increased visibility of disability in American culture during the postwar period, as vast numbers of disabled soldiers rejoined society after suffering what would have in earlier periods been life-ending injuries, and increased focus from the medical and military establishment on identifying bodies that differed from the norm as markers of deviant forms of masculinity. The rehabilitative project of military medicine, though it made great advancements during this time and without question helped countless men adapt to sudden, drastic changes to their bodies and senses of self because of war-related injury or trauma, cannot be easily separated from broad cultural anxieties surrounding the male body in relation to notions of masculine sufficiency that are fundamentally exclusionary in nature.

Modern-day legal understandings of disability attempt to account for the effect of stigma on the lives of disabled individuals by emphasizing that embodiment is only one aspect of disability experience. The Americans with Disabilities Act of 1990 "acknowledges that disability depends upon perception and subjective judgment rather than on objective bodily states: identifying disability as an 'impairment that substantially limits one or more of the major life activities,' the law also states that being legally disabled is a matter of 'being regarded as having such an impairment.'"[34] This late twentieth-century legal understanding of disability attempts to mediate between aspects of disability experience that continue to complicate analyses of disability identity even within the field of disability studies, as scholars parse a mode of being that simultaneously presents as an embodied state and a cultural construction. This book thus argues that disability is best understood as a subject position, informed by embodiment and culture but reducible to neither: a social position produced culturally but experienced—felt—bodily.

In his groundbreaking work *Enforcing Normalcy: Disability, Deafness, and the Body*, Lennard Davis focuses on the construction of normalcy as an ideological concept (rather than seeking to define disability, normalcy's subordinated second term). In general agreement with Foucault, Davis argues that normalcy as a concept emerged roughly between 1840 and 1860. The concept of normalcy differs from the previously predominate notion of the ideal, a word Davis dates to the seventeenth century that "presents a mytho-poetic body that is linked to that of the gods (in traditions in which the god's body is visualized). This divine body, then, this ideal body, is not attainable by the human." Davis argues that "in a culture with an ideal form of the body, all members of the population are below the ideal."[35] Unlike the ideal, the normal becomes a state for which all subjects strive and against which all are measured. First used in the radical feminist periodical *off our backs* in 1981, the word *ableism* has come to name "discrimination in favor of able-bodied people; prejudice against or disregard of the needs of disabled people."[36] Disability studies scholars like Davis have added nuance to the term by incorporating the notion that ableism is predicated on a conception of disability as an "absolute category" rather than a multivalent "descriptive term." In an ableist framework, the disabled body is understood as a "discrete object . . . rather [than] a set of social relations," which "presents itself to 'normal' people through two main modalities—function and appearance."[37]

Although Henri-Jacques Stiker argues that the modern view of disability emerged following World War I with the development of the modern prosthetic device and an accompanying shift to a rehabilitative model of treatment for veterans disabled as a result of military service, the increased cultural awareness of disability precipitated by the unprecedented violence of the war was further complicated by the events of World War II. It is during World War II and the following postwar period that we witness the most pronounced examples of the bifurcated understanding of disability this book examines and the most direct expression of a masculinity in crisis that continues to have profound implications for American culture.[38] Ultimately, the rehabilitative project of military medicine postulates the elevated, ideal masculinity of the soldier-male as a cultural norm and, as such, places the disabled subject in an inescapable double bind: to be considered normal again, the disabled masculine subject is encouraged to gauge his bodily recovery and the recovery of his masculinity against an impossible standard defined at least in part through the capacity to perform violent acts. This work thus examines intertwined contradictions at the heart of our understanding of disability and masculinity that grew to be pervasive in post–World War II America, which still directly inform how the masculine subject is understood today.

This study draws its theoretical framework in large part from feminist and queer theory to examine how disability functions as a subject position and serves as a crucial locus for understanding interconnected notions of wellness, the able body, and heteronormative American masculinity as hegemonically constructed in the twentieth century. Scholars working at the intersection of disability, gender, and sexuality have previously considered the fraught connection between heteronormativity and cultural notions of the able body. Robert McRuer argues that, in the twentieth century, "compulsory heterosexuality is intertwined with compulsory able-bodiedness," noting that "both systems work to (re)produce the able body and heterosexuality." In this formulation, disability and homosexuality become marked and stigmatized categories, allowing both able-bodiedness and heterosexuality to function as unmarked identity categories. As McRuer notes, "able-bodiedness, even more so that heterosexuality, still masquerades as a nonidentity, as the natural order of things."[39]

In reaction to a tendency in disability studies to position disability as a master trope, evinced by still-canonical early works of disability studies, one of my interests in this book is to show how disability comes to be rhetorically impacted on other discourses (particularly those of gender and sexual identity) in a way that complicates but does not subsume other aspects of identity formation for the subject.[40] Alison Kafer argues that "what is needed [from disability studies] are critical attempts to trace the ways in which compulsory able-bodiedness/ablemindedness and compulsory heterosexuality intertwine in the service of normativity; to examine how terms such as 'defective,' 'deviant,' and 'sick' have been used to justify discrimination against people whose bodies, minds, desires, and practices differ from the unmarked norm."[41] While Kafer's *Feminist, Queer, Crip* and other more recent works of disability theory have made important interventions along these lines, the tendency remains to see disability identity as a newly understood transcendental signifier through the logic that disability as a discursive category trumps other minority identities because it is at once minoritizing and universal (since most individuals are likely to experience some form of disabling condition at one point or another during their lives).[42]

I follow Kafer in her formulation of a *political/relational* model of disability that is truly dynamic in its understanding of disability as an identity category. Where medical models of disability have rightly been critiqued for treating disability as a defect located in individual bodies and minds that needs to be cured, often with invasive treatments, and the social model is limited by its failure to fully acknowledge the lived experience of disability due to its focus on disability as an identity produced by social structures, a political/relational model of disability "make[s] room for people to acknowledge—even mourn—a change in form or function while acknowledging that such changes cannot be understood apart from the context in which they occur."[43] Maren Tova Linett notes that "compulsory ablebodiedness allows the non-disabled body to appropriate the neutral condition of invisibility, as do whiteness, maleness, and heterosexuality."[44] It is thus not incidental that whiteness often functions as an unmarked identity category in the specific formulation of masculinity examined here. For many of the male figures present in this book, disability deprives the subject of his presumed entitlement to neutrality, marking as other a previously "unmarked" subjectivity. Sami Schalk has done important work to recenter discussions in disability studies on the perspectives of people of color, noting the ways in which "disability, as an identity, an experience, and a political category, has been conceptualized and approached differently . . . by white activists and intellectuals" than it has by activists and intellectuals of color.[45] This book's focus on instances of disability subjectivity produced by a sudden change in embodiment or mental state for an individual whose identity before their injury or other trauma (perhaps unconsciously) rested on assumptions of normativity and neutrality helps to reveal the central role of the able body as an unmarked category in American culture and its centrality to constructions of white masculine identity that were hegemonic in the mid-twentieth-century United States.

THE STRUCTURE OF THIS BOOK

A particular interest of *The Illegible Man* is the proliferation of supplementary cultural meanings attached to disability, which in the postwar years helped form exclusionary limits through which the American masculine subject was reconstructed following the violent conflicts of the early to mid-twentieth century and their attending cultural crises. In the postwar contexts examined in this study, disability functions as an exclusionary marker in and of itself and also embodies a more generalized form of otherness associated with other stigmatized identity markers thought to be irreconcilable with traditionally understood American masculinity. The disabled masculine subject thus functions, like Benjamin's Angel of History, as a figure positioned to witness the violent forces that give shape to history from the very position that will serve to exclude him from the future born of this moment. The texts this work examines, for the most part produced between 1920 and 1980, often center on just such a figure.

Chapter 1, "Disability, Masculinity, and the Problem of Legibility in Postwar American Fiction," reads Ernest Hemingway's *The Sun Also Rises* (1926) and James Baldwin's *Giovanni's Room* (1956) as texts that are strikingly similar in their depiction of masculinities excluded from normative conceptions of the traditionally gendered family, an exclusion reinforced by the expatriate status of both novels' protagonists. Read together, *Giovanni's Room* and *The Sun Also Rises* demonstrate that, in postwar contexts, disability and illness are seen as preventing male figures from fulfilling the sexually aggressive role associated with masculine figures in heterosexual relationships. This chapter focuses on the subject position created when a putatively able-bodied masculine subject becomes disabled following an unexpected injury but continues to identify with a narrative of able-bodied masculine sufficiency he now perceives as irrevocably lost. Where *The Sun Also Rises* depicts such a subject position specifically and in the context of post–World War I culture, *Giovanni's Room*, through its association of nonnormative masculinity with disease and other forms of physical impairment, demonstrates the workings of a similarly fraught subject position occupied by homosexuality in the post–World War II context. Both texts show ways in which supplemental meanings attached to terms designating individuals or groups as other for exclusionary purposes tend to proliferate and become increasingly pejorative in times of pronounced cultural and political insularity.

Yet where Hemingway renders Jake Barnes's injury, through elision, as beyond representation, Baldwin's David experiences moments of failed recognition as he struggles to decipher the meaning of his homosexual identity through culturally received heterosexist narratives of normative masculine sufficiency and narrates this process directly.

Chapter 2, "From Trust to Suspicion: Disability, Masculinity, and the American Culture of Scrutiny in the War Department Documentary," investigates propaganda images produced by the United States War Department that played a crucial role in regulating normative notions of masculinity in postwar America. It focuses on the documentary films made by John Huston during his enlistment in the US Army during World War II and the unedited footage of Huston's war documentaries deemed too controversial to be released to the public by the military, now housed at the National Archives. This chapter focuses on the final two films Huston made for the War Department, *Battle of San Pietro* (1945) and *Let There Be Light* (1946), both of which were heavily censored by the American military at the time of their release. This chapter deals, in particular, with depictions of rehabilitative medicine in official film documents commissioned by the US military, but it also, more broadly, serves as an investigation of the nature of the documentary medium itself. It uses Mary Ann Doane's theories of cinematic contingency and the archive to examine Huston's films as a case study problematizing our understanding of history through archival material like documentary films. Huston's documentary films occupy a position of transition from a documentary rhetoric based on trust to a rhetoric of suspicion: ultimately unable to reconcile these two impulses, Huston's World War II–era documentary films lay bare the incoherencies structuring official narratives of rehabilitation, reintegration, and masculinity of the mid-1940s.

Chapter 3, "Tactile Visions: Disability, Prosthesis, and the Problem of Recognition in Postwar American Cinema," explores issues of gender and sexuality in conjunction with the depiction of physical disability in William Wyler's *The Best Years of Our Lives* (1946). In the film, protagonist Homer Parrish—played by disabled nonprofessional actor Harold Russell—faces difficulty renegotiating newly altered relationships with his loved ones while adjusting to the physical limitations of being a double amputee. Wyler's film acknowledges the real-life difficulties involved in physical disability while emphasizing how disability often undermines traditional notions of masculinity in postwar American society. The film's visuals, which draw on documentary aesthetics for realism, challenge assumptions about "normal" bodies, anticipating work by theorists of embodiment and subjectivity like Judith

Butler and demonstrating that our bodies cannot be understood apart from the symbolic network of the culture in which we live. In part, this chapter seeks to reconcile tensions in contemporary film theory between traditional scholars who restrict themselves to purely visual analyses of the film medium and work by more recent critics who seek to overturn the "regime of vision" in film studies by focusing instead on the role of physical sensation in the experience of an "embodied" film spectator. This chapter also adopts a transnational perspective to place its discussion of American responses to disability in the wake of war in dialogue with texts produced by European countries that experienced the violence of World War II on their own shores, contrasting the postwar crisis of American masculinity depicted in Wyler's film with the post-fascist masculine subject in Italian neorealism.

Chapter 4, "Returns and Repressions: Economies of Violence and Anxieties on the Home Front," explores how disability interacts with the formation of heteronormative masculinity as constituted through the exclusion of any term seen to destabilize that subject position, adopting an interdisciplinary perspective incorporating both film and literature. The chapter begins by discussing Ann Petry's novel *Country Place* (1947), Richard Brooks's novel *The Brick Foxhole* (1945), and Ted Allenby's narrative from Studs Terkel's "*The Good War": An Oral History of World War II* (1985), three texts that depict the violence elicited by threats to masculine sufficiency as narrowly defined in the latter half of the twentieth century. Where Petry and Brooks's novels depict male subjects who respond violently to external threats to their masculinity, Allenby's interview with Terkel details his use of violence to deal with his own homosexuality while serving as a closeted soldier in the marines and then the navy from the mid-1940s to the early 1960s. The second half of the chapter uses the framework established by its earlier readings of texts from print culture to conduct an extended reading of John Sturges's film *Bad Day at Black Rock* (1955). Sturges's inclusion of a disabled veteran as the protagonist in a Western film set after World War II destabilizes standard narratives of disability and masculinity to such an extent that the film at times loses narrative coherence, both interrogating and betraying anxieties regarding the presence of masculine violence stateside. Like Huston's war documentaries, Sturges's fictional film depicting an ambivalent reclamation of heteronormative masculinity following a disabling injury through the use of violence functions as a key transitional text between mid and late twentieth-century understandings of disability and masculinity.

Chapter 5, "Landscapes of Loss: Disability, the American Wilderness, and the Remasculinization of the Vietnam Veteran," extends the book's investigation of American masculine identity into the Vietnam era, focusing on Michael Cimino's *The Deer Hunter* (1978) and Ron Kovic's *Born on the Fourth of July* as texts that portray disability, masculinity, and male violence in a late twentieth-century context. Cimino's text derives narrative coherence from archetypal signifiers of violent American masculinity that Sturges's film only partially undermines. The chapter shows how the formulation of American masculine subjectivity examined in this project rests on the violent exclusion of feminized alterity at times also associated with the disabled masculine subject. Picking up on an underexamined through line present in many Vietnam-era texts—a fascination with myths of the American wilderness (and their inherent violence) transposed onto the landscape of Vietnam in which Vietnam functions as an external site for testing American masculinity—this chapter concludes the book's main argument. It shows how Vietnam-era texts dealing with wartime disability like *The Deer Hunter*, as well as subsequent depictions of the Vietnam veteran in American popular culture like Ted Kotcheff's *First Blood* (1982), the film version of David Morell's 1972 novel of the same name, reflect an increasing preoccupation in American culture regarding the nature of American masculine identity as it relates to violence: a simultaneous idealization of violence as a necessary cost of supremacy in the postwar world and a self-conscious reflection on a uniquely American fascination with violence itself.

The book's coda, "Disability, Resilience, and the Cost of American Hegemony under Neoliberalism," touches on more recent narratives of combat and recovery in light of the emergence of resilience discourse in the context of neoliberalism identified by critics like Mark Neocleous. Resilience discourse compels the individual to demonstrate the ability to "bounce back" following a trauma in a manner legible as an optimization of self within neoliberal society that ultimately leaves social structures acting on the individual subject uncritiqued. Though contemporary disability narratives like Ellen Spiro's and Phil Donahue's award-winning documentary *Body of War* (2008) treat their subject matter with greater frankness and, at times, more nuance than their earlier counterparts, issues of masculinity and sexuality remain a central concern in texts examining the disabled masculine subject. Spiro's and Donahue's sympathetic portrait of Tomas Young, the disabled veteran turned antiwar activist who committed suicide following the critical success of the film he helped create, presents a complex portrait of the importance and limitations of resilience for the disabled subject. The coda also reads Ben Fountain's 2012 novel *Billy Lynn's Long Halftime Walk* as a text that, through criticism of the cultural and political landscape of the Bush/Cheney years, ultimately demonstrates the pervasiveness of neo-liberal logic in narratives of masculinity, disability, and resilience in early twenty-first-century America. This coda builds on Robin James's recent work reformulating resilience and melancholia in the context of neoliberalism from a feminist perspective. *The Illegible Man* concludes by offering a further critique of melancholic formulations of disability, exemplified by Hemingway, while foregrounding the importance for disability studies to be critical of resilience discourse and its reliance on ableist assumptions structuring narratives of rehabilitation and social reintegration that, on the surface, seem to aid in the integration of individuals with disabilities into society.

Disabled figures have long haunted American literature and culture. Yet the disabled masculine subject, a figure at the center of many cultural productions of the United States, presents more than a convenient trope onto which cultural anxieties surrounding American identity come to be mapped and projected. The disabled male figure functions as a specific cultural location where central questions concerning American masculine identity are staged, interrogated, and—at times—worked through. When the subject of disability is raised in America's narratives, it is almost always the legibility of the American masculine subject itself that is at stake.

NOTES

1. Kovic, *Born on the Fourth of July*, 16.
2. Ibid., 15.
3. Cronon, *Changes in the Land*, 4.
4. Bradford, "Chapter IX: Of Their Voyage," 133; Hawthorne, "Young Goodman Brown," 85.
5. Dickey, *To the White Sea*, 201.
6. Thoreau, quoted in Cronon, *Changes in the Land*, 4.
7. Thompson, "Introduction," 17.
8. Garland-Thomson, *Extraordinary Bodies*, 41.
9. Emerson, quoted in Garland-Thomson, *Extraordinary Bodies*, 41.
10. Garland-Thomson, *Extraordinary Bodies*, 41–42.
11. Baynton, "Disability and the Justification of Inequality in American History," 33–34, 37. As Baynton notes, the *Annual Report of the Commissioner of Immigration* for 1907 states, "The exclusion from this country of the morally, mentally, or physically deficient is the principal object to be accomplished by the immigration laws." The relationship between these terms, this scholar argues, was intensified by the 1924 Immigration Act, which linked disability and ethnicity specifically to help "justify the creation of immigration quotas based on ethnic origin." Ibid., 47.
12. Ibid., 43, 51.
13. Schalk, *Black Disability Politics*, 6.
14. James, *The New Death*, 24–25.
15. Nielsen, *A Disability History of the United States*, 38.
16. Baynton, "Disability and the Justification of Inequality in American History," 33.

17. Nielsen cites data collected by historian Daniel Blackie, who notes that 49 percent of disabled veterans of the American Revolution found work as farmers, 27 percent found work as "skilled laborers such as coopers or blacksmiths," and "a small number with class background sufficient to seek an education became teachers or preachers, skilled labor that required little physical exertion." Nielsen, *A Disability History of the United States*, 55.

18. Ibid.

19. Ibid., 55, 82.

20. Johnson, quoted in Nielsen, *A Disability History of the United States*, 83.

21. Nielsen, *A Disability History of the United States*, 80, 89. One notable aspect of this expanded curiosity in American culture about bodies considered deviant was the phenomenon of the freak show. Beginning "as early as the 1840s" and continuing into the early to mid-twentieth century, "in traveling freak shows, at P. T. Barnum's famous American Museum in New York and similar facilities, on riverboats, at county fairs, in circus side shows and Word Fairs, the exhibition of human bodies considered both wonderous and freakish drew huge crowds. . . . Exhibitors promoted armless wonders, legless wonders, conjoined twins, and humans considered both unnaturally large and unnaturally small." Nielsen contrasts the experiences of white disabled people whose "race and class rendered [them] relatively safe and non-threatening object[s] for public viewing" with the experiences of people of color subjected to similar treatment by "exhibitors" who "presented people of color as particularly exotic" figures assumed to represent "embodied and savage missing links between humans and animals." Ibid., 90.

22. Ibid., 87, 86.

23. Ibid., 104.

24. In the second chapter of *American Ideals*, entitled "True Americanism," Theodore Roosevelt argues that "the mighty tide of immigration to our shores has brought in its train much evil; and whether the good or the evil shall predominate depends mainly on whether these newcomers do or do not throw themselves heartily into our national life, cease to be European, and become Americans like the rest of us" (1138). Roosevelt and other assimilationists feared otherness associated with new arrivals to the country, who remained outsiders unless they met certain narrow criteria for American citizenship.

25. Hickel, "Medicine, Bureaucracy, and Social Welfare," 236, 235.

26. "A temporary or permanent war-related disability rated at 10 percent or more and not due to 'willful misconduct' entitled an individual to compensation," notes Hickel. Hickel, "Medicine, Bureaucracy, and Social Welfare," 240.

27. Ibid., 246.

28. Ibid., 251–52.

29. Linett, *Bodies of Modernism*, 12.

30. Serlin, "Disability, Masculinity, and the Prosthetics of War," 160–61.

31. Ibid., 161.

32. Ibid., 162.

33. Ibid., 170–71.

34. Garland-Thomson, *Extraordinary Bodies*, 6.

35. Davis, *Enforcing Normalcy*, 24, 25.

36. "ableism," *OED Online*.

37. Davis, *Enforcing Normalcy*, 7–8, 11.

38. Stiker, "The Birth of Rehabilitation," 121–24.

39. McRuer, *Crip Theory*, 31, 1.

40. *Rhetorical impaction* is the phrase used by Eve Kosofsky Sedgwick to describe the way in which the term *homosexual* comes to be overdetermined in the knowledge structures and cultural productions of modern society, a phenomenon I discuss at greater length in this book's first chapter.

41. Kafer, *Feminist, Queer, Crip*, 17.

42. Margrit Shildrick's 2009 book *Dangerous Discourses of Disability, Subjectivity, and Sexuality*, for example, performs a complex and nuanced reworking of disability subjectivity, combining insights of phenomenology, psychoanalysis, queer theory, and a Deleuzian investigation of "global corporealities" to ultimately ask "what would it mean, ontologically and ethically, to reposition dis/ability as the common underpinning of human becoming." Shildrick, *Dangerous Discourses of Disability, Subjectivity, and Sexuality*, 10.

43. Kafer, *Feminist, Queer, Crip*, 6.

44. Linett, *Bodies of Modernism*, 11.

45. Schalk, *Black Disability Politics*, 6.

1

DISABILITY, MASCULINITY, AND THE PROBLEM OF LEGIBILITY IN POSTWAR AMERICAN FICTION

AT KEY MOMENTS IN BOTH Ernest Hemingway's *The Sun Also Rises* (1926) and James Baldwin's *Giovanni's Room* (1956), novels of the American expatriate experience written thirty years apart, the protagonist stands naked before a mirror in a room located in France. Early in Hemingway's book, Jake Barnes, alone in a Parisian flat, undresses for bed; as he does, he catalogs the contents of his small room, the sounds of Paris at night floating up from the street. Barnes, who was gravely wounded in World War I, has just parted from Brett Ashley, his unrequited love interest in the novel. As his eyes come to rest on his reflection in the bedroom mirror, Jake stops narrating.

In the corresponding scene in Baldwin's book, the protagonist, David, studies his own visage in the mirror of his bedroom in the rented house just outside Paris where he lives for the duration of the novel, struggling to describe what he sees. His thoughts are preoccupied with the impending execution of his lover, Giovanni, but also with the sight of his own body reflected before him. In the final moments of Baldwin's novel, the first-person narrator struggles to relay the details of both the scene he imagines and the sight reflected before him. David's vision grants him no agency: "The body in the mirror forces [him] to turn and face it." He is compelled to look at—and attempt to understand—what is reflected before him, yet his body in the mirror remains "the incarnation of a mystery." Even his imagination fails to make legible what it conjures in his mind. As he pictures his lover walking to his death, David "cannot read what is in [Giovanni's] eyes: If it is terror then [David has] never seen terror, if it is anguish, then anguish has never laid hands on [him].["1] Baldwin's novel thus concludes with an image that echoes its opening, its protagonist reflected in glass, failing to shape his vision into a coherent narrative. In the corresponding scene of Hemingway's novel, Jake Barnes looks on his own body, injured in a manner that prevents him from engaging in heteronormatively defined penetrative sex, and refuses to describe what he sees.

These two scenes, read in conjunction, are broadly paradigmatic of a representational shift central to the interests of this book. Pearl James argues that American modernist literature responded to World War I through a topos that understood the violence of the war and its effects on male bodies as being "beyond words": not just unspeakable but *unrepresentable* within the conventional modes of representation that fiction and nonfiction writing of the time utilized to present narratives of death and survival in the wake of violent conflict.[2] This chapter's discussion of *The Sun Also Rises* elucidates representational strategies used by Hemingway to present the lasting effects of World War I's violence on his protagonist, notably withholding the specific details of his wounding in a manner that exemplifies the modernist mode of representation that James argues is paradigmatic of early twentieth-century accounts of World War I and its aftermath. This book traces historical developments that led to a movement away from a style of modernist representation accomplished by elision and toward a mode of representation that presents trauma and damage directly, complicating (or, in some cases, preventing) the legibility of the male subject. This new topos of illegibility became increasingly prominent following World War II and ultimately typified the understanding of the American masculine subject in the postwar American culture of the mid to late twentieth century for both "able-bodied" and "disabled" men. In this formulation, "disability" as a discursive category became a central locus of anxieties surrounding the gender identity and sexuality of American men that intensified as disability became more visible in postwar society in the United States.

While the two novels are distinct in their representational strategies, *The Sun Also Rises* and *Giovanni's Room* are consistent in what they demonstrate about the interconnected nature of ableist notions of bodily health and heteronormative understandings of American masculine identity. This chapter examines these two novels as texts of American expatriate experience in which illness or disability cause or stand in representationally for a male protagonist's exclusion from postwar American familial structures as normatively defined—and, by extension, from postwar American society more broadly. Reading these depictions of "impaired" masculinity in conjunction elucidates interconnected notions of wellness, the able body, and heteronormative masculinity in twentieth-century America. These novels' respective protagonists struggle with issues of self-definition tied to an internalized belief that their divergence from masculinity as heteronormatively constructed marks them as fundamentally different from "normal" men. Both figures experience this difference and their exclusion from American society so palpably that it leads to self-imposed exile from their home country.[3]

Moreover, both texts depict their protagonist's deviation from the norm by associating wellness and ability with heteronormative masculinity and American identity. What is distinctive about each text, however, is less how the protagonist understands his exclusion from hegemonic constructions of American masculinity than how each text presents the subject position and uses point of view to represent this subject position.

In *Gender, Race, and Mourning in American Modernism*, Greg Forter argues that socioeconomic changes in America in the late nineteenth and early twentieth centuries—which reduced the autonomy of men, who found themselves embedded in increasingly large bureaucratic structures as wage labor transformed the public sphere—contributed to a discursive shift in the understanding of male gender roles over the same period. From 1830 until 1880, Forter asserts, the separation of the public and private spheres along gender lines obscured inherent contradictions structuring American understandings of masculinity. Men were understood to be innately aggressive and naturally competitive, their personalities defined by an "instinct for dominance that was rooted in the male body." Male traits, if properly channeled, could lead to success in the worlds of work, commerce, and war—but these attributes, which could be socially destructive, needed to be kept in check by qualities seen as inherent only in women. Men could only cultivate "moral compassion, self-restraint, and emotional sensitivity" to a limited extent, and these traits and others thought to be innate to the female gender could "be transmitted to men only by women in the domestic sphere."[4] The understanding that exposure to the domestic sphere could produce a limited synthesis of masculine and feminine traits in males while *male* and *female* remained distinct terms allowed for the belief that men could temper a potentially destructive natural state through integration into the traditionally gendered family without compromising their masculine status. This formulation of gender permeated almost all social relationships and created an illusion of gender stability, rendered legible by historically specific social and economic conditions.

As American society began to transform at the close of the nineteenth century, language describing gender shifted as well, making "a move away from the term *manhood*, defined in opposition to *boyhood*, and toward the term *masculinity*, defined in opposition to *femininity*. What made one a man now was less that one had successfully grown up than that one was persuasively not a woman—a shift that bespoke a heightened need to police the borders between male and female identities." This increased scrutiny of masculine gender identity was in large part a cultural response to monopoly capitalism's transformation of the economy and a corresponding rise of employment for men that "offered neither autonomy nor ownership of productive property"; it produced "a sense of dependence and disempowerment that many men felt as unmanning" and had "explicitly racial meanings as well." New labor markets, which provided limited access to capital for both "ethnic immigrants" and newly freed slaves, "trouble[d] the link between selling one's labor on the open market and experiencing oneself as 'white.'"[5] These developments have clear implications for the corresponding emergence of the modern understanding of disability examined by this book. This chapter explores how, over the course of the first half of the twentieth century, gender, sexuality, health, and ability became increasingly interconnected as sites of anxiety regarding masculine identity.

In *The Sun Also Rises* and *Giovanni's Room*, disability and illness mark the deviance of the text's central male figure from the sexually aggressive position occupied by the male in conventionally structured heterosexual relationships. Hemingway's and Baldwin's novels figure as key texts in this chapter's explication of the connection between the operation of the closet as understood by Eve Sedgwick and cultural understandings of masculinity, the able body, and heteronormativity in ways that are similar but distinct in each text. The fact that *The Sun Also Rises* uses a hidden disability as a cultural signifier for otherness and alienation while *Giovanni's Room* addresses homosexuality and its potentially othering cultural valences makes comparison of the linguistic and rhetorical structures of the two works particularly fruitful rather than contradictory. None of the central characters in *The Sun Also Rises* are explicitly homosexual, yet Jake Barnes's wartime injury and resulting impotence destabilize the masculinity of all male figures in the text—potent or not—to the extent that gender, too, becomes unstable in the novel. Likewise, all the characters in *Giovanni's Room*, heterosexual or homosexual, are depicted as being, strictly speaking, able bodied, yet structures of wellness and straightness are so closely aligned in the novel as to be all but indistinguishable. This is not to suggest that disability identity and homosexuality are functionally one and the same; this work argues, rather, that disability, sexuality, and gender identity became so powerfully overdetermined in American society over the course of the first half of the twentieth century as to be deeply implicated in each other's cultural significance moving forward.

This chapter reads Hemingway's *The Sun Also Rises* as a dramatization of what happens when an unexpected injury transforms a subject's body from "able" to "disabled" and, as such, shifts the individual's subject position *within* the gendering matrix to outside that matrix—this is the heart of Jake Barnes's wound, and his dual identification with both normative and abject positions in postwar society heightens his experience of difference. James Baldwin's evocation of the similarly divided subjectivity of his closeted protagonist is a large part of what makes *Giovanni's Room* such a complex work and has been a source of contentious critical debate surrounding the novel. *Giovanni's Room* was marginalized by the literary establishment at the time of its publication and subsequently within certain circles of literary studies due to the book's homosexual content.[6] Additionally, a good deal of important scholarship has been devoted to unpacking the relationship between race and sexual identity in the novel.[7] Because *The Sun Also Rises* and *Giovanni's Room* both center on characters who simultaneously occupy normative and abject subject positions due to the operations of the closet, this chapter compares these two texts to examine the increased scrutiny of so-called deviant masculinities in the twentieth century and to demonstrate the inherent instability of putatively normative masculine subjectivities in twentieth-century American culture.

Rhetorical Impaction and the Epistemology of the Closet

In *Epistemology of the Closet*, Sedgwick argues that since the end of the nineteenth century, a crisis of homo/heterosexual definition has inflected crucial spaces of knowledge production in modern Western culture to such an extent that the open secret of the closet has come to structure our understanding of both sexual and gender identity in fundamental ways.[8] Sexual identity within the epistemology of the closet rests on a socially determined structure of knowledge and secrecy, acknowledgment and disavowal, that produces in individuals a constant, subtle, and largely unconscious policing of self and other individually (through internalized norms of gender) and intersubjectively (through our daily interactions with friends, lovers, acquaintances, and strangers). Sedgwick foregrounds the extent to which sexual knowledge is not predicated on meaning derived through direct interaction with the world; instead, knowledge of sexuality accrues through supplemental meanings in which hetero/homosexual definition becomes axiomatic as *the* open secret. In this way, sexual identity remains organized around "a radical and irreducible incoherence" despite its cultural centrality.[9]

Sedgwick coins the term *rhetorical impaction* to name the process of signification she describes in her book. In this view, the process through which texts produce and convey knowledge to the reader depends on the production of meanings in addition to those made explicit by the words an author uses to create the illusion of a world that exists beyond the limits of the text's interaction with the reader.[10] This phenomenon of linguistic supplementarity allows texts like Melville's *Billy Budd*, Wilde's *Picture of Dorian Gray*, and James's "The Beast in the Jungle" to meditate on homosexual themes and signify homosexual identity without depicting homosexuality directly or mentioning it explicitly. This type of signification is possible in part because the crisis of homo/heterosexual definition Sedgwick identifies is so pervasive in modern Western culture that its shadow permeates all relationships and many of the texts the culture produces. Sedgwick discusses different ways various literary texts, most notably *Billy Budd* and "The Beast in the Jungle," explore "homosexual panic" in relation to characters' anxieties surrounding tensions between public persona and private identity.

The narrative of "The Beast in the Jungle" is structured around an absent epistemological center, characterized by a deferral of meaning rather than its arrival. John Marcher waits "for the thing to happen that never does happen": an event unnamed in the text that the protagonist has from his earliest days known will someday occur and, in occurring, will fundamentally determine the course of his life. Unspecified within the story and central to James's depiction of his protagonist, this event becomes overdetermined and overinvested with meaning. Sedgwick explains:

> For John Marcher, let us hypothesize, the future secret—the secret of his hidden fate—importantly includes, though is not necessarily limited to, the possibility of something homosexual. . . . Whatever (Marcher feels) may be discovered along those lines, it is, in the view of his panic, *one* thing, and the worst thing, "the superstition of the Beast" (394). His readiness to organize the whole course of his life around the preparation for it—the defense against it—remakes his life monolithically in the image of *its* monolith of, in his view, the inseparability of homosexual desire, yielding, discovery, scandal, shame, annihilation.[11]

James's careful construction of his story in this way foregrounds both the intersubjective nature of identity formation and the extent to which identity formation remains an ongoing process. One can never fully arrive at their identity; one is always becoming themselves and doing so relationally. James depicts the centrality of the perspective of the other to one's sense of self by distributing the shared burden of Marcher's "secret" between the protagonist and his close friend May Bartram. In the story, John Marcher's life centers around his "sense of being kept for something rare and strange, possibly prodigious and terrible, that would sooner or later happen to [him]": an indistinct sense that, in the novel, James references as "the deepest thing within" Marcher himself. Both Marcher and Bartram are said to possess an understanding of Marcher in his essential nature, an understanding which is to some extent shared but, importantly, not identical. This perspectival split is in part what allows James to keep Marcher's secret essentially indeterminate and always, to some extent, deferred within the structure of the narrative.

The relationship created by the knowledge shared between Marcher and Bartram produces a reciprocal structure so central to both their identities that their very status as human becomes the implicit stake of their strange friendship, a relationship that remains pointedly ambiguous throughout the story. Discussing the implications of their relationship, May Bartram tells Marcher, "If you've had your woman, I've had . . . my man." Marcher responds by asking her if she feels this makes her "all right," and she replies, "I don't know why it shouldn't make me—humanly, which is what we're speaking of—as right as it makes you." Of crucial importance in this exchange is the instability it invokes. May Bartram is only *all right*, only *human*, to the extent that her association with Marcher marks her as such.[12]

Crucial to Sedgwick's analysis of "The Beast in the Jungle" is the notion that it evokes homosexual themes even though overt homosexual content remains entirely absent in the text: "This is how it happens that the outer secret, the secret of having a secret, functions, in Marcher's life, precisely as *the closet*. It is not a closet in which there is a homosexual man, for Marcher is not a homosexual man. Instead, it is the closet of, simply, the homosexual secret—the closet of imagining *a* homosexual secret. Yet it is unmistakable that Marcher lives as one who is *in the closet*."[13] Thus, "The Beast in the Jungle" is instructive in revealing the workings of the closet and the extent to which these dynamics structure our daily lives, relationships, and status as human beings. Coming to understand what May Bartram has told him,

Marcher states, "You help me to pass for a man like any other. So if I *am*, as I understand you, you're not compromised." Marcher must "repay" the debt he incurs to May Bartram in this economy, she says, "by going on as you are." Though Sedgwick argues that "the element of deceiving the world, of window dressing, comes into their relationship *only* because of the compulsion he feels to invest it with the legitimating stamp of visible, institutionalized genitality," I would assert (as in my above discussion of Marcher and Bartram's relationship) that the economy of their arrangement *requires* from Marcher his continued closeted appearance, even following Bartram's death.[14]

Various critics have discussed the intertextual relationship between "The Beast and the Jungle" and *Giovanni's Room*, drawing parallels between James's and Baldwin's depictions of closeted homosexual desire. Bryan R. Washington, for example, has argued that *Giovanni's Room* revises "The Beast in the Jungle" by making explicit the homosexual content rendered solely through linguistic supplement in James's text.[15] While critics have in a limited fashion explored parallels between Hemingway and Baldwin's uses of a postwar Parisian setting in *The Sun Also Rises* and *Giovanni's Room* to evoke the dynamics of American identity formation in an expatriate context, unexplored connections remain between these narratives and their reliance on similar linguistic and narrative structures to demonstrate the centrality of the logic of the closet to their narrative coherence. Both Hemingway's and Baldwin's protagonists see themselves as indelibly marked as other by facets of their identities they understand as totalizing. Within each narrative, these identities signify in a manner conflated with markers of deviance associated with European cosmopolitanism that are, at times, rendered metaphorically as contamination or communicable illness; the expatriate status of Jake Barnes and David only intensifies the experience of otherness presented by these texts as a fundamental, inescapable reality for each protagonist. Read together, these texts demonstrate how supplemental meanings surrounding disability and sexuality became increasingly implicated in the policing of masculine identities over the course of the early- to mid-twentieth century.

INVISIBLE DISABILITY, THE CLOSET, AND THE MELANCHOLIC MODERNISM OF *THE SUN ALSO RISES*

The notion of passing—of one's ability to conform in appearance to a category of personhood (e.g., race, gender, or sexuality) while retaining some difference from the way the category is normatively constructed—is a central feature of *The Sun Also Rises* and its depiction of disability identity. The novel tells the story of Jake Barnes, a man injured in World War I who is rendered impotent as a result of his injury and thus prevented from carrying out a romantic relationship with Brett Ashley, a woman he meets and falls in love with during his convalescence in an Italian hospital. The novel follows Jake and his friends, expatriates living in Paris following the end of the war, as representatives of the Lost Generation—individuals identified by the term coined by Gertrude Stein and associated with the widespread dissolution that accompanied the end of World War I. In the novel, Hemingway uses Jake's impotence as a symbol for all that has been lost because of the Great War. Discussing Jake's disability and its broader significance within the narrative of *The Sun Also Rises*, Forter writes, "The war wound clearly stands as the psychic yet physical sign of a lost masculine potency. Precisely because he was once 'whole,' and precisely because he has lost that wholeness in a war dividing the old world from the new, Jake bears an emblematically modern male consciousness, haunted by the memory of a potency and plentitude it cannot recover. The wound defines him as fundamentally lacking, devoid of authentic substance; it suggests that the thing which once gave content to identity by differentiating men hierarchically from women—the penis— is now both literally and structurally inaccessible."[16] On a conscious level, Jake's understanding of his injury exhibits "the conflation of desire with the real" that Judith Butler criticizes in *Gender Trouble* as a central feature of the formation of heteronormative gender identity: "the belief that it is parts of the body, the 'literal' penis, the 'literal' vagina, which cause pleasure and desire [that] is precisely the kind of literalizing fantasy characteristic of the syndrome of melancholic heterosexuality."[17] For this reason, Hemingway can use Jake's injury to signify a metaphorical wounding of all (straight) men as a result of World War I and, more broadly, an epistemological break separating prewar and postwar worlds. In his argument, Forter locates the dissolution accompanying World War I and its ambivalent resolution within the context of social changes that occurred between the end of the 1800s and the early to mid-1900s, as "opportunities for self-making afforded by small-scale capitalism began to disappear [and] men became increasingly reduced to parts in a bureaucratic machine unable to achieve the sense of autonomy so central to the meaning of manhood they inherited." Added to this sense of economic disenfranchisement, Forter notes, was an increased challenge to "middle class male social power . . . by women and ethnic minorities" and a concern regarding the "feminizing effects of modern urban living" produced by these changes.[18] Although Forter is correct in identifying literary modernism as a response to these changes, modernism can be more generally understood as a response to the physical and psychological toll of World War I's unprecedented violence, which ultimately resulted in a near-total loss of faith in the old world's notions of a civilization based on rigid class distinctions and of war as an honorable and noble pursuit.[19]

A crucial element of Jake Barnes's war wound that allows it to function as it does in *The Sun Also Rises* is the way in which it marks Barnes's being as other—entirely changed from his preinjury self—while remaining essentially unnoticeable to others during everyday, casual interactions. Although both the reader and Jake (as well as Jake's close friends) remain constantly aware of the implications of Jake's injury, he is neither scarred nor debilitated in a way noticeable to the casual observer. As such, Jake Barnes functions as a representation of both an impossibly idealized masculinity and its irrevocable absence and loss. Barnes is not subject to the stigmatization that might be elicited by a visible physical disability, yet he remains conscious of the feeling that he no longer qualifies as a man in a sense he understands. By eliding any direct visual representation of Jake's injured body in the novel and referencing the injury for the most part only obliquely, Hemingway's book heightens the effect of this representative strategy, increasing the valences of Jake's disability in the text.

A key moment in the book when Barnes gazes at his injured body utilizes a careful separation of the viewpoint given to the reader through Jake's first-person narration and the character's own view of himself so that the specific details of Jake's injury remain withheld from the reader: "Undressing, I looked at myself in the mirror of the big armoire beside the bed. That was a typically French way to furnish a room. Practical, I suppose. Of all the ways to be wounded. I suppose it was funny. I put on my pajamas and got into bed."[20] Discussing this episode, Forter argues that "the power of the scene derives in part from the fact that Jake declines to name the wound, as well as from his refusal to tell us what exactly he's feeling. Such omissions and understatements load his [subsequent] crying with an emotional intensity that resides in its very lack of specificity."[21] Moreover, even in this instance, the reader retains a view of Jake as *intact*, unscarred. Withholding the sight of Jake's disabled body has the strange effect of heightening our awareness of the contrast between Jake's former able-bodied self and feelings regarding his newly altered sense of identity evoked in this scene.

Forter posits a melancholic relationship between literary modernism and post–World War I masculinity, writing that modernism's responses to crises of gender identity "could be said to remain melancholically fixated on a lost masculine ideal that is fundamentally toxic, and that [modernist authors] themselves show to be unlivable. This fixation makes it impossible to mourn or fully work through their losses—or to see in those losses an opportunity for reinventing masculinity in a less rigidly constrained, less psychically defensive, and less socially destructive fashion."[22] Forter identifies this melancholic understanding of idealized masculinity at work in *The Sun Also Rises*: "a version of manhood Jake's wound has rendered increasingly difficult to sustain . . . a masculinity committed to penetration as the sign of sexual mastery." Hemingway's dependence on such a construction of masculinity in his writing puts his male characters in an inescapable double bind, Forter asserts, wherein "the wound also carries the opposite meaning: the loss of a genteel, sentimental, and implicitly feminine masculinity" problematically associated in the novel with Robert Cohn. "The problem with Cohn," Forter argues, "is that he *has not himself been wounded.*" Though there are many other significant characters in the novel who, like Cohn, have not sustained a literal physical wound of the sort experienced by Barnes, their own experiences of the world have been indelibly marked by their knowledge of Barnes's wound and its broader implications; this knowledge structures their experience of the world in a way it does not for Cohn, and Cohn's behavior in the novel demonstrates his continued belief in the "host of values the wound renders hollow." The version of masculinity constructed by Hemingway in *The Sun Also Rises* (and, more generally, in the rest of his work) is thus fundamentally unstable. Even phallic mastery comes, paradoxically, to represent a kind of loss of potency, as "the absence of the wound works to castrate Cohn. The actual loss of a penis, in contrast, functions paradoxically as the sign of real manliness, saving Jake from . . . the risk of sentimental softening that would render him, in Hemingway's eyes, insufficiently 'hard,' insufficiently modern—and therefore, insufficiently manly."[23]

Hemingway's use of a disability metaphor in his text, though problematic, is thus distinct from the symbolic uses of disability identified by David T. Mitchell and Sharon L. Snyder in *Narrative Prosthesis: Disability and the Dependencies of Discourse*. Mitchell and Snyder examine how disability frequently functions in texts as a cultural signifier for otherness wherein "disability provides a common formula for differentiating a character's uniqueness through the identifying features of physical 'quirks' or idiosyncrasies" such that "disability cannot be accommodated within the ranks of the norm(als), and, thus, the options for dealing with the difference that drives the story's plot is twofold: a disability is either left behind or punished for its lack of conformity." Mitchell and Snyder mention *The Sun Also Rises* in passing in their wide-ranging study, arguing that "the novel deviates from the prototypical modernist equation of disability with social collapse. In this way Hemingway accomplishes a full-fledged disability critique of contemporary society when his protagonist openly refuses to 'work up' his disability into a metaphor for the lost generation at the suggestion of his fishing buddy."[24] This assertion decontextualizes Jake's disability, divorcing its significance in the text from the novel's deeply troubling attitude toward nearly all forms of otherness and alterity; moreover, reading Jake Barnes's impotence as *narrative prosthesis* elides disability's actual function in the novel, which is to mark the protagonist simultaneously as entirely other *and* as an everyman figure.

The version of masculinity Hemingway promotes in his work, and in *The Sun Also Rises* in particular, is fundamentally exclusionary: the author is unable to let go of the idealized version of masculinity his book attempts to mourn, and as such, the text forecloses the possibility of offering a more empathetic, inclusive version of male identity. "Phallic manhood has been idealized *as lost*," Forter argues, "but only once it has been displaced from a psychic content or meaning to a style." By eliding direct references to emotion his text, the author of *The Sun Also Rises* attempts to evoke immense loss without falling prey to the sentimentality marked as "soft" and "un-modern" in his text.[25] Hemingway's minimalist writing style and the strategy of elision through which it functions rest on a Derridean economy of supplement, which creates in the text a dense web of significations centered around Jake Barnes, the novel's disabled protagonist. Barnes's impotence acts literally as the obstacle preventing him from living what he considers to be a normal life and figuratively to evoke the aimlessness and desolation of the entire Lost Generation. Hemingway's choice to give Jake Barnes an injury that renders him unable to engage in sexual intercourse but remains unnoticeable in most public social situations allows the disability to function discursively in the text in multiple ways, despite being rarely referenced directly.

This injury, its effect on Barnes, and its broader symbolic resonance are illustrated in the text early on in an exchange between the protagonist and a young sex worker named Georgette, who only appears briefly in the novel. The pair, who have just met, drink imitation absinthe and flirt after Barnes catches Georgette's eye when she passes his table on the outdoor terrace of a café, later sharing an intimate cab ride on the way to meet Jake's friends. As the scene moves from the public space of the outdoor café to the relative privacy of a Parisian cab, Hemingway underscores the way Jake's injury has changed his life and sense of self, evoking themes the text relates to Jake's disability throughout the rest of the novel. Cuddled against the protagonist in the cab's backseat, the young woman looks up at him, expecting to be kissed. When she touches Jake, he pushes her hand away. At first, he only references his injury obliquely: the woman asks, "What's the matter? You sick?" Jake responds, "Yes," to which she replies, "Everybody's sick. I'm sick, too." This exchange plays with different inflections of illness in the text, one of the central metaphors in *The Sun Also Rises*. Initially, when the young woman asks if Jake is sick, she likely means him to take her question literally, yet she might be asking if the protagonist's lack of desire for her indicates a homosexual identity. Jake's affirmative response to Georgette, however, as a tacit admission of his impotence, connects disability to metaphorical notions of illness that pervade the text. The woman's statement "Everybody's sick. I'm sick, too" extends the metaphor to encompass an indication, one can assume, of feelings of general malaise on her part and perhaps a literal reference to venereal disease. A bit later, after talking indirectly about Jake's previous comment acknowledging his "sickness," Georgette asks him directly what is wrong, and he replies, "I got hurt in the war," to which she responds, "Oh, that dirty war." In Barnes's first-person narration, Hemingway continues, "We would have probably gone on and discussed the war and agreed that it was in reality a calamity for civilization, and perhaps would have been better avoided."[26] Through this dialogue and narration, the novel introduces its preoccupation with Jake's disability and the character's continual awareness of the injury's effect on his relationships with women, as in the previously described scene in which Jake enacts a pickup ritual that he does not carry to its completion due to his feelings about his injury.

Through this scene, Hemingway begins to build negative associations among notions of illness, filth, disability, and various forms of nonnormative sexual identity, associations that become pervasive subsequent to the novel's introduction of a series of binary oppositions in its opening that structure the text and its understanding of otherness and alterity. Hemingway's writing draws contrasts by pairing and opposing the terms *clean/dirty*, *health/illness*, *ability/disability*, *youth/age*, *masculine/feminine*, and *heterosexual/homosexual*, among others. Working in this way, Hemingway presents his readers with a world that is starkly and cruelly divided.[27] In this context, Jake Barnes's disability and impotence signify his fall from a state of able-bodied potency prior to his war injury, a fall Hemingway metaphorically extends to all of post–World War I society through Georgette's recognition of herself in Jake's "illness."[28]

This metaphorical transference occurs again later in part one of the novel, in a scene between Jake and Brett Ashley that mirrors Jake's earlier exchange with Georgette. Following a brief interlude in which Jake introduces Georgette to Brett, Robert Cohn, and Cohn's wife, Frances, at a restaurant, Jake and Brett leave the restaurant and take a cab around Paris and have an oblique but loaded conversation about the status of their relationship in light of Jake's injury. After they separate for the night, Brett returns, intoxicated, to Jake's hotel. They talk briefly and part again after the following exchange:

> [BRETT] "Good night, darling."
> [JAKE] "Don't be sentimental."
> [BRETT] "You make me ill."
> We kissed good night and Brett shivered. "I'd better go," she said. "Good night darling."

As in the previous scene between Jake and Georgette, the literal significance of Brett's reference to illness remains indeterminate. Her shiver could be an involuntary display of pleasure, but her reference to illness just before the kiss subtly undermines this reading. Brett shivering after kissing Jake almost seems to mark a physical transference of contamination. Brett's statement reiterates Georgette's association of Jake's character with illness in the earlier scene, and her involuntary shiver further reinforces this relationship as being *reciprocal*. The book restages this scene between Jake and Brett several times, most notably at its conclusion, as Brett laments the lost potential of their unconsummated relationship.[29] This exchange, shared in private moments by Jake and Brett throughout the narrative, may thus be read in part as symptomatic of a malfunction in the stabilizing function of the private sphere for gendered relations identified by Forter, cited at the start of this chapter.[30] What prevents the couple from successfully coupling in each case is ostensibly Jake's inability to perform sexually, but the failure depicted in this scene has implications beyond the physical limitations of the novel's central character and what they portend for the relationship.

In addition to repeated oblique references to Jake's injury, at several moments the novel either displays or stages his trauma indirectly, displaced through metonymic substitution. The first notable instance of this practice occurs in a scene that constructs an intimate association between Jake Barnes and Count Mippipopolous through triangulation with Brett Ashley. Unlike the relations of triangulation described by Sedgwick in *Between Men: English Literature and Male Homosexual Desire*, this connection of two men mediated through the third term of a female character signifies not coded homosexual desire but connection of two men through physical scars retained from war wounds and the emasculation that results from them.[31] Following an exchange in which Brett tells Jake in veiled terms that she could not live in a relationship with Jake that does not include penetrative sex, she goads the count—a current lover—into showing off his scars from arrow wounds received in the course of his involvement in "seven wars and four revolutions." In this scene, Brett and the count assert that they are like Jake in that they have all "been around a great deal" and "seen a lot." The imprecision of their euphemistic language renders the meaning of their statements pointedly indistinct. When the count asks Brett and Jake if they have ever seen arrow wounds, Brett replies, "Let's have a look at them," and the count complies:

> The count stood up, unbuttoned his vest, and opened his shirt. He pulled up the undershirt onto his chest and stood, his chest black, and big stomach muscles bulging under the light.
> "You see them?"
> Below the line where his ribs stopped there were two raised white welts. "See the back where they come out?" Above the small of the back were the two same scars, raised and thick as a finger.
> "I say. Those are something."
> "Clean through."

Following this exchange, Brett turns to Jake and says, "I told you he was one of us," reinforcing the connection established among the three characters earlier in the scene.[32] The passage's language eroticizes the count's display of his wounds, and the physicality of his description emphasizes masculine characteristics, but the count remains essentially emasculated in his relationship with Brett. She often implies that his age complicates physical intimacy, reproducing in their relationship a similar dynamic to the one preventing Jake and Brett's successful coupling. Moreover, the intimate connection created in this scene between Jake and the count via their relationship with Brett allows the count's performance to act as the display of Jake's own wound to Brett, to Jake himself, and to the reader of the novel, albeit indirectly. The scene thus accomplishes multiple aims for Hemingway, establishing Brett's attraction to and complex relationship with figures of wounded masculinity while forcing Jake (and through him, the reader) to examine in a mediated fashion the wound that (for the protagonist) defines his character. Hemingway's act of substitution in the scene allows him to reveal the physical site of Jake's wound in a sense, ultimately leaving that revelation deferred. Brett's implication of herself in this equation through her use of the pronoun "us" lets the scene to do more than simply link the two male figures through the bodily cost of past violence. Brett's assertion that, like Jake and the count, she has "seen a lot" implies intimate understanding on her part of the two men's private pain and the emotional cost paid as Brett has come to "know" these men.

A similar act of substitution occurs later in the book, further structuring the novel around the absent center of Jake's injury. As the novel progresses, Jake continues to be burdened by his feelings for Brett and becomes increasingly troubled as he passively observes her displays of affection to a host of other men, in particular Robert Cohn and Pedro Romero, a young bullfighter with whom she becomes involved when the group of expatriates travels to Pamplona for the Fiesta of San Fermin and the running of the bulls. Brett's lovers fulfill her sexual needs but do not replace the feelings of love she still clearly harbors for Jake. *The Sun Also Rises* is a novel of very little action, and the undercurrent of violence running through the section that takes place during the fiesta is, for the most part, expressed in a controlled fashion by the bullfighting scenes in which Romero carefully executes bulls through the choreography of the fight. Uncontrolled violence, however, erupts in several important moments, two of which result from Robert Cohn's anger at learning Brett has begun sleeping with Romero and one involving a secondary character, a young husband and father killed during the running of the bulls.

The first instance of violence is notable because it is Jake—a figure usually characterized by passive responses to events in the novel—who instigates an altercation with his friend. Provoked by Cohn's anger regarding Brett's promiscuity, Jake swings at Cohn, who we have previously learned was once a middleweight boxing champion at Princeton, and he responds by badly beating Jake. Later in the same chapter, the group witnesses the goring of a young stranger during the bull run, in a scene not depicted in the novel. Back in town, Jake explains the scene to a waiter, detailing how the man was hurt: "'Here.' I put one hand on the small of my back and the other on my chest, where it looked as though the horn must have come through. The waiter nodded his head and swept the crumbs from the table with his cloth."[33] Jake's gesture demonstrating the manner of the young man's injury directly recalls the count's display of his scars for Jake and Brett. The waiter reacts in disgust, explaining that he feels such displays of violence are a meaningless waste of life.

Although this death may seem unimportant to plot of the novel, its inclusion sets up what becomes a key passage detailing the significance of Jake's disability when Jake recounts for the reader the young man's obituary from the local paper: "He was twenty-eight years old, and had a farm, a wife, and two children." This description of what the dead man has left behind serves as a list detailing the heteronormative life Jake believes he can no longer have due to his impotence—a life symbolized by property and family. The waiter's reaction, that the young man, named Vincent Girones, died "all for sport. All for pleasure . . . Just for fun," recalls the cynical tone of Jake's earlier reference to World War I and its effects on both his life and society more broadly, one of the novel's few explicit references to the conflict. More often, the text references the effect of that historically specific violence on Jake's body, his life, and his sense of self indirectly, as in the following passage: "The bull who killed Vincent Girones was named Bocanegra, was Number 118 of the bull-breeding establishment of Sanchez Taberno, and was killed by Pedro Romero as the third bull of that same afternoon. His ear was cut by popular acclamation and given to Pedro Romero, who, in turn, gave it to Brett, who wrapped it in a handkerchief belonging to myself, and left both ear and handkerchief, along with a number of Muratti cigarette-stubs, shoved far back in the drawer of the bed-table that stood beside her bed in the Hotel Montoya, in Pamplona."[34] This passage extends the connection established between Girones and Jake in his previous conversation with the bartender in a way that is paradigmatic of Hemingway's mode of writing and, as such, is notable for both its form and content. The passage, made up of two sentences, represents a departure from the author's generally terse prose and creates a sequence of relationships that signify Jake's injury while ultimately withholding its revelation from the reader by building between key phrases a series of associations, the symbolic resonance of which intensifies over the duration of the second sentence. The uncharacteristically long second sentence focuses on a series of transactions: the killing of the bull and the taking of its ear by Romero, his gift of the ear to Brett, and her wrapping of the ear in a handkerchief that once belonged to Jake, given to her by the protagonist in a gesture that, though purely utilitarian in the context of the narrative, resonates as one of affection.

The bull's ear, clearly phallic, can be seen as yet another veiled reference to Jake's castration, and the wrapping of that object in Jake's handkerchief—a traditionally feminine token of affection—inverts and destabilizes the association of penetrative mastery with masculine sufficiency on which the text insists, underscoring Jake's emasculation and the impossibility of the relationship he and Brett desire. These two tokens of love, hidden in the back of Brett's bed table drawer, one wrapped within the other, conjure for the reader an image of Brett in solitary mourning, smoking and crying over an ideal of romantic love that, for her, remains unrequited for the novel's duration.[35] Working in this way, Hemingway utilizes the logic of supplemental meaning to once again show the site of Jake's trauma while keeping it hidden. It is "through this sequence of supplements [that] a necessity is announced: that of an infinite chain, ineluctably multiplying the supplementary mediations that produce the very thing they defer: the mirage of the thing itself, of immediate presence, of originary perception."[36] Yet, for this reason, meanings that accrue through supplement must by their nature exceed and surpass the author's intent in writing. Moreover, by relying so completely on the logic of supplement to signify Jake's injury and its accompanying destabilization of heteronormative masculinity, Hemingway heightens the extent to which signification is always already unstable: as a result, *The Sun Also Rises* depends for its creation of meaning on binary oppositions the novel invokes but is unable to sustain.

The unstable logic of Hemingway's text unravels as it proceeds, lending a slipperiness to the author's language seemingly contradictory to the realist tendencies of his writing that depart from other examples of literary modernism. In certain instances, Hemingway takes advantage of this linguistic excess to elicit multiple meanings from his language. Arriving in Spain, Jake, Bill, and Robert Cohn decide to spend a night in Bayonne before continuing on to Pamplona in the morning, where they will wait for the arrival of Brett and Mike. According to Jake, "it was a nice hotel, and the people at the desk were very cheerful, and we each had a good small room."[37] In the morning, the three men tour the city. Barnes initially describes Bayonne as "a very clean Spanish town," and Hemingway, through the voice of the narrator, subsequently repeats the adjective *nice* several times in describing the town and its various attributes—a pointedly indistinct term with mostly positive connotations.[38] The trio rent a car to take them to Pamplona and, after stopping for drinks, Cohn goes ahead to the hotel while Jake and Mike arrange for their luggage to be sent down. At this point, Jake makes an apparently innocuous observation: "While we were waiting [for Cohn] I saw a cockroach on the parquet floor that must have been three inches long. I pointed him out to Bill and then put my shoe on him. We agreed he must have just come in from the garden. It was really an awfully clean hotel."[39] Here, Hemingway modifies the adjective *clean* with the particularly loaded modifier *awfully*, adding a cynical comment on the previously established cleanliness of Bayonne characteristic of Jake's world-weariness. The modification also subtly demonstrates the unsustainability of both Hemingway and his narrator's efforts at understanding the postwar world through simple divisions.[40]

Naming the Beast: Disability and
Sexuality in *The Sun Also Rises*

Close analysis of Hemingway's language in the rest of *The Sun Also Rises* reveals a similar pattern at work throughout the novel, as characters repeatedly attempt to define their lived experiences in an untenably black or white fashion. This epistemological instability extends most notably to the construction of masculine *and* feminine gender categories. Of particular note is the early passage that introduces Brett from Jake's point of view as she enters the bal musette where Jake has taken Georgette after encountering her on the street. Brett arrives by taxi accompanied by a group of young gay Parisian men: "A crowd of men, some in jerseys and some in their shirt-sleeves, got out. I could see their hands and newly washed, wavy hair in the light from the door. The policemen standing by the door looked at me and smiled. They came in. As they went in, under the light I saw white hands, wavy hair, white faces, grimacing, gesturing, talking. With them was Brett. She looked very lovely and she was very much with them."[41] Critics discussing this passage tend to focus on what its representation of homosexual males, taken from Jake's point of view, tells readers about the protagonist's attitude toward nonnormative formations of masculinity. Daniel S. Traber notes "that Jake essentializes homosexuals—'They are like that'—so as to configure them as another negative example supporting his social philosophy."[42] Nancy R. Comley and Robert Scholes argue that Jake's vision "disembodies" the figures accompanying Brett, seeing them "synechdochically, as fragments of men" in an effort to disassociate from the otherness they represent: "The homosexuals are built like 'normal' men yet (Jake might think) do not choose to be 'normal,' while Jake, who has a 'normal' man's sex drive, has been left only fragments of sexual apparatus. He cannot perform, though he desires to do so, while the homosexuals can perform and yet do not desire 'normal' heterosexual sex."[43] Similarly, Wolfgang E. H. Rudat argues that "in order to tolerate himself as he is with regards to sexual status, Jake will have to learn to tolerate other men who have a sexual preference different from his own."[44] Yet it is important to note the emphasis placed on Brett in the passage through repetition. She is identified (somewhat ambiguously) as being "with" these men, a status that is emphasized and invested with meaning through the subsequent phrase, "She looked very lovely and she was very much with them." One assumes Brett has not been "with" these men in a carnal sense, so the passage implies an association of similarity with the men rather than one that is sexual: she is described as "lovely" and as being "very much with" a group of men who defy normative gender construction as defined within the novel. One might argue that Brett's femininity is *reinforced* through association with other potentially feminized figures, yet the passage associates Brett's physical attractiveness with a depiction of nonnormative femininity that reinforces the heterosexism of the text (these men are not "men" in the traditional sense) and undermines the stability of Brett's gender. For Forter, the passage "places the homosexual on a continuum with the prostitute and the New Woman as causes of the 'lostness' indexed in the first epigraph and metaphorized by the penis."[45]

Although the dominant critical perspective on this section of *The Sun Also Rises* accounts for Jake's attitudes toward otherness and alterity, feelings in no way unique to his character in the novel, viewing the bal musette scene solely in this way elides the larger implications it has for gender as constructed in the novel. Traber notes that "the encoded smile [Jake] shares with the policeman when Brett's crowd enters connotes [Jake's] attempt to salvage a sense of stability," but Brett's own gendered appearance as described by Jake highlights both her conscious flouting of traditional femininity through adoption of a flapper's short hair and unconventional clothing and a more fundamental gender instability inscribed at the level of language, as in this passage: "Brett was damned good-looking. She wore a slipover jersey sweater and a tweed skirt, and her hair was brushed back like a boy's. She started all that. She was built with curves like the hull of a racing yacht, and you missed none of it with that wool jersey."[46] Jake's gaze objectivizes Brett, but not in a straightforward fashion. He finds her "damned good-looking" in spite (or perhaps because) of her boyish hair, and her depiction here recalls Jake's previous description of the gay men who accompany her entrance. Additionally, the passage accentuates Brett's feminine body through a simile lending her appearance a touch of the masculine: her clothes (a jersey—like the ones worn by her male companions—with a skirt), presumably not straightforward women's attire, fail to hide a body with "curves like the hull of a racing yacht." The specificity of this simile lends a strangeness to it and complicates the traditional association of ships and the feminine with phallic notions of competitiveness and mastery. Together, the above passages may thus be taken to demonstrate how gender operates as "the repeated stylization of the body, a repeated set of acts within a highly rigid regulatory frame that congeal over time to produce the appearance of substance, of a natural sort of being."[47] What is most notable about Hemingway's linguistic objectification of Brett, however, is how the use of repetition actually denaturalizes Brett's gendered body, much in the same way the Steinian repetition in the previous passage fragments and denaturalizes male bodies.

In Butler's view, normative bodies emerge as a product of discourse through a process of materialization impelled by the regulatory effects of a culture's power structures. Central to Butler's argument is the notion that gender materializes as the effect of a reiterative citational practice, so the normative gendered body always remains in process, never fully realized: "That this reiteration is necessary is a sign that materialization is never quite complete, that bodies never quite comply with the norms by which their materialization is impelled."[48] Many of Hemingway's descriptions of gendered bodies evoke just such an instability—the failure of even the most carefully chosen language to fully comply with the regulatory force of law the author attempts to inscribe on the bodies he depicts—to such an extent that this instability of signification pervades the text of *The Sun Also Rises*, and not just in the author's descriptions of physical embodiment. As a modernist text, *The Sun Also Rises* is, at heart, about a group of characters struggling to make sense of a world in which outdated modes of knowledge production no longer suffice. This is why so many of the concerns of the novel (and its characters) are, on a fundamental level, epistemological: the status of knowledge itself is of central importance to the novel and its thematic elements. Characters, most notably Jake Barnes, repeatedly try and fail to create fixed identities for themselves and others throughout the narrative, a narrative that often questions how, precisely, one is supposed to *be* a man or *be* a woman in a new, postwar world.

One facet of this thematic concern is the importance of proper names, which are used to provide subtle commentary on the role of various characters in the book. Hemingway, for example, gives Robert Cohn's domineering wife, Frances, a name that could be masculine *or* feminine, presumably to underscore what the author views as her inappropriately masculine role in her marriage to Cohn, highlighting Cohn's inability to constrain her nonfeminine behavior.[49] The most complex example of this phenomenon in the text involves the gendering through naming of Lady Brett Ashley, who—as the novel repeatedly explains—gained her royal title through marriage. This background, in fact, has direct bearing on how we are to read Brett's romantic relationship with Jake. Cohn, already infatuated with Brett early in the book, requests Jake tell him about her, asking, "What do you know about Lady Brett Ashley, Jake?" He replies, "Her name's Lady Ashley. Brett's her own name. . . . She's getting a divorce and she's going to marry Mike Campbell." In this same scene, Jake reveals to Cohn the circumstances surrounding the relationship Jake and Brett shared following the end of the war: she was a Voluntary Aid Detachment nurse in the hospital where he convalesced following his wartime injury. Later in the novel, we learn from a conversation between Mike Campbell and Jake the story behind her receiving a royal title and the details of her previous marriage to Lord Ashley, which shed important light on Jake and Brett's relationship: "Ashley, chap she got the title from, was a sailor, you know. Ninth baronet. When he came home he wouldn't sleep in a bed. Always made Brett sleep on the floor. Finally, when he got really bad, he used to tell her he'd kill her. Always slept with a loaded service revolver. Brett used to take the shells out when he'd gone to sleep. She hasn't had an absolutely happy life, Brett. Damn shame, too. She enjoys things so."[50] This scene, detailing the circumstances behind Brett's unsuccessful first marriage, is noteworthy for its similarity to what little we know about Jake and Brett's own relationship in that it reinforces Brett's pattern of being drawn to figures of impaired masculinity.[51]

More notable, however, is the extent to which heteronormative marriage in this case fails to create a fixed gender identity for Brett through her acquisition of her husband's surname. Like many other notable female characters in the text, Lady Ashley's given name, Brett, more commonly names a man than a woman.[52] Similarly, Lord Ashley's surname is often used as a woman's first name but sometimes as a man's name. Thus, the full name "Lady Brett Ashley," though it denotes a feminine aristocratic title, complicates the heteronormative gendering function traditionally accomplished by a woman's married name, rendering it pointedly androgynous. The specific phrasing of Cohn's question to Jake early in the novel is thus particularly loaded. When Cohen asks, "What do you know about Lady Brett Ashley, Jake?" the arrangement of words linearly on the page creates further ambiguities characteristic of a text that constantly undermines the binary oppositions through which it assigns, in particular, gender identity. To better visualize the effect, it helps to rewrite Cohn's question as *What do you know about Lady/Brett Ashley/Jake?* The question remains unchanged when spoken, but when read in this fashion, the revised sentence accentuates how Hemingway's words undermine the gendering effect they attempt to perform by troubling the binary opposition of gender on which meaning in his text rests. Separating the sentence into the binary sets *Lady/Brett* and *Ashley/Jake* reveals how both the masculine and feminine as constructed in the novel by necessity contain the trace of the opposing term. We might thus read Robert Cohn's question ("What do you know about Lady/Brett Ashley/Jake?") as the central question of the novel itself, a novel that again and again insists that its characters designate both themselves and others through a process of cognitive differentiation that fails by its own design. As such, the central question asked by

Hemingway's novel about disability is functionally the same question structuring the epistemology of the closet as described by Sedgwick and explored by Baldwin in *Giovanni's Room*.

SUBJECT FORMATION, ILLEGIBLE MASCULINITY,
AND BALDWIN'S *GIOVANNI'S ROOM*

Another Country, Baldwin's formally ambitious 1960 follow-up to *Giovanni's Room*, problematizes the experience of legibility for its characters from the start. In the opening of the first section of the novel, Rufus, the novel's initial protagonist, stands in Times Square facing Seventh Avenue. He is palpably aware of the gaze of a policeman and other passersby and fears that he will be recognized if happened on by someone who knows him, despite a disheveled state resulting from frequent hangovers. Where Jake Barnes looks to the gaze of a policeman at several key moments in *The Sun Also Rises* for recognition and to legitimize him as a heteronormative masculine subject, Rufus, aware that his race and sexuality position him as other in midcentury America, views the policeman who appears intermittently but pointedly in the first section of Baldwin's novel as a potential threat. In this context, Rufus rejects the value of legibility and "hope[s] he [will] not be recognized."[53]

Legibility and its role in subject formation is also a central concern of *Giovanni's Room* from the start of the novel. Baldwin's second novel narrates the expatriate experience of David, a closeted gay man who leaves America in the 1950s and pursues a romantic relationship with a man named Giovanni while living in Paris. While critics like Reid-Pharr note how Giovanni's southern Italian heritage allows Baldwin to explore the erotic and social implications of the characters' interracial homosexual relationship, the novel's setting (foreign yet uncannily familiar for Baldwin's protagonist) allows the novel to demonstrate the complex interrelationship of heteronormative understandings of the body, wellness, masculinity, and sexuality following World War II. As noted, the homosexual relationship around which *Giovanni's Room* centers is often understood in racial terms. Although David can be seen as a stand-in for Baldwin himself, the character's whiteness is emphasized in the opening pages of the book, as the character looks at himself in a mirror: "My reflection is tall, perhaps rather like an arrow, my blonde hair gleams. My face is like a face you have seen many times. My ancestors conquered a continent, pushing across death-laden plains, until they came to an ocean which faced away from Europe into a darker past."[54] The novel opens, somewhat jarringly, with David's acknowledgment of "his complicity in racial conquest. And this recognition marks the beginning of an associative pattern compelling the reader to explore the connections linking Giovanni's persecution with the African Americans."[55] As such, the novel can be seen as a meditation on racial oppression despite the absence of further explicit references to race. Reid-Pharr's analysis of the novel foregrounds identity formation as a central concern of *Giovanni's Room*, arguing that the author's use of first-person perspective subtly conflates the identities of the author and his protagonist despite their racial difference. In Reid-Pharr's reading, the novel's prominent inclusion of a mirror in its opening and closing scenes also demonstrates Baldwin's broader interest in "the relationship of the Object to the Inverse, the One to the Other. David is indeed the *real life* (American) character who considers the fate of the already, or almost already dead Giovanni. In the process, he faces away from Europe, away from whiteness, and from received notions of masculinity and sexuality to a nebulously darker past."[56]

While the book certainly deals with interactions between heteronormativity and race, as the protagonist "struggles with the erotic and social implications of choosing either 'the white woman,' Hella, or 'the colored man,' Giovanni," Baldwin's writing also demonstrates how metaphors of illness often figure in the operation of the closet.[57] Through its narrative, *Giovanni's Room* evokes mid-twentieth-century metaphorical notions of illness as described by Susan Sontag, while the metaphors Baldwin uses to signify his protagonist's fraught relationship to his sexuality evoke the operation of the closet as understood by Eve Sedgwick. The dislocation provided by the novel's Parisian setting forces David to confront his homosexuality, which he views as an illness, a taint deep inside him that has invaded his body like a cancer, making him different in essence from "normal" men. Although he clearly seeks to identify with American notions of heteronormative masculinity, only in Paris can David confront the fundamental instability characterizing normative notions of maleness, wellness, and sexuality.

Giovanni's Room can thus be seen as one of many texts produced following World War II that express a fundamental unsettling of normative conceptions of gender and sexuality in this postwar context without necessarily dealing explicitly with World War II or its aftermath. These texts and American society more broadly sought to ameliorate this gender trouble by reinforcing the traditionally gendered nuclear family as central to both American identity and social structures.[58] In *Giovanni's Room*, Baldwin's protagonist undergoes a crisis of identification while living in Paris in the 1950s precisely because of the strength of dominant postwar narratives informing sexual identity formation. David clearly identifies with heteronormative constructions of American masculinity even as he is excluded from them: "The vision I gave my father was exactly the vision in which I myself most desperately needed to believe," he says, longing to conform to a vision of masculine identity defined by wife and family.[59]

Baldwin's repeated invocation of vision as a trope in *Giovanni's Room* clearly differs from the metaphors of impaired sight used by Wright and Ellison after World Wars I and II. In *Native Son*, Richard Wright uses the trope of blindness, most notably in the ever-present ghostlike and sightless Mrs. Dalton, to represent a white America that, though clearly dangerous to those it marks as racially other, remains willfully blind toward outsiders like the African Americans living in Chicago's "black belt."[60] Moreover, Henry Louis Gates Jr. notes that Ellison signifies on Wright in *Invisible Man* "with *invisibility* as an ironic response of absence to the would-be presence of blacks and natives."[61] If Baldwin's metaphors can be said to be signifying on works of his predecessors in *Giovanni's Room*, then Baldwin signifies as a man who is gay as well as Black, riffing on earlier metaphorical formulations of the closet-as-room like Genet's prison cell as depicted in *Our Lady of the Flowers*.

In *Giovanni's Room*, both David and his father understand maleness in narrowly heteronormative terms: David attempts to prove his manhood in part through heavy drinking, a pursuit the elder figure tacitly approves of as it aligns with the specific notions of masculinity David's father—a drinker and a womanizer—upholds. Discussing his son with a concerned family member, David's aunt, his father states, "All I want for David is that he grow up to be a man. And when I say man . . . I don't mean a Sunday school teacher." It is precisely David's desire to conform to American notions of normative masculinity that compels him to leave his country in order to "find [himself]," an impulse the narrator describes as uniquely American and doomed, in his case, to fail. David states, "I think now that if I had any intimation that the self I was going to find would turn out to be only the same self from which I had spent so much time in flight, I would have stayed home."[62] As Reid-Pharr notes, "David has run away already from 'America,' which in this instance refers not simply to a geographical location of a complex of political and social structures but also a patriarchal economy that produces maleness as the lack of lack, a fiction that David is never able to maintain."[63] Despite David's ultimate inability to escape himself in another country, he initially attempts to conform to heteronormative masculinity during his time abroad, asking his girlfriend, Hella, to marry him before she departs Paris for Spain. David's wish to be with Hella stems from his broader desire to conform to the heteronormative gender role of an American male, which a relationship with her seems to offer.[64] Deeply conventional, David's fiancée seems out of place in the bohemian world David comes to inhabit—albeit with some ambivalence—while living in Paris.

Even after beginning his relationship with Giovanni, David writes his father to say he intends to marry Hella, despite the fact that, deep down, he has no intention of doing so. Yet when David initiates his relationship with Giovanni, a bartender at a Parisian gay bar he begins frequenting after Hella's departure for Spain, the narrator's experience of newfound freedom in a foreign setting becomes increasingly fraught as he is unable to reconcile his homophobia with his feelings for Giovanni. Initially, David attempts to distance himself from the gay men he meets in Paris, creating in his mind a strict separation between himself and men who express their homosexuality openly; Baldwin reflects this separation in the language David uses when discussing other male homosexuals. Describing one of the patrons of the gay bar he frequents in Paris, David states, "It looked like a mummy or a zombie—this was the first, overwhelming impression—of something walking after it had been put to death . . . It carried a glass, it walked on its toes, the flat hips moved with a dead, horrifying lasciviousness." The dehumanization evident in David's use of the pronoun *it* to describe this man becomes more explicit in his description of Guillaume, the owner of the bar: "His utter grotesqueness made me uneasy; perhaps the same way the sight of monkeys eating their own excrement turns some people's stomach. They might not mind so much if monkeys did not—so grotesquely—resemble human beings." Here, we see David's attempt to construct the gay men he meets in Paris as entirely different in essence than himself, another species that, for David, represents "a receptacle of all the world's dirt and disease."[65]

Illness serves particularly well as a metaphor for the protagonist's fraught understanding of homosexuality because it recalls homophobic notions that homosexuality can be transmitted like a contagion. Jacques, an elder American businessman born in Belgium who also frequents the bar where Giovanni works, comments presciently on the effect of homophobic social structures on David's understanding of himself and his relationship with Giovanni: "You are afraid it may change you," he says, warning David that his internalized homophobia, if not addressed, will isolate and alienate him from human connection. In his brief exchange with David, the older man uses the word *dirty* five times to characterize the protagonist's understanding of his homosexuality, stating, "You can make your time together anything but dirty; you can give each other something which will make both of you better—forever—if you will *not* be ashamed, if you will only *not* play it safe." In this passage, we see a critique of the increasingly pejorative discourse that marked nonnormative formulations of masculinity in the twentieth century, in which imagery associated with dirt and disease comes to be associated broadly with nonnormative formulations of masculinity, as in Jacques's final warning to David: "'You play it safe long enough,' he said, in a different tone, 'and you will end up trapped in your own dirty body, forever and forever and forever—like me.'"[66]

Susan Sontag observes the emergence in the twentieth century of an understanding of illness and its treatment in terms of "metaphors [that] contribute to the stigmatizing of certain illnesses and, by extension, of those that are ill."[67] This formulation demonstrates a clear shift from metaphorical understandings of illness in earlier periods: while "the Romantics invented invalidism as a pretext for leisure, and for dismissing bourgeois obligations in order to live only for one's art," illness in the twentieth century came to be seen as "a ruthless, secret invasion" to be countered by aggressive medical treatments. Over the course of the twentieth century, illness and other bodily impairments became markers of nonnormativity irreconcilable with masculinity as traditionally constructed. These metaphors often signify the threat nonnormative masculinities pose to straight society and the social order.[68]

Romantic notions of illness made men singular, but they were still men; moving into the twentieth century, illness and disability made the "impaired" masculine subject different in essence from the images of normative masculinity surrounding him on all sides, as notions of illness became irreconcilable with masculinity as normatively constructed.[69] Throughout Baldwin's novel, David remains unable to conceptualize his relationship with Giovanni outside of a heteronormative framework. Contrasting his life with Giovanni with the relationship he imagines he could have with Hella, David tells Giovanni, "What kind of life can we have in this room? What kind of life can two men have together, anyway? All this love you talk about—isn't it just that you want to be made to feel strong? You want to go out and be the big laborer and bring home the money, and you want me to stay here and wash the dishes and cook the food and clean this miserable closet of a room and kiss you when you come in through the door and be your little girl." David has dated and slept with women, but his male lovers figure in his imagination as proof of his own inscrutable difference from other men. Recalling his first sexual experience with a man, David states, "For a while he was my best friend. Later, the idea that such a person *could* have been my best friend was proof of some horrifying taint in me. . . . I cried for not understanding how this could have happened to me, how this could have happened *in* me."[70] This description corresponds both to Sontag's understanding of twentieth-century notions of illness as a ruthless, secret invader and to Sedgwick's description of homosexuality as constructed within the epistemology of the closet. David worries that something deep within himself makes him "different in his essential nature than the normal men around him"; it is, he says, a thought that lies "at the bottom of my mind, as still and awful as a decomposing corpse."[71] Both Sedgwick and Foucault historically locate the origins of the epistemological crisis they discuss in social changes culminating in European culture in the late nineteenth century.[72] For Foucault, this historical moment marks the emergence of a homophobic understanding of homosexuality as "a new specification of individuals . . . a species" whose essence becomes definable by even a single sex act, a notion that emerged roughly concurrently with the earliest changes in cultural understandings of illness identified by Sontag.[73] Sedgwick writes, "Foucault among other historians locates in about the nineteenth century a shift in European thought from viewing same-sex sexuality as a matter of prohibited and isolated genital *acts* . . . to viewing it as a function of stable definitions of *identity* (so that one's personality structure might mark one as *a homosexual*, even perhaps, in the absence of any genital activity at all)."[74] Baldwin's representation of his protagonist's internalized and often self-directed homophobia resonates with the Foucauldian understanding of modern constructions of homosexuality, as David's first gay experience marks for him a moment of change the narrator identifies as both awful and irrevocable, imagined as a form of contagion. Yet the effect of this understanding of homosexuality is to produce a binarism that undermines heteronormativity as well, even on the level of language. Linguistic surplus in Baldwin's text often works in a manner similar to Hemingway's own (at times) indistinct diction in his prose. When he learns that Giovanni has had relationships with both men and women, for example, David states that he, too, is "sort of queer for girls."[75]

As the novel concludes, Hella finds David in a gay bar in the company of a new lover after searching for him for several days. No longer able to hide his sexuality from the woman he once planned to marry, David confesses that he has had sexual relationships with men, and Hella ends their relationship, telling him she plans to return to the United States. Yet in the closing of *Giovanni's Room*, we see the evidence and perhaps, ultimately, the failure of "confession as one of the main rituals we rely on for the production of truth."[76] Structuring Baldwin's novel is his protagonist's compulsion to confess. David begins the novel stating a wish to repent, although for what, he does not specify.[77] The end of *Giovanni's Room* demonstrates not only the instability of the knowledge system produced by the epistemology of the closet but also the unavoidable incoherence of the narratives it produces as, ultimately, David's sexuality remains, for him, inscrutable, and Baldwin emphasizes the futility of the protagonist's attempt to find himself. At the moment of his final effort to embrace heteronormativity by severing his relationship with Giovanni to commit to a marriage to Hella, David feels palpably his separation from the dominant fiction with which he has sought to conform, and the novel closes as it began—with David gazing at himself in a mirror. "My mind was empty," Baldwin writes, "or it was as though my mind had become one enormous, anaesthetized wound."[78]

Unable to let Hella "be a woman" through a relationship with him, David stands alone at the novel's end, facing a body in the mirror he cannot reconcile with his own. "And I look at my body," he says, "which is under a sentence of death. It is lean, hard, and cold, the incarnation of a mystery. And I do not know what moves in this body, what this body is searching. It is trapped in my mirror as it is trapped in time and it hurries toward revelation."[79] Joshua Parker notes a correspondence between the concluding scene of Baldwin's *Giovanni's Room* and the scene in *The Sun Also Rises* previously discussed in this chapter in which Jake stands naked before his hotel room mirror gazing at the injury Hemingway uses to define him. Describing the two authors' similar use of a Parisian setting, Parker argues that "each narrator . . . builds a city of words while describing the irremediable impediment of his sexual relations with an Anglo woman."[80] Baldwin, however, allows his protagonist to do what Hemingway forbids: unlike Barnes, David freely describes what he sees, for the most part directly. Yet what David sees nevertheless remains to him uninterpretable, and the novel ends not with the revelation of truth but merely "the revelation of the confession . . . coupled with the decipherment of what it said."[81] Baldwin's narrative ends with an impaired vision, a distortion in a mirror, a wound still seeking closure. For Reid-Pharr, at the novel's conclusion, "Again we see the reference to death, the site at which the distinctions between the inside and out, the self and the other, give way, allowing only the articulation of ghost-like subjectivities. Strikingly, David's ghost body becomes inexplicable. He can no longer fashion a narrative by which to describe it. It is distinct from the self, which remains victim to a type of body logic that he cannot yet understand."[82] The concluding pages of *Giovanni's Room* thus posit a relationship between the novel's protagonist and his embodiment, providing an apt demonstration of

the extent to which legibility emerges as a central obstacle to identity formation for the masculine subject in the late twentieth century. Contemplating
the reflection of himself, David states, "My own hands are clammy, my body
is dull and white and dry. I see it in the mirror, out of the corner of my eye."[83]
Here, the first sentence foregrounds the physicality of David's body and his
awareness of and intimate identification with it as such. David refers to his
hands as "my *own*" and understands his relation to them proprioceptively
via his body's sensory perception of itself as a distinct object in the physical world. The second sentence, by comparison, is remote and distant and
focuses on a visual mode of perception foregrounded as doubly mediated.
David sees himself not directly but "in the mirror, out of the corner of [his]
eye": David's is a sense of self inflected by external perception and by his own
subjective interpretation of this recognition, both perspectives necessarily
informed by culturally constructed attitudes toward his sexuality even if not
directly referenced in this specific instance. That these various perspectives
fail to cohere into a self-image legible to Baldwin's protagonist is precisely
the point of the end of the novel.

Nevertheless, David's position at the end of *Giovanni's Room* is not identical to that of James's protagonist in Baldwin's source material. "In the last
scene of 'The Beast in the Jungle' John Mercier becomes," in Sedgwick's reading, "not the finally self-knowing man who is capable of heterosexual love,
but the irredeemably self-ignorant man who embodies and enforces heterosexual compulsion. In this reading, May Bartram's prophecy to Marcher
that 'You'll never know now' (390) is a true one."[84] In the corresponding
end scene of *Giovanni's Room*, the insight into knowledge is different. Self-
knowledge is not actively denied: it is revealed as impossible to possess or,
at the very least, as incredibly difficult to attain, mediated by social forces
preexisting the subject's formation that, in this case, prevent legibility.[85]

Raymond Williams notes how use of the term *subject* in contemporary
criticism departs from its primary archaic use, which denoted "a person under the dominion of a lord or sovereign." It is informed by more modern
uses developed in the late seventeenth century "especially from Descartes,
[who] proposed the thinking self as the first substantial area of knowledge—
the subject—from the operations of which the independent existence of all
things must be deduced—as objects thrown before the consciousness."[86]
For theorists interested in the effects of ideological power on the subject,
the term retains traces of its original meaning, naming a position subject to
discipline and coercion while referencing the disciplinary effects of oppressive social structures rather than those imposed by a sovereign ruler. Kaja

Silverman has traced the way the concept of the subject position has thus developed into an understanding of subjectivity "not as an essence, but as a set of relationships."[87] Key to this notion of subjectivity is Althusser's concept of interpellation, wherein successful subject formation is constituted through a moment of recognition that plays out intersubjectively and within a society's dominant ideologies. Interpellation is described by the critic using the metaphor of a police officer calling to an individual in the street. It is through the act of mutual recognition that occurs when the individual turns to meet the officer's hail that a person "*becomes* a *subject*. Why? Because he has recognized that the hail was 'really' addressed to him, and that 'it was *really him* who was hailed' (and not someone else)."[88]

Jake Barnes's pointed interactions with policemen in *The Sun Also Rises* can be read as almost literal stagings of this description of subject formation. In the previously discussed bal musette scene, the look shared by Jake and the policeman emphasizes the reciprocal nature of subject formation. Jake's masculinity fails in that instance precisely because he feels he has been *misrecognized*: the policeman recognizes him as a heteronormative masculine subject only because he remains unaware of Jake's disabling injury and its implications. As Hemingway's novel ends, the book restages this interaction and the previously repeated scene in which Jake fails to enact a heteronormative coupling ritual. Jake and Brett are together again in the back of a Parisian taxicab as Brett laments the lost potential of their failed heteronormative relationship:

> "Oh Jake," Brett said, "We could have had such a damned good time together."
> Ahead was a mounted policeman in khaki directing traffic. He raised his baton. The car slowed suddenly pressing Brett against me.
> "Yes," I said. "Isn't it pretty to think so?"[89]

The ending of *The Sun Also Rises* renders the novel both cyclical and melancholic as Jake remains conscious of the loss that now structures all his relationships but cannot be mourned and thus assimilated into a coherent sense of self.[90] Jake's final statement, also the final words of the novel, is both an idealization of his fantasy of retained wholeness and an acknowledgment of its loss, which he will continue to revisit—a reminder to him that he can no longer answer the hail of a society that seeks to acknowledge maleness through exclusion of the alterity associated with a disabling injury.

The key differences between the representational modes of the Hemingway and Baldwin texts focused on in this chapter demonstrate the broader implications of this book's argument concerning the policing of masculine identities in the postwar contexts of the twentieth century: the move from a post–World War I modernist aesthetic of elision to a post–World War II aesthetic of illegibility that looks on nonnormative masculine figures as objects to be deciphered, which is representative of the culture of scrutiny that became increasingly prevalent as the United States moved into the Cold War and can be seen as one phenomenon producing greater incoherence in the understanding of disability and masculinity over the course of this time period. The remainder of this book examines different vectors through which this representational shift can be seen, including documentary and fictional feature film, oral history, and memoir. In each case, American understandings of masculinity must be renegotiated following individual and collective traumas with physical, emotional, or cultural consequences for the masculine subject as normatively constituted. This renegotiation complicates the legibility of the American masculine subject even as identity categories excluded from the hegemonic construction of American masculinity due to race, sexuality, and/or ability became more visible in postwar American society. This book contends that the legibility of American masculinity as normatively constructed has always relied on exclusionary myths of American identity.

Notes

1. Baldwin, *Giovanni's Room*, 168, 166.
2. James, *The New Death*, 5.
3. King Vidor's 1925 film *The Big Parade*, which presents the narrative of a man who loses a leg after prematurely leaving a field hospital to find a French woman he has fallen in love with, may seem to be a counterexample of the representational trope of elision Pearl James explicates in *The New Death* in that the protagonist is shown on-screen with a missing limb. However, at the conclusion of the film, Jim Alperson (John Gilbert) returns from the war to a less than welcoming reception from his family and goes back to France, presumably to live out the rest of his days as an expatriate. Though the character is reunited with his love on his return to France, the film's conclusion clearly implies that there is no place in America for this disabled figure. As such, *The Big Parade*'s treatment of its disabled protagonist is largely in line with the two expatriate figures focused on in this chapter.
4. Forter, *Gender, Race, and Mourning in American Modernism*, 1–2.
5. Ibid., 2.
6. As Josep M. Armengol explains, Alfred A. Knopf rejected Baldwin's second novel after publishing *Go Tell It on the Mountain* due to concerns over the homosexual content of *Giovanni's Room*. Armengol notes the novel's cool reception with critics at the time of its release as well: "Many reviewers in the mainstream press described Baldwin's new novel as sexually deviant, [and] African American critics saw it as racially deviant as well." Armengol, "In the Dark Room," 671.
7. Robert Reid-Pharr has argued that viewing the novel "as Baldwin's anomaly, the work with no black characters" has long caused scholars to disregard the significance of Blackness

within the text; Reid-Pharr, in contrast, sees racial identity as one of the text's central concerns, arguing "that the question of blackness, precisely because of its very apparent absence, screams out at the turn of every page" of a novel in which "race is one of the central signifiers." More recently, Josep M. Armengol has discussed connections between Blackness and homosexuality as constructed by Baldwin in *Giovanni's Room*, arguing "that in *Giovanni's Room*, as in *Another Country* . . . , race is deflected onto sexuality with the result that whiteness is transvalued as heterosexuality, just as homosexuality becomes associated with blackness, both literally and metaphorically." Reid-Pharr, "Tearing the Goat's Flesh," 125, 103; Armengol, "In the Dark Room," 673.

8. Drawing heavily on late Foucauldian thought, Sedgwick argues that this crisis of knowledge is marked by (but not reducible to) a specific definitional impasse produced by increased policing of sexual identity beginning in the late eighteenth century and culminating in the nineteenth century in Europe in particular. Sedgwick, *Epistemology of the Closet*, 72.

9. Ibid., 85.

10. Ibid., 97.

11. Ibid., 253, 205.

12. Ibid., 257.

13. Ibid., 205.

14. Ibid., 258, 206.

15. Washington, *The Politics of Exile*, 71.

16. Forter, "Melancholy Modernism," 60.

17. Butler, *Gender Trouble*, 96. Judith Butler began using they/them pronouns in 2020. Although all of the works written by Butler cited in *The Illegible Man* were published prior to this date, I use they/them pronouns when referring to this author out of respect for their up-to-date pronoun preference.

18. Forter, "Melancholy Modernism," 56.

19. This book's third chapter discusses Judt's *Postwar: A History of Europe Since 1945*, focusing in particular on the contrast the historian implicitly draws in his book between a feminized postwar Europe reduced to rubble and a United States remasculinized by war and newly arrived as a world power following the war's conclusion. Judt, *Postwar*, 5.

20. Hemingway, *The Sun Also Rises*, 38.

21. Forter, "Melancholy Modernism," 66.

22. Ibid., 59.

23. Ibid., 67, 60–61.

24. Mitchell and Snyder, *Narrative Prosthesis*, 10, 56, 165.

25. Forter, "Melancholy Modernism," 65.

26. Hemingway, *The Sun Also Rises*, 24–25.

27. See Barbara Johnson's "Translator's Introduction" to Jacques Derrida's *Dissemination*, which notes, "Western thought, says Derrida, has always been structured in terms of dichotomies or polarities. . . . These polar opposites do not, however, stand as independent and equal entities. The second term in the pair is considered the negative, corrupt, undesirable version of the first, a fall away from it." Johnson, "Translator's Introduction," viii.

28. In *Gender, Race, and Mourning in American Modernism*, Forter reads this scene a bit differently, writing that "at one level, of course, the characters mean quite different things by the word 'sick': Georgette is speaking of venereal disease, Jake of his phallic injury. But the novel also works to suggest that these are not so different after all. It introduces the prostitute as a way of indicating that this is a world in which desire itself has become a sickness." Additionally, this scene could be read as paradigmatic of the phenomenon Elizabeth Outka explicates in her book *Viral Modernism: The Influenza Pandemic and Interwar Literature*, which reads references to illness as evidence of the "absent presence" of the influenza pandemic of 1918–19 in transnational modernist literature. Forter, *Gender, Race, and Mourning in American Modernism*, 61; Outka, *Viral Modernism*, 5.

29. Hemingway, *The Sun Also Rises*, 42, 251.

30. Forter himself reads this scene as a further generalization of Georgette's "sick" desire "to more respectable women as well." Forter, *Gender, Race, and Mourning in American Modernism*, 62.

31. In *Between Men*, Sedgwick "attempted to demonstrate the immanence of men's same-sex bonds, and their prohibitive structuration, to male female bonds in nineteenth-century English literature. . . . *Between Men* focused on the oppressive effects on women and men of a cultural system in which male-male desire became widely intelligible primarily by being routed through triangular relations involving a woman." Sedgwick, *Epistemology of the Closet*, 15.

32. Hemingway, *The Sun Also Rises*, 67.

33. Ibid., 201.

34. Ibid., 202–3.

35. For Forter, Brett's hiding of the bull's ear in her bedside table is part of a process of "memorial desecration" depicted by Hemingway's text, wherein a totemic representation of "sacred, meaning-conferring power" is emptied of meaning, first by its transfer to a woman and second by its "encystment within an entirely private, non-communal system of significance (the souvenir)" that withdraws the object from the signifying system Hemingway constructs in his novel. Forter, *Gender, Race, and Mourning in American Modernism*, 84–85.

36. Derrida, ". . . That Dangerous Supplement. . . ," 157.

37. Hemingway, *The Sun Also Rises*, 95.

38. Ibid., 96.

39. Ibid., 97.

40. Recall the count's earlier statement that the arrows that wounded him went "clean through" his body, an instance rendered more significant by the author's fraught usage of the word *clean* later in the book, the implication being that the count's masculine body was not only penetrated as a result of his wounding but also in some sense contaminated.

41. Ibid., 28.

42. Traber, "Whiteness and the Rejected Other in *The Sun Also Rises*," 245.

43. Comley and Scholes, *Hemingway's Genders*, 44.

44. Rudat, "Hemingway on Sexual Otherness," 174.

45. Forter, *Gender, Race, and Mourning in American Modernism*, 63.

46. Traber, "Whiteness and the Rejected Other in *The Sun Also Rises*," 245; Hemingway, *The Sun Also Rises*, 29–30.

47. Butler, *Gender Trouble*, 45.

48. Butler, *Bodies That Matter*, 2.

49. Take, for example, the following sentence describing Robert Cohn's relationship with Frances: "The lady who had him, her name was Frances, found toward the end of the second year that her looks were going, and her attitude toward Robert changed from one of careless possession to the absolute determination that he should marry her." Hemingway, *The Sun Also Rises*, 13. Here, the author's awkward use of passive voice displaces Cohn as the subject of the sentence and emphasizes his wife's unusual name, structurally reproducing the character's passivity in his relationship with "the lady who had him."

50. Hemingway, *The Sun Also Rises*, 46, 207.

51. The pattern is repeated when Brett nurses an injured Pedro Romero following his violent altercation with Robert Cohn on Cohn's learning that Romero also slept with Brett, an incident Hemingway uses to further demonstrate what he views as Cohn's improperly directed masculine energy. In this instance, the reader learns that Mike's relationship with Brett began because "she was looking after [him]" following an injury. Ibid., 205–6.

52. E.g., Frances. Georgette, as a feminized form of the masculine *George*, would also fit this category.

53. Baldwin, *Another Country*, 4.
54. Baldwin, *Giovanni's Room*, 3.
55. Washington, *The Politics of Exile*, 72.
56. Reid-Pharr, "Tearing the Goat's Flesh," 126.
57. Reid-Pharr, *Once You Go Black*, 110. Discussing the significance of Giovanni's Italian heritage in Baldwin's novel, Josep M. Armengol explains, "Italians began to be considered white only upon their arrival in the United States. As James R. Barrett and David Roediger (1997) note, it was in part through organized labor activity that previously nonwhite groups became white." Armengol further explains, "In the early twentieth century, Italians immigrating to the United States, like all others arriving on America's shores, were asked to fill out a standardized immigration form. In the box for race, they were given two choices: North Italian or South Italian. By World War II, however, the only option they had for the race question was 'white.' In this context, then, Giovanni, as an Italian in Europe, may be considered nonwhite or black." Armengol, "In the Dark Room," 678. Baldwin's designation of Giovanni's racialized identity in the novel thus further unravels the binary oppositions on which David attempts to anchor his identity at the start of the novel. As an American living in the 1950s, David would be unlikely to consciously recognize Giovanni's southern Italian identity as Blackness, despite Giovanni's minority status in European society at the time.
58. Silverman, *Male Subjectivity at the Margins*, 54. *The Illegible Man*'s third chapter includes an in-depth discussion of Kaja Silverman's work on fraught postwar masculinity, in which she uses the term *dominant fiction* to reference an understanding of reality that is exclusionary by nature and labels nonnormative those masculinities not included in the traditionally gendered equation of family. Ibid., 16.
59. Baldwin, *Giovanni's Room*, 20.
60. Wright, *Native Son*, 85.
61. Gates, *The Signifying Monkey*, 106.
62. Baldwin, *Giovanni's Room*, 21.
63. Reid-Pharr, "Tearing the Goat's Flesh," 131.
64. Baldwin, *Giovanni's Room*, 5.
65. Baldwin, *Giovanni's Room*, 40, 54. With perhaps intentional irony on Baldwin's part, David's quite conscious dehumanization of the gay men he associates with monkeys bears a striking relationship to Marlow's dehumanizing, animal-like descriptions of Congolese natives with "faces like grotesque masks," who are said to "crawl on all fours . . . black and naked." Marlow often perceives them as a single, undifferentiated entity, "a mass of hands clapping, of feet stamping, of bodies swaying, of eyes rolling . . . a black and incomprehensible frenzy" that Marlow similarly seeks to constantly differentiate himself from in Conrad's *Heart of Darkness*. Conrad, *Heart of Darkness*, 1963, 1964, 1979.
66. Baldwin, *Giovanni's Room*, 57.
67. Sontag, *Illness as Metaphor and AIDS and Its Metaphors*, 99.
68. Ibid., 5, 33–34.
69. Ibid., 216.
70. Baldwin, *Giovanni's Room*, 6.
71. Sedgwick, *Epistemology of the Closet*, 92; Baldwin, *Giovanni's Room*, 16.
72. Sedgwick, *Epistemology of the Closet*, 1.
73. Foucault, *The History of Sexuality*, 42–43.
74. Sedgwick, *Epistemology of the Closet*, 82–83.
75. Baldwin, *Giovanni's Room*, 30.
76. Foucault, *The History of Sexuality*, 58.
77. Baldwin, *Giovanni's Room*, 6.
78. Ibid., 145.
79. Ibid., 168.

80. Parker, "Hemingway's Lost Presence in Baldwin's Parisian Room," 53, 40.

81. Foucault, *The History of Sexuality*, 66.

82. Reid-Pharr, "Tearing the Goat's Flesh," 132.

83. Baldwin, *Giovanni's Room*, 168.

84. Sedgwick, *Epistemology of the Closet*, 210.

85. For Sedgwick, the true source of panic elicited by the epistemology of the closet is the need to respond violently when presented with a subject whose illegibility in heterosexist society compels a moment of recognition that renders one's own legibility suspect.

86. Williams, *Keywords*, 309.

87. Silverman, "From Sign to Subject, A Short History," 52.

88. Althusser, quoted in Silverman, "From Sign to Subject, A Short History," 49.

89. Hemingway, *The Sun Also Rises*, 251.

90. Freud, "Mourning and Melancholia," 586–87.

2

FROM TRUST TO SUSPICION

Disability, Masculinity, and the American Culture of Scrutiny in the War Department Documentary

THE WELL-KNOWN INCIDENT IN WHICH General George S. Patton physically assaulted a soldier suffering from what is today known as posttraumatic stress disorder (PTSD) during a tour of a field hospital in Italy—which was widely reported and was dubbed "Patton's Slap" in a December 6, 1943, article in *Newsweek*—demonstrates the violence inherent in the policing of heteronormative gender roles. As the *Newsweek* article explains, Patton struck the man after learning that the convalescent soldier had been relieved of duty following a traumatic experience in battle despite not having been physically wounded. Although military doctors had been aware of the effects of shell shock since at least World War I, Patton did not believe that the soldier's condition warranted medical care. The article explains:

> In the thick of the Sicily campaign and not far from the front, Patton was touring hospital tents near San Stefano. He went the rounds commending the wounded soldiers. Then he came upon one who sat on the edge of his cot. "Where are you wounded?" asked Patton. The soldier, a "shell shock" case, mumbled something about hearing shells that never landed and guessed it was his nerves. Well known for his disbelief in the reality of "shell shock," Patton flew into a rage, called the soldier "yellow-bellied," and gave him a back-handed cuff that knocked off the man's helmet lining. A nurse lunged at the general but was restrained and led away weeping. As he was leaving, he heard the soldier sobbing. He strolled back and slapped the private again. At about the same time, Patton similarly unbraided another "shell-shock" victim.[1]

59

Although the report does not reference gender or sexuality directly, the masculinity of both the soldier struck by Patton and Patton himself are the implicit stakes of the exchange, which—importantly—plays out through triangulation with a female figure: the nurse who attempts to defend the traumatized soldier when Patton first physically assaults him. "Patton's Slap" is a physical act, but it also has rhetorical force, marking the recipient as deficient in his performance of heteronormative masculinity in opposition to figures of proper masculinity, who bear physical injuries with quiet stoicism.

The exchange between Patton and the soldier recalls the structure of the climactic moment of Melville's *Billy Budd*, in which the title character is compelled to maintain his position of heteronormative masculine superiority by striking and killing Claggart, the master-at-arms of the HMS *Bellipotent*, a figure Eve Sedgwick has argued represents the closeted homosexual in a coded fashion in the story. In *Epistemology of the Closet*, Sedgwick writes that in the moment of Melville's *Billy Budd* when Billy strikes and kills Claggart as Captain Vere watches, "the reader is both threatened with and incited to violence" by their implication in the act precisely because it cannot be seen as a simple act of violence: the true violence of Budd's act is its marking function, which forces Claggart into a position of subjection before the eyes of Vere and the reader.[2] Like "Melville's Fist," "Patton's Slap" enacts the violence of signification through a physical act, but Patton's assault of his subordinate as recounted by *Newsweek* modifies the dynamics of the episode depicted by Melville, altering the trajectory of the violent signification the general performs through his act of violence.[3] Where Billy Budd's closed fist acts to signify his adherence to heteronormative masculinity, marking Claggart as other in a gesture that designates Budd as adequately masculine through violent performance, Patton's open-handed slap works to designate the crying soldier as deficient in his masculinity through a performance mocking the recipient's perceived effeminacy. The presence of the female nurse, and her attempt to defend the assaulted soldier, furthers the emasculating nature of the episode for the soldier in question, whereas Vere's presence in Melville's scene illustrates the fraught nature of the masculine authority from which Billy Budd's significatory act derives its power. Yet in both the fictional telling of a shipboard murder from the late nineteenth century and the news magazine account of an actual incident of violence taken from the 1940s, the boundaries of heteronormativity are policed with violence.

William C. Menninger addressed the American military's concerns regarding the masculinity of its fighting men in the lead-up to World War II in his book *Psychiatry in a Troubled World: Yesterday's War and Today's*

Challenge. He attributes the increased incidence of war-related psychological trauma during World War II as compared to World War I to "the fact that the country went into the most pathological of human activities—war—against its desire and without preparation. Men who had been ill-prepared for war by peaceful life in our democracy had to face a tough, hard, long, costly conflict."[4] Published in 1948, the book is an account of military psychiatry based on Menninger's time as chief consultant in neuropsychiatry to the surgeon general of the army, a position he held from 1943 to 1946; as such, Menninger's book provides an example of the tone and rhetoric of the American War Department in the lead-up to World War II, a response informed by the socioeconomic upheaval of the previous decade as well as the United States' sudden entry into active combat in the early 1940s following the Japanese attack on Pearl Harbor. Discussing World War II–era propaganda, Erik Barnouw identifies the filmmaker's task as such: "as to the faithful, to stir the blood, building determination to the highest pitch; as to the enemy, to chill the marrow, paralyzing the will to resist." Yet the implicit purpose of American war documentaries in the lead-up to war following the Depression was more complex than a simple "stir[ring] of the blood." According to Barnouw, when General George Marshall outlined to Frank Capra the purpose behind what would become the well-known *Why We Fight* series, he specifically mentioned concerns regarding the masculinity of his recruits, many of whom had been drafted into service. Barnouw writes, "The General explained that in the American army, civilians would outnumber professional soldiers by fifty to one. The Germans and Japanese were sure, the general said, that these American boys would be too soft for war; but Marshall felt they would fight like tigers—if they knew why they were in uniform."[5]

This chapter examines the three War Department documentary films made by John Huston while he was embedded with the United States Army during the Italian campaign of World War II. The chapter seeks to demonstrate how these films not only represent physical disability and mental trauma in the context of wartime violence but also exemplify changes to the documentary film form. These changes began to emerge in the late 1940s in the context of cultural and technological developments that helped shift the representational strategies common to documentary films produced by the US government during and just after World War II. Films produced for the Office of War Information by Hollywood filmmakers working to support the war effort differed significantly in form and content from state-sponsored documentaries made by a variety of governmental agencies during the Great

Depression, as the US military sought to exert more control over the messaging and ideology presented by the films it produced than did the various agencies that produced Depression-era social documentaries. These new documentary films were designed to inspire public support for the American military during the war, and after the war, they presented narratives that sought to assuage public concerns about returning veterans and their capacity to reintegrate successfully into American society following the war's violence. In these films, as in many other texts examined in this study, the implicit and at times explicit stakes of reintegration into society following wartime service are the individual serviceman's capacity to successfully achieve or reclaim status as head of household by reintegrating into the heteronormative nuclear family.

Like many prominent Hollywood filmmakers of the 1940s, John Huston enlisted in the military during World War II to make films for the Office of War Information. Although his wartime output—three films produced between 1943 and 1946—represents only a small fraction of the director's filmography, critics and biographers alike tend to agree that Huston's military experiences profoundly affected his life and shaped his film career, despite Huston's well-known contentious relationship with military brass during his enlistment. While *Report from the Aleutians* (1943), the first film Huston made for the military, is generally consistent both ideologically and formally with the broader canon of American wartime propaganda produced during World War II and features only a few references to US casualties, the two subsequent films Huston made during his enlistment were initially not well received by his superiors. Where *Battle of San Pietro* (1945) was censored by the US government to limit Huston's intended graphic depiction of American injuries and casualties, *Let There Be Light* (1946), which deals with the treatment of psychological trauma in returning veterans, was originally suppressed entirely. According to a much repeated story, after watching an early version of *San Pietro*, the generals overseeing the project angrily accused Huston of using his position as a military filmmaker to make an antiwar film and demanded the director remove many of the more graphic scenes in his initial cut.[6] The official reason given for the suppression of *Let There Be Light* (which went unseen by the general public until the 1980s) was concern for the privacy of the combat veterans who appeared in the film and fear on the part of the army that the film's release might negatively impact future recruitment.

The objective of this chapter is to place these particular War Department films in the broader context of documentary scholarship largely missing from previous discussions of Huston's War Department documentaries. Moreover, the chapter seeks to examine these films as cultural objects that demonstrate how ableist notions of heteronormative American masculinity were codified in the postwar period in part through collaboration between the US government and the Hollywood filmmakers the military enlisted to produce propaganda images. Prominent scholars of American documentary Jonathan Kahana and Paula Rabinowitz both focus their interventions in the field of documentary studies on historical periods known for producing social documentaries that tend toward revolutionary or, at least, progressive aims. Choosing to concentrate primarily on films made either during the 1930s or between the 1960s and 1980s, these critics purposely leave aside the military-sponsored films of the 1940s in their analyses. Kahana writes that he chose not to discuss the American documentaries of the World War II period in *Intelligence Work: The Politics of American Documentary* "because other moments better demonstrate how emancipatory energies of social documentary inspire formal and technological innovation, or vice versa."[7] Similarly, Rabinowitz writes in her introduction to *They Must Be Represented: The Politics of Documentary* that her aim is to focus on instances of documentary production linked to periods of pronounced radicalism in the United States, elucidating the relationship between "the major political issues galvanizing radical critiques during the twentieth century—the Depression, the Vietnam War, civil rights and decolonization, women's and gay and lesbian liberation . . . and documentary rhetoric."[8] This chapter therefore seeks to historically situate the documentary output of the US War Department during World War II in relation to the documentary forms and strategies that preceded it and those that developed following World War II. Additionally, this chapter uses Huston's War Department films as a test case to examine understandings of physical disability and mental illness that emerged during and after World War II, which operate in large part via exclusion of nonnormative forms of masculinity from the traditionally gendered equation of wife and family.

The fraught relationship between disability and masculinity present in Huston's war films has gone largely unexamined. Scholarship on Huston's war documentaries tends to focus on the constraints the director faced while working for the military, discussing his reenactment of combat footage in *San Pietro* in particular and the effect of this restaging on that film's historical value. Lance Bertelsen's essay "San Pietro and the 'Art' of War," published in *Southwest Review* in 1989, remains the only substantial scholarly treatment of *San Pietro* archival footage. The article discusses Huston's staging of most of the on-screen violence for the documentary and the censorship the film was subjected to at the hands of generals overseeing Huston's shooting of the film.[9] Greg Garrett makes a similar argument in his 1993 essay published in *War, Literature, and the Arts*, stating that "knowing that many of *San Pietro*'s battle scenes were consciously composed, our knowledge and respect for John Huston the filmmaker increases, and, paradoxically, his artful, created scenes give us the best idea of the terror and exhilaration of actual infantry combat."[10] Garrett's analysis of *Let There Be Light* continues this trend, examining Huston's final War Department documentary in the context of his fictional films and speculating that the film's suppression was rooted in the director's subversive adaptation of film noir aesthetics in his documentary practice.[11] The depiction of the psychoneurotic soldier's masculinity in the film, however, has received almost no consideration in the surprisingly brief scholarly treatment of *Let There Be Light*. For example, Lesley Brill discusses the importance of homecoming in the narratives of recovery presented in the film, eliding the extent to which these narratives rely on heteronormative notions of masculinity that excluded many individuals from military service and, more broadly, society at large.[12] This chapter argues that the documentary work done by John Huston for the United States War Department during World War II elucidates the relationship between masculinity and ableist notions of both physical and mental health in American culture of the 1940s.

Physical disabilities and mental trauma related to war were both seen as potential impediments to successful reintegration into family and social structures for men following World War II, as demonstrated by widespread public concern about the fate of veterans in the United States after the war. Huston's wartime documentaries became increasingly fraught in their depiction of the American soldier during and after the war, and the films were increasingly censored by the US military as a result. This censorship took place in the context of a growing culture of scrutiny that emerged in America following the war, which stigmatized deviance from heteronormative norms of masculinity, particularly related to concerns about the employability and, more basically, the emotional and physical health of American veterans. This chapter argues that these themes are expressed obliquely in the formal shifts in documentary film the chapter examines. Huston's films present a striking example of these changes as they occurred, before these formal elements became codified as part of the cinematic language used to connote documentary realism subsequent to World War II. Scholars of documentary film note the development during the Depression of a documentary film form and rhetoric aimed to construct a relationship of trust between the filmmaker and the viewer. Social documentaries created during and after the Cold War tended to approach subjects from a position of suspicion and used new visual rhetorics to convey a more cynical take on the subjects they examined. These filmmakers presented perspectives that were often more critical of the US government and other aspects of the American establishment than the perspectives of Depression-era social documentary. This chapter argues that Huston's War Department documentaries present a transition between what Raymond Williams would call two distinct "structures of feeling": the first associated with trust and the second associated with suspicion.[13] Huston's films attempt to synthesize official governmental narratives of World War II and its aftermath with a more critical take on the war and its effects, a stance that becomes increasingly difficult to sustain with each successive film. While Huston's films retain the didactic presentation of War Department aims common to most, if not all, World War II–era Office of War Information documentaries, the filmmaker's use of representational strategies that became more common later in the development of the documentary genre reveal inconsistencies in these official narratives. Huston's battle reenactments and his strikingly forthright representation of American casualties in *The Battle of San Pietro* are presented in a style that anticipates later documentaries that convey realism by foregrounding the capacity of film to create an archival record of contingency. This aesthetic dramatizes immediacy through camera movements eventually codified as a presentation of "reality" through the use of an unstable vantage point created by a handheld camera and the inclusion of "accidents" and chance occurrences as part of the film's narrative. Huston's depiction of violence and its effects on wartime and postwar American masculinity cannot be reconciled with the didactic narratives his films were ultimately made to present, and the filmmaker's attempt to adopt a more realistic documentary style that prefigures certain elements of direct cinema cannot be easily separated from this formal and thematic tension. As the prevalence of disability and psychological trauma following World War II began to present challenges to the legibility of the American masculine subject, Huston's films began to incorporate elements that shifted the ground of what was legible within the documentary film genre itself. The result is a series of films that, in one sense, become increasingly unsuccessful in presenting a coherent narrative. Nevertheless, these films are of particular interest to this study as they demonstrate the increasingly illegible nature of the American masculine subject over the course of the twentieth century, an illegibility reflected in the shifts in documentary representation that this chapter traces and more broadly in the transition from trust to suspicion reflected by developments in documentary film form.

The story of American documentary film during World War II can be understood in part as a transition from films produced by relatively autonomous artists—government-funded filmmakers working under the auspices of the New Deal who nevertheless retained a good deal of creative and ideological independence—to War Department propaganda made by Hollywood filmmakers who enlisted in the military to work as a part of the war effort. Although most well-known documentary films made during the Depression and later during wartime were government sponsored, the close relationship of the culture industry and the emerging military-industrial complex that characterized American film production during World War II contributed to an abrupt shift in the ideological content of state-sponsored documentary film in the lead-up to the official entry of the United States into the war. During the Depression, the Roosevelt administration's New Deal policies were developed and implemented by a variety of government organizations that "often overlapped and competed with one another" as they sought to ameliorate the various crises that arose from the economic and agricultural instability of the 1930s.[14] Various scholars have noted how this decentralization fostered a complicated relationship between the state administering New Deal policies, the filmmakers working to promote these policies, and the general public addressed by social documentary of the period. As Kahana notes, the social documentaries of the New Deal era aimed to do more than simply inform viewers about important issues or government services; they moved beyond an "instrumental address" of the audience to a more complex relationship with viewers characterized by the goal of the "creation of publics" and the exertion of "corrective pressure on the institutions that spoke for the masses, from organs of capitalism to the government and the left in its organized forms." In this way, Depression-era American social documentary sought to do more than instruct the masses or influence public opinion. During this period, documentary "serve[d] not only the didactic functions of pedagogy or promotional functions of propaganda or publicity but also the generative function of the public sphere," building the case for the policies it promoted by attempting to create a unified sense of purpose among the individuals who made up its audience.[15] Documentaries represented state interests, but not exclusively. In addition to presenting the point of view of their government sponsors, artists like Pare Lorentz and Dorothea

Lange sought to put pressure on the state on behalf of ordinary Americans; generally speaking, the documentary practice of the 1930s sought activist goals of social change. Rabinowitz notes that, in this context, "the implicit meaning of documentary is not only to record but to change the world—to evince material effects through representation—and to do so through highly personal interventions into public life."[16]

As the 1930s drew to an end, however, changes in America's foreign policy and the accompanying emergence of the military-industrial complex exerted an increasingly direct influence on American culture. Jack C. Ellis and Betsy A. McLane note that, even before the United States officially entered the war, the Roosevelt administration's material support of allies like the British through lend-lease programs necessitated a more unambiguously positive depiction of United States agriculture than was provided by films like Robert Flaherty's *Power and the Land*. As these authors note, though *Power and the Land*'s narration argues that modern production methods will only increase crop yields, "images . . . of despoliation created by cutting down the timber and cultivating all of the available land, like those in *The Plow That Broke The Plains*, carry dramatic weight," undermining the film's intended depiction of America as the "breadbasket of democracy."[17] Kahana notes that images from *The Power and the Land* "remained virtually unseen in the United States—the film was shelved by the government when the American entry into World War II made its grim view of agricultural capitalism untimely."[18] Thus, while a decentralized apparatus of production provided individual artists a forum for personal and political expression under the New Deal, mobilization for war in the early 1940s restricted the autonomy of filmmakers working on behalf of the United States government. When America officially entered World War II, US government control of state filmmaking was centralized, first by President Roosevelt's appointment of Lowell Mellet to the position of coordinator of government films in 1941 and second by the creation of the Office of War Information by presidential executive order in 1942.[19] This centralization of film production under military supervision (rather than through a variety of individual government agencies like the Farm Security Administration) reduced the level of autonomy for state filmmakers that had been afforded Depression-era social documentarians. The character of the collaboration between the federal government and the filmmakers it employed also changed more fundamentally when Hollywood partnered with the War Department to produce newsreels, feature-length nonfiction films, and short documentaries for internal military use and release to the general public. Government collaboration with Hollywood initially met with skepticism from figures like Lorentz, who believed a relationship between the federal government and Hollywood would compromise the integrity of the government's documentary film project: "It's not easy," Lorentz argued, "to step out and find men who are trained in the recording of facts. There is a great deal of difference between recording facts and recording fiction and drama."[20] In fact, what came to distinguish the military-sponsored documentary films of the World War II period was their use of narrative conventions common to Hollywood's fiction films.

Though wartime propaganda is generally invested in heteronormative notions of masculinity, the American War Department's documentary project began with issues of masculinity specifically in mind, in part because of the undermining of American masculinity by socioeconomic realities of the previous decade. Because body ideals are bound up in both intimate notions of personhood and public notions of national identity, the well-being of a nation is often linked to the bodily well-being of the individual subject. Rabinowitz argues that Dorothea Lange's Depression-era photos turned the bodies of their subjects into images consumed publicly as metaphors for the Depression, connecting individual bodies to a "disabled" national body. Rabinowitz writes:

> Lange not only figured the publicity of the private, but in her discovery of the intimate moments of individuals standing apart from a social apparatus and coiled within their own bodies according to Sally Stein's complex reading of the meanings of bodily harm and pain in both the national and Lange's imagination, Lange found a visual language for conveying physical pain and exhaustion. In a nation focused on FDR's crippled body as a metaphor for the economic paralysis facing the nation, Stein argues, Lange, a crippled woman, foregrounded isolated bodies leaning on feeble supports to suggest the ruinous effects of social forces on individuals.

As the private pain of disability became a public metaphor for America's "paralysis" during the Depression, the masculinity of both individual men and the nation as a whole became intertwined with America's economic struggles. Lange's photographs in particular evoke the personal and collective implications of the harsh realities of the Depression on American family life. Rabinowitz writes, "In her attention to the individual face, Lange presents the connections between 'human' and 'erosion' in a way that Lorentz does not. Here the plow breaks up more than the plains—the land—it destroys a community, a way of life, families and individual bodies and finally alters the nation as a whole."[21]

As the Depression came to an end and the United States mobilized for war, notions of the documentarian as "itinerant intellectual" gave way to the figure of the embedded filmmaker who (at least in theory) lived and worked alongside the troops and functioned as part of the military.[22] Collaboration between the War Department and Hollywood filmmakers seemed to close down the space of critical inquiry opened up by progressive social documentarians in the previous decade: if the impulse of the social documentaries of the 1930s was to document the effects of the Depression on the lives of individuals and families and, hopefully, to serve as a catalyst for positive social change, the purpose of documentary films produced for the US military by the Office of War Information was quite different. These films belied the cultural anxieties of a nation that found itself moving swiftly into war following a decade that had undercut traditional masculine gender identity and destabilized the heteronormative family by undermining men's ability to perform as breadwinners and, by extension, heads of households.

From Trust to Suspicion: Documentary Rhetoric and the Military-Industrial Complex

Report from the Aleutians, the first (and most traditional) of Huston's war documentaries, can be read as a straightforward narrative of American masculinity reclaimed through war similar in style and aim to other American propaganda films of the era that were part of the War Department Historical Series. In his discussion of Huston's war trilogy, Edgerton aligns Huston's early film with American war propaganda films like those directed by Frank Capra, which the critic argues sacrifice artistic integrity for compliance with the wishes of the military. Of Huston's film, Edgerton writes, "The primary impressions that the movie imparts are 'morale is first-rate . . . and getting stronger,' and that the Japanese are being kept at bay in the North Pacific while the Americans rapidly rebuild their sea power after the tragedy of Pearl Harbor."[23] The film tells a story of soldiers remasculinized, transformed by their incorporation into the machinery of war. *Report from the Aleutians* places little emphasis on individual men and focuses instead on the way the soldiers now function as a cohesive unit. Early in the film, the narrator underscores this collectivity, explaining that "bookkeepers, grocery clerks, college men [and] dirt farmers" have been changed through enlistment in the military into "soldiers now, as though all their lives they've been nothing but."[24] The film references casualties anonymously and after the fact, and individual accomplishments, when singled out, are highlighted in the context of images of the war machine to emphasize each man's relation to a larger whole.

Yet despite the similarity of *Report from the Aleutians* to more standard examples of wartime propaganda produced by Hollywood filmmakers in collaboration with the American War Department, Huston's work as a documentary filmmaker differs from better-known examples of World War II–era propaganda in important ways. Though likely given by chance, Huston's assignments were in some sense more complicated than those of other filmmakers working for the Office of War Information. Where John Ford was tasked with documenting the turning point of the Pacific Theater in his award-winning film *The Battle of Midway*, the conflicts depicted in both *Report from the Aleutians* and *Battle of San Pietro* required extensive shaping by Huston's hand to produce narratives aligned with the propagandistic aims of the Office of War Information. In his discussion of *Report from the Aleutians*, Edgerton notes that Huston was asked by the War Department to dramatically recreate the film's final scene to depict a "completely successful mission," eliding the loss of several warplanes during the actual bombing run restaged in the film's finale.[25] Despite Huston's elision of casualties from *Report from the Aleutians*, the filmmaker's time at this remote outpost was largely uneventful, and the resulting film focuses mainly on the banal day-to-day experiences of American soldiers.[26]

Battle of San Pietro, in contrast, depicts the harrowing nature of infantry combat during World War II and, unlike *Report from the Aleutians*, has been noted for emphasizing the individual soldier as a method of heightening dramatic tension. Bertelsen writes that early in the film, "Huston constructs a generalized, heroic image of the infantry . . . but as the moment of actual attack approaches, the soldiers of the 143rd regiment are strongly individualized. They are shown separately, full face, close-up—smiling, talking, worrying, their eyes full of deference and humor and fear—in a way that makes disturbingly clear their humanity and the non-military aspect of their being."[27] Gilles Deleuze has discussed the role of the close-up in encouraging viewer identification and empathy in the cinematic viewing experience. Close-up shots arrest the viewer's attention, momentarily pulling them out of the "chain of narrative events" otherwise made seamless through the combination of "perception-image" and "action-image," wherein "the perception of a situation leads to a (motivated) action which in turn leads to another action" through the logic of continuity editing.[28] The close-up, which Deleuze calls the "affection-image," constitutes a unity all its own, which "abstracts it from [the] spatio-temporal coordinates" created by the editing of individual shots into a coherent representation of a specific time and place.[29] Huston's use of close-ups, like Lange's contemplation of the face in her photographs, focuses attention on the personal, human aspect of events, so that *San Pietro*'s individual scenes tend to undermine the depersonalization of violence present in many propagandistic depictions of combat.

The individuation Huston accomplishes in specific moments of *San Pietro* through the rupturing effect of the close-up is elaborated by the structure of the film itself, as sound and image combine to extend Huston's focus on the individual face in certain shots to the film as a whole. The film's spoken prologue establishes *San Pietro*'s somber tone, addressing the high cost of American operations on the Italian peninsula in 1943 and emphasizing the necessity of taking the Liri Valley by force from German control at a time when the attention of the US Armed Forces was focused on England. The film's narrative is framed with an acknowledgment that the divisions depicted were undersupplied and that their objective was one of diminished expectations "conducted on an extremely limited scale." Concerning the liberation of the village of San Pietro, the prologue's narrator states, "We took it, and the cost in relation to the later advance was not excessive. By its very nature, this success worked bitter hardships upon each individual soldier, calling for the full measure of his courage and devotion."[30] The ambivalent tone established by the prologue remains as the film's narrative progresses.[31] Moreover, where *Report from the Aleutians* (like most American war documentaries of the period) encourages broad yet depersonalized public identification with the goals and aims of a wartime state, *San Pietro* encourages viewer identification with the individual soldier rather than with a monolithic construct. The film's voice-over, read by John Huston himself, departs from the "Voice of God" narration typified in propaganda films of the period and uses the pronoun *we* when describing the effects of events on the infantrymen depicted in the film. Thus, the viewer is further encouraged to identify with the men on a more intimate, one-to-one basis than more authoritarian models of documentary filmmaking allow.

Huston's aim of humanizing individual soldiers and emphasizing personal connection to their hardships in *San Pietro* is similar to the rhetorical strategy used by Depression-era New Deal filmmakers working to construct a public sphere they hoped would facilitate dialogues through which progressive change could be realized. One of the defining characteristics of Depression-era social documentary, Kahana asserts, is its frequent use of deictical voice-over: "In deixis, the speaker makes overt reference to the physical context that joins the speaker and listener, by a set of markers that include personal and demonstrative pronouns, adverbs marking time and location, and verb tenses. Deictical speech, which Christian Metz describes with the formula 'I-Here-Now,' emphasizes the immediacy of communication and the reversibility of the speaker's and the listener's positions. A deictical utterance is one in which the identity of the 'I' and the 'you' are determined by the present act of speaking." As Kahana argues, New Deal social documentaries of the early 1930s adopted an informal conversational tone "to make the voice-over commentary humane and sympathetic [by] giving the awesome phenomenon of state power a local and familiar character. Its aim was to reduce the sense of the state as a transcendent authority over the people and establish, in its place, the eminence of governmental power."[32] Deictical address represents an attempt by the filmmaker to cultivate a sense of shared cultural experience between the film's annunciator and its viewer.[33] In *San Pietro*, Huston's voice-over retains some—but not all—of the informality of deictical address, allowing the viewer to empathize with the infantrymen while retaining a degree of distance from the events taking place on-screen. Huston's image and soundtrack work together in *San Pietro* to create a startling intimacy with his subjects; ultimately, however, the viewer is neither addressed directly by the voice-over nor encouraged to feel as if they are participating in the events depicted on-screen. Although Huston's narration does impose an "official" ideological position onto his film on behalf of the military (a didactic specificity direct cinema would later attempt to counteract by creating an impression of spontaneity in its narratives), the informality of *San Pietro*'s address collapses the comfortable distance from on-screen events afforded to the viewer by Voice of God narration. As critics of documentary like Charles Wolfe note, Voice of God narration implies observation from "an indefinite and unstable 'elsewhere,' relative to the world of the image and the screen" rather than the "position of omniscience" suggested by the technique's name.[34] In this way, *San Pietro*'s voice track emphasizes the immediacy of the images shown on-screen by presenting a perspective closer to that of the participants in the battle than that of a more distant, impartial observer.

Huston's nonmythologizing depiction of the common infantryman makes the film's violence unsettling to watch; the film itself is generally incompatible with the aims of the War Department documentary project of the World War II period, even though its narrative was altered at official request prior to its release to lessen this effect in the cut eventually seen by the public. As Edgerton explains, Huston initially intended the film to end with a sequence composed "of several easily recognizable American soldiers now being placed into body bags as their previously recorded words are heard in voice-over speaking about what they thought the world would be like after the war."[35] In contrast, the coda of the released version of *San Pietro* takes place after the battle has ended and juxtaposes the hardships of the soldiers previously depicted in the narrative with reassuring images of liberated San Pietro villagers; nevertheless, these images subtly underscore the cost of violence on the civilian population of San Pietro. Able-bodied men are conspicuously absent in footage of a village now populated mainly by women and children: the only adult male shown in the film's final sequence is an elderly man limping amid the rubble, aided by a cane. Yet despite the traces of carnage that remain unmistakable in this final sequence, its tone is markedly different from the bleakness that characterizes the rest of the film. In the coda, the film's perspective shifts from the infantrymen to the liberated civilians, in particular the children of the village. Adopting the perspective of one of the young children shown wandering through the village rubble, the narrator states, somewhat naively, "Tomorrow, it will be as though the bad things never happened."[36] Cultural notions of the normative family are thus subtly inscribed in the narrative closure of Huston's film as *San Pietro* gestures implicitly to the return of a time before war disrupted the lives of the village's children, despite the conspicuous absence of able-bodied adult men in the film's final sequence.

Despite the graphic nature of the released version of *San Pietro*, the official version is selective in the elements of wartime carnage it makes visible to the audience. The unedited footage shot by Huston during the Italian campaign available for view at the National Archives includes long sequences of reenacted battle footage demonstrating the extent to which Huston intended to focus his film on graphic images of death. One particular reel of footage, for example, contains several shots of a slow pan from the backdrop of the peaceful landscape of Italy down to a helmet, pierced by a bullet hole, beside the hand of a fallen soldier (fig. 2.1). Another reel contains a more extensive series of sequences in which soldiers repeatedly enact death scenes: one unit can be seen advancing again and again across the same field as one solider and then another fall to the ground, apparently shot by an unseen enemy (figs. 2.2 and 2.3). The soldiers advance, fall, and then get up and advance again. Yet despite the clear intent to show battlefield casualties evinced by this footage, different footage completely excised from the final film indicates the extent to which Huston's editing process limited the film's depiction of the lasting effect of disability on the veterans of the Italian campaign. National Archives holdings related to *San Pietro* contain newsreel footage shot by Huston during the Italian campaign, including two differently edited sequences of comedian Joe E. Brown entertaining convalescent troops outside of a field hospital. In the first version of the sequence, Huston's footage foregrounds the presence of injured soldiers in the crowd while Brown does a comedy routine mimicking a pitcher at a baseball game; in the second version of the sequence, only soldiers in the crowd without visible injuries can be seen, and Huston shifts focus from the servicemen to the comedian and his routine (figs. 2.4, 2.5, and 2.6). Likewise, in the official version of *San Pietro*, heroic deaths are shown in a surprisingly graphic nature, but the film's narrative carefully elides any depiction of lasting damage done to living human bodies. Paradoxically, it seems more threatening to show the viewer images of a grave injury survived at great cost to one's body than to show death itself.

Viewing unedited archival footage of *San Pietro* affords the opportunity to see the results of Huston's "battlefield" shoots prior to the influence of his military overseers and, moreover, without the narrative shaping Huston imposed on the images through editing and voice-over. In his 1931 essay "A Short History of Photography," Walter Benjamin anticipates the primacy of the photographic image as a cultural signifier for realism in the twentieth century but cautions that in an increasingly image-saturated culture, it is not the image but its caption that becomes "the most important part of the photograph": photographs do not stand on their own, instead depending on historical and political context for meaning.[37] Scholars of documentary film extend Benjamin's concept of captioning to explain this form's rhetorical principles. Documentaries embed meaning in the relationships they create through selective editing and the juxtaposition of sound and image: "reality" does not reside in isolated images. Likewise, raw footage is film divorced from intentionality, an object that can only make meaning in relation to itself.

Silent and uncaptioned, the footage of the Huston archive exudes an uncanny voyeurism only partially suppressed in the finished film by the communalism inscribed on the film's images through voice-over. In shooting *San Pietro*, Huston often composed shots with the camera's view partially obscured: soldiers depicted in combat tend to be seen from the vantage point of a camera operator hidden behind tree branches, barbed wire, or other objects that clutter the visual field. At times, shots seem to simulate the point of view of an infantryman observing the battle from a position of cover, but the context of these images changes when the camera's gaze records footage of apparently fallen soldiers from a position of assumed safety, implicating

Figure 2.1. Discarded helmet with a bullet hole next to the hand of an American soldier. National Archives at College Park, Maryland.

Figure 2.2. Troops moving across a field toward a farmhouse. One soldier mimics being hit by enemy fire. National Archives at College Park, Maryland.

Figure 2.3. Troops continue moving across a field toward a farmhouse. A second soldier mimics being hit by enemy fire. National Archives at College Park, Maryland.

Figure 2.4. An audience of wounded soldiers watches comedian Joe E. Brown perform a comedy routine. National Archives at College Park, Maryland.

Figure 2.5. Close-up of a wounded soldier in the audience sitting in a wheelchair. National Archives at College Park, Maryland.

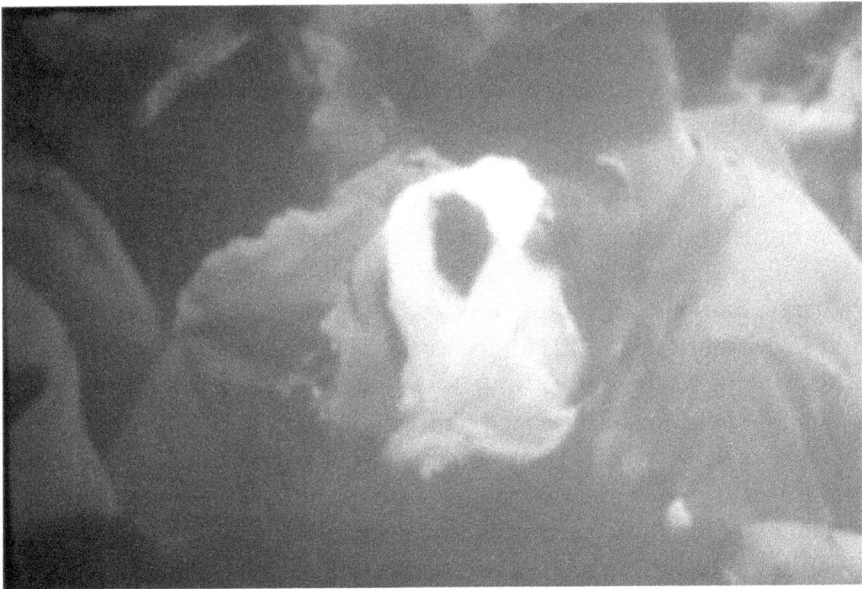

Figure 2.6. Close-up of a wounded soldier in the audience with a bandaged head. National Archives at College Park, Maryland.

the viewer in an uncomfortable act of surveillance. A particularly striking sequence of unused footage shows a soldier from medium distance, viewed from behind as he kneels over the body of a man, apparently a fallen comrade. As the camera pushes in for a clearer shot, the soldier turns his head several times, acknowledging the camera's presence with eye contact before briefly cradling the fallen man's head in his arms (figs. 2.7, 2.8, and 2.9). The meaning of this sequence is essentially indeterminate, as it lacks the structure and documentary captioning that present viewers of *San Pietro*'s finished cut with narrative cues shaping the reception of the included images. Nevertheless, the voyeuristic tone of these shots is unmistakable, and viewing the scene seems to violate the privacy of both the living and the dead.

Where close-ups early in the released version of the film generally encourage an empathetic identification with the soldiers depicted, reinforced by the informality of Huston's narration, this scene—viewable only as a silent image—complicates the I-Here-Now formulation through which the New Deal voice-over sought to bridge the gap between viewer and subject. When the kneeling soldier looks back at Huston's camera, his action functions primarily as acknowledgment of the filmmaker's presence in the moment being recorded. The soldier's return of the gaze also marks a moment that undermines the connection between viewer and subject the finished film attempts to construct, presenting a viewing dynamic that both illustrates and challenges the power imbalance inherent in Huston's privileged viewing perspective. The difficulty inherent in reading the archival outtakes of Huston's film, however, is inseparable from their lack of caption. As Rabinowitz explains, caption is particularly important in scenes involving ethical issues related to the representation of the body. She writes, "History is where pain and death occur but it is in representation that the facts and events gain meaning. As 'star' of the documentary, the presence of the body, especially the body in pain, signifies truth and realness which seem to defy contextualization," yet without caption, "the camera's view is disembodied and so dehistoricized, while filmed bodies are simultaneously overinvested with meaning yet deprived of agency." As the critic notes, "raw footage needs editing, bodies need historicizing."[38]

In *Intelligence Work*, Kahana traces a shift in the ideology and rhetoric of American documentary film—"a simple historical shift between two structures of feeling, from trust to suspicion," reflecting increased cynicism regarding political and social structures in Cold War–era America.[39] In the previously described outtake, Huston's camera moves in a way that would, in subsequent years, become coded to indicate covert surveillance, implying

Figure 2.7. Two soldiers concealed in thick brush, shown from a distance. National Archives at College Park, Maryland.

Figure 2.8. Medium shot of two soldiers concealed in thick brush. One soldier looks over his shoulder, momentarily acknowledging the presence of the camera. National Archives at College Park, Maryland.

Figure 2.9. Medium shot of two soldiers concealed in thick brush. One soldier cradles the head of his apparently dead or wounded comrade. National Archives at College Park, Maryland.

an ideological position of cynical distance from events subjected to critique by the filmmaker's gaze. In both *San Pietro*'s official form and in the fragments that exist as archival holdings, we see the emergence of visual tropes that would eventually be codified within the canon of documentary rhetoric as indicating a perspective of suspicion or surveillance. Both Kahana and Edgerton point out how documentary movements of the 1960s and 1970s like direct cinema emerged in part as a result of technical innovation in film and sound recording equipment during World War II.[40] Edgerton points out that *San Pietro*'s final cut blends the authoritarian elements of World War II–era documentaries made by the Office of War Information with "formal elements that are closely associated with the *cinéma vérité* movement of the 1950–1960s, such as longer takes, hand-held and mobile camerawork, and on-the-spot interviewing." He argues that these elements allow Huston—like practitioners of direct cinema—to adopt a more objective point of view, letting "these pictures stand on their own without interpretation."[41] Yet objectivity in documentary cinema almost always proves to be an illusion or, at best, a rhetorical strategy. Kahana explains that, as a result of the codification of documentary practice during the Depression, "by the end of the 1930s, documentary named not only a form but a position" and presented an accompanying awareness that "no image of the world [is] a neutral one." Kahana thus argues that the "blossoming of forms and methods in documentary [following World War II] is matched, however, by increasing suspicion of the concept of the public, and the public sphere, in American culture; indeed, publicness began to be constituted . . . by a discourse of suspicion."[42]

When viewing *San Pietro* in its totality—both in its form as a refined object of calculated state filmmaking and as unshaped artifacts housed in a government archive—one sees the contradictory impulses of a filmmaker pinned between two historically specific positions of documentary rhetoric: trust and suspicion. Depriving the viewer of the anchoring presence of an authoritarian voice-over, *San Pietro*'s narrative structure heightens the extent to which the film overinvests violent imagery with meaning, an effect furthered by the absence of soundtrack in the archival footage. Cinematic signification always involves surplus, and this is particularly true in the case of "nonfiction" film precisely because traditional documentary narrative generally asserts a one-to-one fidelity between actuality and the events shown on-screen. Despite the presumed reality of their films, documentary filmmakers select the images we see and leave out others; moreover, through editing, film constantly produces meanings and associations beyond the filmmaker's control. As a result, the viewer remains aware that they are only shown a partial picture, in effect heightening the extent to which images on-screen constantly produce and are overinvested with meaning.

San Pietro also tells us something larger about the documentary film project itself. In *The Emergence of Cinematic Time*, Mary Ann Doane argues that "the significance of cinema . . . lies in its apparent capacity to perfectly represent the contingent, to provide a pure record of time." Doane writes that the actuality, the documentary form that was the earliest form of cinema itself, "appeared to capture a moment, to register and repeat 'that which happens.'" Doane asserts that the actualities made by early filmmakers like the Lumières "produced continual evidence [of] the drive to fix and make repeatable the ephemeral."[43] Documentary rhetoric itself (especially the specific forms of documentary rhetoric that emerged following World War II) signifies the real precisely by enacting for the viewer the seemingly contradictory purpose of cinema: as staged actuality, documentary conveys an urgent sense of immediacy through the dramatization of contingency. The complexity of this impulse, however, is made particularly apparent by moments in the staged archival footage from *San Pietro* when contingency erupts from a scene, as in the previously discussed moment when an American soldier spontaneously returns the gaze of the state's vision, destabilizing the ideological position of state documentary and the subject/object relationship of cinema itself.

PSYCHOLOGICAL TRAUMA, THE "VETERAN PROBLEM,"
AND JOHN HUSTON'S *LET THERE BE LIGHT*

The physical health and mental stability of returning veterans was a concern for both the military and the American public even prior to the end of World War II, and depictions of soldiers suffering from psychological trauma in entertainment culture and news media following the war were often less than sympathetic. Films like George Marshall's *The Blue Dahlia* (intended by scriptwriter Raymond Chandler to tell the story of a murder committed by a mentally disturbed ex-bomber pilot prior to censorship under the Hays Code at the request of the army) and newspaper articles with headlines like "Veteran Beheads Wife with Jungle Machete," "Ex-Marine Held in Rape Murder," and "Sailor Son Shoots Father" transformed diffuse cultural anxieties about returning vets into specific fears of violence.[44] Although stories like these were largely exaggerated, media scares regarding the potential for returning soldiers to commit acts of violence against their own families reveal the extent to which public fears about emotional trauma in returning veterans were rooted in deeper, more subtle anxieties regarding the fate of the American family and the ability of American men to regain their place in society. Concerns about the fate of American men coming home from war were not entirely unfounded: returning from a violent conflict, the American GI faced a variety of very real challenges in the second half of the 1940s. Rabinowitz cites Louis L. Bennett's study published September 1944 in the social work journal *Survey Midmonthly*, indicating that "some 'problems' noted by the director of Veterans' Service Center in New York included 'family difficulties,' 'education and jobs,' 'housing,' and 'emotional disturbance and instability.'"[45] The results of this study highlight the multifaceted nature of the issues facing veterans who sought to reenter civilian life following the war. While the American public remained preoccupied with sensational accounts of rare and isolated incidents of violence among returning soldiers, the United States government enacted programs to deal with the emotional duress and socioeconomic dislocation experienced by many veterans, at times conflating the two issues in ways that stigmatized physical disability and psychological trauma. Rabinowitz argues that despite the feminization of the American welfare state in contemporary discussions of the government's responsibility to support vulnerable members of society, American welfare programs were originally conceived in part as investments in individual men—and in the stability of the country.[46] She writes, "These GIs had left a far different America—one reeling from a decade of depression, which forced the first unified federal welfare programs to secure Social Security and unemployment insurance, as well as provide 'relief' for poor, unemployed urban families and displaced rural farmers. During the 1930s, welfare was understood as a response to a crisis—as a defense against social disarray, anarchy and fascism, and as a relief from privation. By the time the United States entered the Second World War, welfare was officially trumpeted as a national defense."[47] Underlying this sort of official rhetoric was the idea that the American populace, and American men in particular, represented a valuable and threatened national resource. National programs aiding returning veterans buttressed the masculinity of American men and, by extension, the security of the country. In this context, physical disability and mental illness signified a threat to American safety and prosperity, and these anxieties were only exacerbated by the socioeconomic realities faced by America's veterans as they returned from war to a now unfamiliar America. Rebecca Jo Plant notes that, as a result, "in the aftermath of World War II, commentators routinely linked the issues of mental health and democratic viability, and mental illness emerged as a major preoccupation, even something of a cause célèbre." Pressured by the attention focused on mental illness following the war, Congress passed the National Mental Health Act in 1946, the first government effort to fund the research and treatment of mental illness in the United States. Plant argues that "the sense of urgency which informed these developments stemmed from a widely held conviction that mental health constituted a critical—and critically endangered—national resource. . . . If mental illness made America vulnerable to external enemies, it also threatened to erode the nation's democratic order from within."[48] Thus, the US military's own efforts to understand and treat mental trauma in enlisted men reveal different valences of the concerns also preoccupying the American public.[49]

In 1948, Menninger, chief of army psychiatry during World War II, published *Psychiatry in a Troubled World: Yesterday's War and Today's Challenge*, a book assessing the effectiveness of army psychiatry in dealing with psychological issues before, during, and immediately following the war. The book represents an attempt on Menninger's part to account for the shortcomings of the military's response to mental trauma experienced by soldiers in wartime; though Menninger's fraught relationship to the psychiatric establishment in the United States is reflected in some of the book's more ambivalent moments, the book tends to portray the United States military sympathetically and deflect criticisms of the United States Army, army psychiatry, and the majority of American soldiers despite the high incidence of cases of mental trauma during and after World War II. The book accomplishes this aim in part through comparison of World Wars I and II, through which Menninger underscores the increased severity of World War II's violence in comparison to the previous conflict and emphasizes the advances made by psychiatry in the period between 1918 and 1941.[50] Presumably written for a military rather than popular readership, the book does not concern itself with sensational fears regarding the safety risk veterans might present to their loved ones but rather addresses the belief that "in their great numbers," psychologically wounded soldiers might become "ruthless robbers of manpower."[51] In the buildup to war, the military had been concerned draftees were feigning mental deficiencies to be excused from military service; following the war, this concern shifted to a belief that those traumatized by violence overseas might return home unwilling or unable to work.

Huston's third War Department documentary, *Let There Be Light*, belongs to a subgenre of nonfiction films commissioned by the Office of War Information that document the military's efforts to rehabilitate soldiers following physical wounds or war-related psychological traumas, often addressing specific concerns potential employers might have about the employability of returning veterans. As such, the film participates in the post–World War II military discourse surrounding mental trauma through a narrative that links mental stability to physical well-being, emphasizing a sound mind and an able body as necessary preconditions for reintegration into a normative family unit and productive postwar life. While *Let There Be Light* clearly intends to present a sympathetic depiction of its subjects, the film often conflates physical disability and the effects of mental trauma in troubling ways in order to accomplish this aim. As part of this strategy, the film includes a prologue that minimizes the role of psychological wounds in the displacement experienced by returning solders. Text displayed at the start of the film states that treatment techniques shown in the film "have been particularly successful in acute cases, such as battle neurosis" but that "equal success is not to be expected when dealing with peacetime neuroses which are usually of a chronic nature," emphasizing that wartime psychological traumas are temporary conditions unrelated to the character of the soldier himself. The written prologue concludes by affirming the film's objectivity and documentary value: "No scenes were staged. The cameras merely recorded what took place in an Army hospital."[52] In this way, the prologue sets up and betrays the film's divided purpose and bifurcated point of view. While individual sequences seem to make conscious use of the tropes of documentary verisimilitude later codified in direct cinema (keeping the cameras rolling so they "merely record" actual events) and portray the patients of Mason General with startling vulnerability, the film's broader narrative arc is presented through narration that at times directly contradicts what the viewer sees on-screen in order to conform with the reassuring thesis put forth at the start of film—that psychological trauma in returning veterans, though widespread, can be dealt with easily and effectively.

Huston structures *Let There Be Light* as a three-part narrative: the arrival and initial evaluation of soldiers who will be treated at Mason General Hospital; treatment through a combination of individual talk therapy, group therapy sessions, and psychopharmacology; and rehabilitation, which concludes when the men reunite with their families and loved ones at the film's end. The first section focuses particular attention on the intake interviews army psychiatrists conduct with the soldiers whose treatment the film will detail. These interviews highlight the primary obstacles to be addressed in the film through therapy: survivor's guilt, homesickness, and more acute traumas that elicit physical symptoms in the men. First introducing the men as a group, the narrator's voice-over highlights the physical symptoms of trauma the initial in-depth interviews only touch on: "Here are men who tremble, men who cannot sleep. Men with pains that are nonetheless real because they are of mental origin. Men who cannot remember. Paralyzed men whose paralysis is dictated by the mind. However different the symptoms, these things they have in common: unceasing fear and apprehension, a sense of impending disaster. A feeling of hopelessness and utter isolation." The narrator's initial description of the men entering treatment at Mason General emphasizes the physical manifestations of emotional trauma— although the description does highlight the emotional hardship and isolation felt by soldiers experiencing posttraumatic stress, these men are identified, first and foremost, as "men who tremble." The above quoted passage is the first of many instances in the film in which physical and mental effects of wartime trauma are conflated in order to elide the lasting effect of trauma, which often goes unseen. Later in the film, the narrator explains, "Modern psychiatry makes no sharp division between the mind and the body. Physical ails often have psychic causes, just as emotional ails might have a physical basis."[53]

Although mind and body certainly exert a mutual influence on each other, Tobin Siebers has noted the care taken by the disability community to parse the differing effects and cultural registers of physical disability and mental illness. Advocates for the physically disabled have expressed concern regarding the conflation of physical and mental disabilities, fearing that the "misrepresentation [of a physical disability] as a mental condition will have a detrimental effect on [the disabled individuals'] ability to organize themselves politically." Siebers writes, "The tendency of the social model [of disability] to refer to physical states as mental ones . . . is a political, and hardly a neutral one, because it often represents impartment as the product of mental weakness. . . . Behind the ideal that physical disability may be cured by acts of will or the imagination is a model of political rationality that oppresses people with mental disabilities."[54] The conflation of the effects of physical and mental trauma in *Let There Be Light* is analogous to the position criticized by Siebers, logic born out in a subsequent scene depicting a man suffering from psychosomatic paralysis, or "conversion hysteria," described thus: "organically sound, his paralysis is as real as if it were caused by a spinal lesion."[55] Though this dialogue underscores the reality of impairment caused by mental trauma for those who suffer from it, the scene's progression links the man's recovery nearly completely to the loss of his condition's visible symptoms—his physical impairment. Edgerton notes that "several critics have rightly pointed out that the above described scenes in *Let There Be Light* create the strong impression that many of these patients are quickly and miraculously cured despite several sections in the narration that qualify the dramatic turnabouts on the screen as merely the first steps toward rehabilitation. The major flaw in the film certainly is this strong disposition to believe in the unfailing powers of the various military psychiatrists at Mason General."[56] Yet Edgerton's own analysis elides the connection between physical impairment and mental illness sustained throughout the film. While Huston does clearly attempt to "assert that a psychoneurotic impairment is no more disgraceful than a physical injury," as Edgerton argues, this analysis oversimplifies the relationship between mind and body understood in *Let There Be Light*. While treating the above-mentioned soldier for the "purely psychological" roots of his paralysis, the psychiatrist asks him to discuss his anxiety related to life as a soldier, the effect of his absence on his family back home, and his recent crying spells. The soldier in question discusses his difficulty "holding things in," and the army psychiatrist responds, "Well, we can help you do that." During the treatment that follows, the soldier is given sodium amytal and undergoes a regression while in "a state similar to hypnosis." The drug is said to provide "a shortcut to the unconscious mind" so that the military psychiatrist can more easily "remove through suggestion those symptoms which impede the patient's recovery":

the physical manifestation of the soldier's emotional trauma that prevents him from walking without assistance.[57]

Rather than discuss the wartime experiences that led to the soldier's treatment, the army psychiatrist inquires about the soldier's anxieties regarding his father's ability to maintain authority within his parents' marital relationship. The cursory working through of these familial dynamics, rather than the addressing of any specific war experience, is shown to lead directly to the soldier's recovery of his motor skills, and the soldier's legs are rendered "good and strong" by the conclusion of the brief interaction depicted on-screen. The score swells, heightening dramatic tension as the psychoneurotic soldier regains his ability to walk almost miraculously. Although the narration does note that "the fact that he can now walk does not mean that his neurosis is cured," the soldier himself is told, "When you wake up, you'll keep on walking perfectly well."[58] This example is typical of the structure of the film. While one element might acknowledge the limitations of army psychiatry's treatment of the men in its care, other elements enforce a radically different interpretation of events. They convey a narrative that minimizes the role of the war in the difficulties experienced by returning veterans and present the working through of any trauma that occurred as a straightforward and entirely successful process. Although some scenes in the film do show soldiers working through specific wartime experiences with the aid of an army psychiatrist, the moments emphasized in the narrative as significant breakthroughs either directly portray or strongly imply that a patient is as good as cured if his physical symptoms can be alleviated and generally avoid specific discussion of soldiers' wartime experiences.

In the event soldiers were deemed too traumatized to reintegrate into society following treatment, the psychiatric discourse of the period took pains to place the blame on individual men for their troubles rather than address that wartime experiences accounted for their feelings of distress. Though not explicitly mentioned in Menninger's book, the draft was clearly implicated in the anxieties surrounding mental trauma in returning soldiers. "We [were forced to take in] men with strong neurotic disposition[s]," Menninger writes in *Psychiatry in a Troubled World*: "[These men] were placed in the Army where they did not want to be; they were subjected to many stresses, both physical and psychological. With both a weak motivation and a weak personality the Army did not have much chance of making good soldiers out of such men."[59] The official voice of *Let There Be Light* often expresses these sentiments in describing soldiers' responses to their course of treatment; toward the end of the film, again emphasizing the role of alleviating physical symptoms of trauma in the recovery process, the narrator explains, "All those symptoms, like being unable to speak, stuttering, they have an underlying anger and resentment in the deeper parts of the personality [of the individual soldier]. You could almost say it like this: Underneath 'I can't,' you can find 'I won't.'"[60] *Let There Be Light* thus undertakes a project of elevating army psychiatry that works hand in hand with the film's overall goal of minimizing the role of the war itself in the dislocation experienced by returning psychoneurotic veterans.

Let There Be Light's narrative also illustrates the extent to which the understanding of recovery presented by the film relies on heteronormative cultural notions of the nuclear family. According to the film, central to the psychically wounded soldier's convalescence and eventual reintegration into society is his recovery of a feeling of "personal safety" to bring him "out of his isolation" and make him feel "like other people." The soldier accomplishes this task by regaining an "experience of safety" that, according to the army psychiatrist in charge of Mason General's group therapy sessions, "stem[s] from childhood safety" that "itself would stem from the parent's safety." The key to reintegration into wider society is, implicitly, reintegrating into a normative family unit and working out any neuroses that might prevent such reintegration from being successful. This dialogue occurs immediately following the scene depicting the "cure" performed on the soldier experiencing hysterical paralysis and reinforces the logic of the earlier scene. It demonstrates the extent to which group therapy sessions at Mason General rely on the same narrative of oedipal displacement demonstrated when the paralyzed patient regains his ability to walk after a cursory confrontation of his feelings toward his father, who he is told was unable to adequately exercise authority in a heteronormative familial triangle. At this point in the film, the psychiatrist warns the soldiers attending group therapy not to keep their emotional difficulties to themselves, contradicting earlier instructions given in individual therapy sessions, and asks several men previously shown undergoing one-on-one psychiatric treatment to discuss anxieties felt during childhood rather than recent traumas related directly to war. The film explains that "the basic method of psychiatric treatment" is "discussion and understanding of the underlying causes of the symptom," but such discussion rarely addresses the direct causes of a soldier's trauma, instead relocating the cause of each individual's traumatic response onto a site less problematic for the military: formative childhood experiences the psychiatrist interprets as producing weak character traits in the adult patient.[61]

Deleuze and Guattari note the extent to which psychoanalysis can rely on just such narratives of oedipal displacement: "We have seen, following Foucault how nineteenth century psychiatry had conceived of the family as both cause and judge of the illness, and the closed asylum as an artificial family charged with internalizing guilt and with instituting responsibility, enveloping madness no less than its cure in a father-child relationship everywhere present." Deleuze and Guattari's criticism of psychoanalysis—its tendency to impose a narrative of familial dysfunction onto the patient's experiences, reducing a complex web of socially produced desires to the oedipal relationship—is useful to consider in relation to the psychotherapy sessions depicted in *Let There Be Light*, which substitute family neurosis for the historically specific trauma of combat. The end result of this process is the relocation of blame for the trauma of war from the military or combat itself onto individual soldiers and their families. "Sick desire stretches out on the couch, an artificial swamp, a little earth, a little mother," Deleuze and Guattari write of the patient of psychoanalysis, quoting *Aaron's Rod*, D. H. Lawrence's depiction of Europe following World War I: "Look at you, stumbling and staggering with no use in your legs. . . . And it's nothing but your wanting to be loved that does it. A maudlin crying to be loved, which makes your legs go all rickey."[62] Mason General's treatment of hysterical paralysis literalizes Lawrence's metaphor, creating a repeatable script into which the particulars of each patient's life are inserted, diagnosed as rooted in familial dysfunction, and cured through a cursory working through of the psychiatrist's narrative. By focusing on physical manifestations of psychological trauma and locating the cause of physical symptoms in the soldiers' upbringing, army psychiatry as depicted in *Let There Be Light*—despite its best intentions—creates the impression that any lingering effects of combat on a soldier are the shameful result of a personal failing rooted in a family dynamic that does not conform with the social norms reinforced by the film's narrative.

Where many of *Let There Be Light*'s sequences employ narrative techniques like continuity editing and montage to reinforce the film's official logic, the long, unedited scenes portraying psychiatric interviews with individual soldiers, like Huston's close-ups in *San Pietro*, present a rupture that almost entirely undermines the didacticism of *Let There Be Light*'s storyline, as psychiatrists "listen to the stories of the men, who tell them the best they can."[63] In these scenes, Huston gives primacy to the men's individual stories, and we see firsthand the difficulty involved in self-narration not only following a specific trauma but also under the conditions of modernity more generally. In *The Emergence of Cinematic Time*, Doane uses the concept of "shock," which Walter Benjamin understands as the paradigmatic experience of modern subjectivity, to describe the role of cinema in "conceptualizing contingency in modernity." Doane notes that, in Benjamin's argument,

> First, shock is specified as that which is unassimilable in experience, a residue of unreadability. In being parried by consciousness, it never reaches the subjective depths (of the unconscious, of experience) that would confer upon it stable meaning. Second, shock is defined in terms that associate it with pathology. The subject must defend himself/herself against it at the risk of losing psychical integrity or equilibrium. Consciousness is above all "protective." Third, the defense against shock embodies a privileged relation to time. The rationalization of time (its division into discrete entities—seconds, minutes hours, and its regulation by the clock) is a symptom of the foreclosure of meaning in the defense against shock (an incident is "assigned a precise point in time in consciousness at the cost of the integrity of its contents"). Rationalization supplants, displaces, or, in a sense, *mimics* meaning.

The narrativizing impulse of army psychiatry depicted in *Let There Be Light* is thus best understood as a process that mimics rather than produces meaning, foreclosing for the subject the possibility of working through traumatic experiences through therapy. Doane explains that "shock is not to be avoided or rejected in a historically regressive nostalgia for the auratic. Instead, it must be *worked through*."[64] The difficulty inherent in parsing the significance of *Let There Be Light* lies, in part, in the fact that the film does depict isolated moments in which individual soldiers work through specific war-related traumas. But these instances do not merge seamlessly with the overarching message on which the film insists. Early in the film, one soldier is told by his psychiatrist that "a display of emotion is all right" and "sometimes very helpful," but only after he nearly discontinues his treatment after breaking down and crying in front of Huston's camera.[65] It is difficult to know the extent to which the presence of a film crew influenced the unfolding of the treatment witnessed in the film. As the soldiers recall their experiences at the request of psychiatrists at Mason General, they also perform their neuroses for the camera. Yet in these sequences, it is the startling moments of genuine insight on the part of the patients that stick with the viewer rather than the tidy didactic narratives psychiatrists inscribe on these experiences through analysis, often with the aid of pharmacology. As the men undergoing treatment at Mason General attempt to regain a sense of stability by narrating their war experiences, their progress in working through trauma is often arrested by official army psychiatry's insistence on surface narratives emphasizing closure at the expense of true insight—and on regaining legibility as a masculine subject within postwar society.

This insistence on surface rather than depth in the treatment of the psychoneurotic soldier is reproduced in the structure of the film itself, particularly at its conclusion. The final sequence of *Let There Be Light* underscores the relationship constructed by the film among notions of mental stability, the able body, and heteronormative masculinity. The soldiers complete their final group therapy session, reunite with their wives and girlfriends, and then, importantly, demonstrate their physical health. The viewer is shown the now-rehabilitated vets playing a baseball game, intercut with flashbacks highlighting not the soldiers' psychological trauma but the physical impairment it caused: the "kid at bat" no longer suffers the tremors he did just eight weeks prior and runs the bases with ease, and the young man who was treated for hysterical paralysis scores a home run his first time up at bat. The narration preceding this coda underscores that the one thing that will surely cure the psychoneurotic soldier is for him "to find someone . . . that [he] can learn to feel safe with," a romantic partner to substitute for the missing safety of childhood.[66] Thus, we see that the overall effect of *Let There Be Light* is to reproduce the narrative repeatedly extolled by the army psychiatrists at Mason General. The surface narrative of Huston's *Let There Be Light* attempts to fulfill a similar purpose for its viewers as the narrative given to the soldiers by their doctor, yet the film's authentic moments of self-disclosure remain unresolved by this narrative arc and are at odds with the didactic nature of the film. The end result is a film that cannot construct a stable meaning for the viewer. Psychiatrists give conflicting advice at different points, and many individual moments undermine the stability of meaning the film tries to create through the clear-cut narrative of rehabilitation it is unable to successfully maintain.

World War II–era War Department documentaries remain important documents for what they show about the relationship between Hollywood and the American military during and immediately following World War II, particularly due to the central role these films played in regulating and enforcing masculine norms during wartime and in the postwar period. The films John Huston produced for the American War Department between 1943 and 1946 are additionally notable for what they demonstrate about the documentary film project itself. Reading Huston's war documentaries against the grain not only reveals the conflicted ideological position of the last two films in the series but also opens up a space of inquiry into emerging modes of documentary representation that took a more cynical perspective on their subject matter and belied the increasingly invasive scrutiny to which masculinity was subjected in the years following the end of World War II.

NOTES

1. "Patton's Slap," *Newsweek*, December 6, 1943, quoted in Edgerton, "Revisiting the Recordings of Wars Past," 32–33.
2. Sedgwick, *Epistemology of the Closet*, 99.
3. The term "Melville's Fist" comes from an article written by Barbara Johnson entitled "Melville's Fist: The Execution of *Billy Budd*," in which Johnson examines the rhetorical effects performed by Melville's story: "It is a dramatization of the twisted relations between knowing and doing, speaking and killing, reading and judging, which make political understanding and action so problematic." As Johnson asserts, "the 'deadly space' or 'difference' that runs through *Billy Budd* is not located *between* knowledge and action, performance and cognition: it is that which, within action, prevents us from ever knowing whether what we hit corresponds to what we understand." Johnson, "Melville's Fist," 599.
4. Menninger, *Psychiatry in a Troubled World*, 133.
5. Barnouw, *Documentary*, 139, 157.
6. A number of scholars who have worked on Huston's War Department output reference this episode in their scholarship, including Edgerton, Garrett, and Bertelsen. Huston himself describes the episode in his autobiography, *John Huston: An Open Book*, explaining that on seeing the film for the first time, his supervisors accused him of making an antiwar film, to which Huston tells us he "replied that if I ever made a picture that was pro-war, I hoped that someone would take me out and shoot me." Garrett and Bertelsen both repeat the story more or less exactly as Huston tells it in his autobiography. Edgerton, "Revisiting the Recordings of Wars Past," 30; Garrett, "John Huston's *The Battle of San Pietro*," 9; Bertelsen, "San Pietro and the 'Art' of War," 249; Huston, *John Huston*, 119.
7. Kahana, *Intelligence Work*, 35.
8. Rabinowitz, *They Must Be Represented*, 8.
9. Bertelsen, "San Pietro and the 'Art' of War," 230–56.
10. Garrett, "John Huston's *The Battle of San Pietro*," 9.
11. Ibid., 31–32.
12. Brill, *John Huston's Filmmaking*, 111–19.
13. First coined by Williams in his 1954 "Preface to Film," the term *structure of feeling* names the distinct "effect of the totality" of a given historical period as it "is expressed and embodied" in a culture during a specific historical period, which "is only realizable through the work of art itself, as a whole." The structure of feeling of an era is the sum total of the impression created by the various elements of a culture that, when viewed as a whole, allow us "to reconstruct, with more or less accuracy, the material life, the general social organization, and, to a large extent, the dominant ideas." Williams, "Preface to Film," 611.
14. Ellis and McLane, *A New History of Documentary Film*, 80.
15. Kahana, *Intelligence Work*, 96.
16. Rabinowitz, *They Must Be Represented*, 102.
17. Ellis and McLane, *A New History of Documentary Film*, 89.
18. Kahana, *Intelligence Work*, 91.
19. Doherty, *Projections of War*, 42–43. The United States Film Service, a short-lived effort at organizing US government film production under one roof, was established by Roosevelt in 1938. Placed under the direction of Pare Lorentz, it was "intended to make films propagandizing the policies and activities of all departments of government" but was shut down in

1940. According to Ellis and McLane, film scholar Robert Snyder blames the termination of this service on congressional opposition to the New Deal and lack of sustained support for the program from President Roosevelt, as well as Hollywood opposition to the program and a negative reaction from the public to the bleak portrayal of the western and southwestern United States by Lorentz in films like *The Plow That Broke the Plains*. Ellis and McLane, *A New History of Documentary Film*, 86, 90.

20. Lorentz, quoted in Kahana, *Intelligence Work*, 121.

21. Rabinowitz, *They Must Be Represented*, 88, 87.

22. The phrase *itinerant intellectual* is Kahana's term naming the vocation of Depression-era New Deal documentarians. Kahana, *Intelligence Work*, 58.

23. Edgerton, "Revisiting the Recordings of Wars Past," 28.

24. Huston, *Report from the Aleutians*.

25. Huston, quoted in Edgerton, "Revisiting the Recordings of Wars Past," 29.

26. Edgerton, "Revisiting the Recordings of Wars Past," 29.

27. Bertelsen, "San Pietro and the 'Art' of War," 234.

28. Deleuze's taxonomy of the cinematic image, developed in his two-volume study of film focused largely on the postwar cinematic canons of Europe and the United States, distinguishes between the *movement-image*, created by the cinematic syntax of classical Hollywood continuity editing to produce an illusory coherence of both space and time from individual, isolated shots, and the *time-image*, characteristic of the cinemas of post–World War II Europe, which attempts to present a direct representation of the passage of time through long static shots anchored in a single locality and temporality. The close-up, or *affection-image*, is one type of shot that Deleuze argues can be used within the movement-image paradigm to momentarily arrest the viewer's attention to produce various effects. Elsaesser and Hagener, *Film Theory*, 60. A more detailed discussion of the movement-image and the time-image is found in this book's third chapter.

29. Balázs, quoted in Elsaesser and Hagener, *Film Theory*, 60.

30. Huston, *The Battle of San Pietro*.

31. Though the military intended the film to be made "specifically for American audiences on why the advance of the US Army in Italy had slowed to a virtual halt," and some (including the generals in charge of the project) interpreted it as a work of subversive protest, Huston said he undertook the project as a tribute to America's fighting men, stating that "it was anything but done out of hatred of war on my part. It was done out of a profound admiration for the courage of the men who were involved in the ghastly thing." Edgerton, "Revisiting the Recordings of Wars Past," 30; Huston, quoted in Edgerton, "Revisiting the Recordings of Wars Past," 30.

32. Kahana, *Intelligence Work*, 110, 113, 107.

33. Kahana references the FERA informational short *The New Frontier* as a prime example of deictical voice-over, citing lines of narration such as "While we're down this way, we'll drop in on one of the neighbors" and "Wanna know where the water comes from? All right, we all know the answers: here's the community water works" as examples of deictical speech's subtle emphasis of the "temporary hierarchy of speaker and addressee" characteristic of narration in New Deal social documentary. Kahana, *Intelligence Work*, 110.

34. Ibid., 107.

35. Edgerton, "Revisiting the Recordings of Wars Past," 30.

36. Huston, *The Battle of San Pietro*.

37. Benjamin, quoted in Rabinowitz, *They Must Be Represented*, 21. Benjamin also discusses the role of the caption in his essay "The Author as Producer," writing that "it goes without saying that photography is unable to say anything about a power station or a cable factory other than this: what a beautiful world! . . . For it has succeeded in transforming even abject poverty, by recording it in a fashionably perfected manner, into an object for enjoyment. . . . What we

require of the photographer is the ability to give his picture a caption that wrenches it from modish commerce and gives it a revolutionary useful value." Benjamin, "The Author as Producer," 230.

38. Rabinowitz, *They Must Be Represented*, 21, 22.

39. Kahana, *Intelligence Work*, 35, 38.

40. Kahana, *Intelligence Work*, 39; Edgerton, "Revisiting the Recordings of Wars Past," 31.

41. Edgerton, "Revisiting the Recordings of Wars Past," 30. While formally similar, direct cinema and cinéma verité are philosophically distinct. Barnouw notes the distinction in the following manner: "The direct cinema documentarist took his camera to a situation of tension and waited hopefully for a crisis; [in *cinéma verité*, the director] tried to precipitate one. The direct cinema artist aspired to invisibility; the . . . *cinéma verité* artist was often an avowed participant. The direct cinema artist played the role of uninvolved bystander; the *cinéma verité* artist espoused that of provocateur." Barnouw, *Documentary*, 255.

42. Kahana, *Intelligence Work*, 63, 38.

43. Doane, *The Emergence of Cinematic Time*, 22.

44. Edgerton, "Revisiting the Recordings of Wars Past," 33.

45. Rabinowitz, *Black & White & Noir*, 278.

46. Ibid., 158.

47. Ibid., 159.

48. Plant, "William Menninger and American Psychoanalysis," 183.

49. Additionally, Plant notes, "In large measure, this conviction arose from the experiences of World War II, when the U.S. Selective Service rejected a staggering number of men (1,100,000) on psychological and neurological grounds. Yet despite this extensive screening, during the war nearly 40 per cent of all medical discharges were for neuropsychiatric reasons (Herman, 1995). Frequently reiterated in the popular press, these alarming statistics created an image of a weak and emasculated citizenry, psychologically unfit to defend the nation (Furnas, 1945; Hersey, 1945; Lynch, 1945)." Plant, "William Menninger and American Psychoanalysis," 183.

50. Menninger, *Psychiatry in a Troubled World*, 5.

51. Ibid., 121.

52. Huston, *Let There Be Light*.

53. Ibid.

54. Siebers, *Disability Theory*, 79.

55. Huston, *Let There Be Light*.

56. Edgerton, "Remembering the Recordings of Wars Past," 35.

57. Huston, *Let There Be Light*.

58. Ibid.

59. Menninger, *Psychiatry in a Troubled World*, 131.

60. Huston, *Let There Be Light*.

61. Ibid.

62. The Lawrence quotation Deleuze and Guattari discuss here is taken from a scene in Lawrence's novel in which Lilly and his wife criticize Jim Bricknell for his repeated infatuations with younger women. Deleuze and Guattari, *Anti-Oedipus*, 359, 334.

63. Huston, *Let There Be Light*.

64. Doane, *The Emergence of Cinematic Time*, 13, 14.

65. Huston, *Let There Be Light*.

66. Ibid.

3

TACTILE VISIONS

Disability, Prosthesis, and the Problem of
Recognition in Postwar American Cinema

IN AN INTERVIEW PUBLISHED IN the *New York Times* on November 17, 1946, William Wyler states that his primary goal in making *The Best Years of Our Lives* was to create a realistic depiction of the struggles veterans faced in returning from World War II, claiming that "great pictures can't be entirely fictitious." In the interview, Wyler continues, "The trouble with Hollywood is that too many of the top people responsible for pictures are too comfortable and don't give a damn about what goes up on the screen so long as it gets by at the box office."[1] *The Best Years of Our Lives* was, in fact, both a commercial and critical success despite a frank treatment of postwar American realities that is fairly unique within the canon of post–World War II Hollywood cinema. Wyler's desire for historical verisimilitude led him to cast a disabled nonprofessional actor, Harold Russell, as one of the film's three protagonists. Although he had not acted in commercial films prior to *The Best Years of Our Lives*, Russell appeared in a 1945 War Department documentary, *Diary of a Sergeant*, that depicts the rehabilitation of a soldier who learns to use metal prosthetic hooks in place of his hands following a training exercise injury and subsequent double amputation. Though Russell's name is not specifically mentioned in the film, it draws on the circumstances of his injury in presenting a narrative of physical rehabilitation in line with the broader goals of the American War Department documentary project. This documentary, released a year before *Let There Be Light*, follows a narrative trajectory similar to Huston's film; although *Diary of a Sergeant* depicts the rehabilitation of physically disabled veterans rather than a recovery narrative for individuals suffering from the psychological wounds of war, both films rely on similar cultural notions of masculinity in constructing their plots.

Wyler takes up themes present in *Diary of a Sargent* with more complexity in *The Best Years of Our Lives*, focusing on World War II's destabilization of notions of family and masculinity as normatively constructed in postwar America. Although the film portrays the experiences of three men returning from the war, each of whom faces his own struggles reentering society, Wyler focuses in particular on the exclusion Russell's character experiences due to his physical difference from other men around him. The ex-military man's disability stages a renegotiation of masculinity in a subject whose physicality once epitomized maleness, challenging assumptions about the boundaries demarcating normative bodies and demonstrating that masculinity cannot be understood apart from the symbolic network of an ableist culture. Unresolved formal tensions within *The Best Years of Our Lives* complicate the film's genre classification and its presentation of both normative and nonnormative masculinities through the representational excess created by Wyler's casting of a disabled nonprofessional actor to play Homer Parrish, the film's physically disabled protagonist.[2]

In *The Best Years of Our Lives*, Homer Parrish's disabled body serves primarily as a visual marker of difference from cultural norms of heteronormative masculine identity, provoking discomfort in other characters (and potentially in viewers) as a disruption of specular masculinity constructed within traditional cinema. For this reason, this chapter considers at length the implications of presenting a disabled protagonist for notions of cinematic identification within the primarily visual system of signification described and critiqued by feminist psychoanalytic film theory. When I turn to a phenomenological understanding of film spectatorship near the end of the chapter, I aim not to invalidate a former body of scholarship but to consider an additional dimension of experience in specific moments of *The Best Years of Our Lives*, moments in which an able-bodied spectator might be both encouraged and challenged identify—on a corporeal level—with a body visually marked as different from theirs.

This chapter also serves as a counterpart to chapter 2 of *The Illegible Man* in that it turns to rehabilitation narratives focused on physical rather than psychological trauma—and the depiction of these narratives in Hollywood feature film rather than in War Department documentary film. Whereas the previous chapter of this book discussed John Huston's borrowing of devices from fictional film narratives to tell the stories of subjects drawn from real life, this chapter touches on Wyler's incorporation of documentary aesthetics in his filming of a fictional narrative in *The Best Years of Our Lives*. These two chapters, taken together, thus present a limited investigation of the increased use of documentary coding in fictional film as a device to convey filmic verisimilitude, a trend that informs the war film genre in particular even today. Ultimately, however, the aim of this chapter is to continue to advance this book's primary argument regarding disability and masculinity as increasingly fraught intertwined sites through which American national identity was both contested and reconstituted in hegemonic terms following World War II.

REMASCULINIZATION AND REHABILITATIVE MEDICINE IN *DIARY OF A SERGEANT*

From the start, *Diary of a Sergeant* consciously aestheticizes the events it presents, beginning with a prologue dramatizing the amputation of Harold Russell's hands. Viewers are introduced to the film's protagonist abruptly— we see the soldier's face briefly as a trauma team rushes him into an operating room on a gurney, anesthetizes him, and prepares him for surgery. The details of the operation are only implied. Low angle shots approximate the point of view of the patient as he lies on his back, the top of his head in view at the bottom of the frame, his face obscured by the bulky facemask of a World War II–era anesthesia vaporizer. The sequence ends with a dissolve transitioning to an image of a hand writing in the pages of a diary dated June 6, 1944. A voice-over explains, "This was the day I lost both my hands," and a quick cut introduces the startling sight of Russell lying prone in a hospital bed with his handless arms bandaged and suspended above him in a position reminiscent of a gesture of surrender.[3]

The opening sequence of *Diary of a Sergeant* foregrounds Russell's dependence on others and the physical limitations he now faces as a double amputee. When the camera returns to the previous shot of the protagonist in bed, we see that a female nurse writes Russell's diary entries for him; a voice-over emphasizes the sailor's helplessness, explaining, "On this June day in 1944, someone else's fingers were writing down my words in my diary. But there just weren't any words for many of the things I thought of."[4] Ironically, the film also deprives Russell of speech, as the voice we hear speaking the man's words throughout the film is not his own but that of an anonymous voice actor, a narrative choice on the part of the film's director that literalizes one of the primary modes of representation working to stigmatize disability: "from folktales and classical myths to modern and postmodern 'grotesques,' the disabled body is almost always a freakish spectacle presented by the mediating narrative voice."[5] The film's monologue further highlights the young man's sudden feelings of lack as he reinterprets memories from his past from this new perspective: "Like remembering a kid's party where they tied my hands behind my back and made me take a bite out of an apple hanging by a string. I thought of the time in the meat market where I worked before the war, when I sliced the tip of my right middle finger and had to get along with my left hand for a week. Just the tip of one finger, and I was fifty percent helpless." Here, Russell's words generate pathos by hinting at the fragility of all bodies while emphasizing the permanence of the young man's new condition. Like most able-bodied people, Russell has experienced temporarily disabling situations in the past, but his old memories take on a new horror as they come to underscore that this disability is not a temporary condition. He wonders how he will get by "now, with stumps instead of fingers, and palms, and wrists. . . . How would it be," he asks, "when I couldn't even handle a cigarette by myself?" This sense of helplessness is made more palpable by the envy the protagonist feels toward disabled veterans who "got theirs in combat," unlike Russell, whose injury resulted from a stateside training exercise that ironically occurred on D-Day. Unlike the wounded men he meets in rehab, Russell notes, "I didn't have a German scalp hanging from my belt. I didn't have a purple heart. I didn't even have an overseas ribbon—all I had was no hands."[6]

The implicit purpose of the film's extended prologue is to emphasize the emasculating nature of Russell's disability and the newfound difference he feels from his old self; like *Let There Be Light*, the narrative of *Diary of a Sergeant* is one of masculinity reclaimed through rehabilitative medicine following war-related trauma. Initially, Russell resigns himself to a life of feminine pursuits like "knitting sweaters for the Red Cross . . . with [his] feet" until he sees a War Department short documentary feature, *Meet McGonegal*, about a disabled veteran of World War I who uses prosthetic hooks to do "all the everyday things [Russell] never thought [he'd] do again." Inspired by the promise of living a "normal" life, Russell throws himself into rehabilitation.[7] Garland-Thomson argues, "The meanings attributed to extraordinary bodies reside not in inherent physical flaws, but in the social relationships in which one group is legitimated by possessing valued physical characteristics and maintains its ascendency and self-identity by systematically imposing the role of cultural or corporeal inferiority on others. Representation thus simultaneously buttresses an embodied version of normative identity and shapes a narrative of corporeal difference that excludes those whose bodies or behaviors do not conform."[8] By including a sequence in which convalescent soldiers watch a visibly disabled man work his prosthetics on-screen as a part of their own rehabilitation, *Diary of a Sergeant* dramatizes the role of received images and cultural narratives in the rehabilitative process and, more generally, the process of identity formation itself: not until Russell's character in the documentary is shown a depiction of what successful rehabilitation looks like is he able to even conceive of living a fulfilling life with his new disability, let alone to begin his process of reintegration into society. The remainder of the film details Russell's physical rehabilitation and accompanying social readjustment to a life with prosthetics. A crucial aspect of this narrative is thus Russell's reclamation of his sense of masculinity. Part of the rehabilitative process depicted in the film is a social hosted by the military on behalf of the convalescent men during which amputees learn to dance on their prosthetic legs. In fact, the film confronts with surprising frankness the effect of Russell's disability on his confidence with women. During a sequence in which the protagonist receives a furlough from his rehab to return home, Russell considers approaching a young woman who shares his train car but decides against it for fear that his prosthetics might frighten her; here, he confronts the dilemma of having to choose between his functional prosthetic hooks and ornamental "dress hands that look natural covered with gloves," which might be less off-putting visually but would render him largely helpless.[9]

Once home, however, Russell displays for the camera a superior control of his utilitarian prosthetics—in sequences like those depicted in *Meet McGonegal*—as he is shown showering, washing his face, and brushing his teeth. The film's only reference to the lasting aftereffects of the war's violence occurs when the narrator notes that "there aren't many men left in our neighborhood since the war" and that, for this reason, no one has been present to help his mother perform masculine tasks in her son's absence. Ventriloquizing Russell, the narrator takes care to explain: "Nothing [else] had changed at home . . . Everything else was the same" as before the war.[10] Yet despite the documentary's upbeat conclusion, this sequence obliquely references many ways the United States *has* been changed by the events of World War II, and the entire film subtly underscores the extent to which notions of the normative family and the masculinity of both individual soldiers and the nation as a whole are at stake in this new, uncertain world.

GENRE TROUBLE: HISTORICAL TRAUMA AND
THE GENDERING OF MELODRAMA

Wyler decided to cast Russell in *The Best Years of Our Lives* after seeing *Diary of a Sergeant*. Impressed with the young man's performance in the documentary, the director became interested in the soldier's personal narrative, incorporating elements of Russell's experiences depicted in the documentary into the fictional narrative of his film. Discussing the circumstances surrounding the film's conceptual development with Thomas M. Pryor, a writer for the *New York Times*, Wyler states, "We decided to take up this boy where *Diary of a Sergeant* left him and show him returning home fully readjusted and determined to live among other people and to act like them in every respect. We wanted to show people that these disabled men were thoroughly capable of doing ordinary things with artificial hands; that we, in fact, are the ones who are maladjusted, since we annoy and embarrass them with our patronizing attentions." Although Wyler's comments anticipate aspects of a constructivist view of disability—locating America's "disability problem" following the war in the fabric of society rather than in the individual bodies of wounded veterans—his remarks nonetheless emphasize the importance that normative conceptions of the body retain in narratives of rehabilitation, in which the disabled soldier's goal is to "live among other people and act like them in every respect."[11] In Wyler's narrative, Homer Parrish (Russell's character) returns home after losing his hands in an aircraft carrier fire that ends his military career; he encounters difficulty negotiating newly altered relationships with his loved ones while adjusting to the physical limitations he, like his real-life counterpart, now faces. While the fictional film borrows a number of elements from its documentary precursor in its depiction of the physical effects of the main character's disability, Wyler's narrative emphasizes to a greater degree the notion of disability as a complexly embodied, culturally located identity that destabilizes normative conceptions of masculinity, as Parrish is troubled more by altered relationships with his loved ones than by the physical limitations of a double amputee.

Wyler's desire to create a film "written by events" within the Hollywood studio system creates formal tension in the film itself, which plays out both aesthetically and narratively.[12] *The Best Years of Our Lives*, notable among post–World War II American films for its frank and nuanced depiction of physical disability, uses conventions of melodrama to explore how wartime injuries destabilize notions of gender and sexuality in the postwar world, despite Wyler's use of a documentary aesthetic in shooting parts of the film. By using melodrama to explore the hardships faced by a disabled veteran, *The Best Years of Our Lives* inverts the gender dynamics of a genre that has traditionally explored women's issues since World War II; this subversion of genre underscores Parrish's fraught relationship to his masculinity as he learns to live with a dependence on others that runs counter to the self-sufficiency emphasized in his military background. Yet all three protagonists in the film face problems conforming to the normative masculine roles awaiting them on return to the United States following their military service. Where Homer Parrish must reclaim his masculinity through marriage, Fred Derry and Al Stevenson must reclaim theirs through integration into the postwar economy, which has been transformed by social changes that occurred while they were away at war. Heightening all three men's struggle to take up the mantle of postwar masculinity are their individual difficulties processing wartime traumas: Stevenson has developed a drinking problem that prevents him from functioning in his upper-class position as a bank manager and Derry clearly suffers from posttraumatic stress, but Parrish is the character most pointedly excluded from reintegration into postwar life due to his physical disability.[13] Linking all three protagonists' postwar experience in *The Best Years of Our Lives* is frustration with feelings of passivity running counter to heteronormative notions of masculinity.

While Homer Parrish's struggle to reintegrate into postwar life following his injury is the most pronounced source of conflict in *The Best Years of Our Lives*, the character's disability (and the passivity it signifies) stands in for a broader crisis of masculinity also faced by Fred Derry and Al Stevenson, the film's other male protagonists, who encounter similar—if seemingly more surmountable—challenges as they try to rejoin the lives and families they left behind. All three veterans must, ultimately, prove their ability to establish their position as head of a normative family unit within the changing landscape of postwar America despite the obstacles they face as a result of their war experiences. While Wyler presents Derry's and Stevenson's recoveries from psychological wartime traumas as inseparable from their reintegration into the world of work, his film links Parrish's recovery of his masculinity almost exclusively to the success of his relationship with Wilma; other aspects of his new life as a civilian, such as work, remain largely unaddressed.

Following World War II in particular, the physical and mental trauma of war, as well as the unique challenges faced by returning veterans like Parrish, irrevocably altered our understanding of both the male body and masculinity as an identity category. Kaja Silverman argues that the violence of World War II, coupled with the conflict's broader social effects, caused the fundamental breakdown of masculinity as a stable epistemological category precisely because "our 'dominant fiction' or ideological 'reality' solicits our faith above all else in the unity of family, and the adequacy of the male subject" as normatively constructed.[14] Returning from war, men subjected to traumas (both historical and personal) found they could no longer recognize themselves in the cultural narratives they once easily inhabited: in the postwar world, it was difficult, especially for the "family man," to come home.[15] Melodramas of the post–World War II period responded to this historical moment by expressing these anxieties obliquely through depictions of the domestic sphere, incorporating an ideological dimension at times overlooked in considerations of the genre that focus on its visual elements, such as the frequent use of a color-saturated mise-en-scène to express the emotional inner lives of its (often female) protagonists. Christine Gledhill argues that post–World War II melodrama often concerns "a bourgeoisie 'decaying from within' in Eisenhower's America," while Susan Hayward notes how these postwar films reflect "the social order . . . through the personal" to express different valences of oppression experienced within postwar family dynamics.[16] As it centers on the fraught nature of the American family following World War II, *The Best Years of Our Lives* certainly qualifies as a melodrama, yet the film's focus on male characters negotiating their relationships to redefined masculine roles in the postwar context pushes the boundaries of the genre by bringing out contradictions present in the gender roles inhabited by the film's protagonists. Like later postwar melodramas such as those made by Douglas Sirk, *The Best Years of Our Lives* shows clear concern with a loss of faith in the very notions that constitute the American dream of postwar prosperity. Yet where Mary Ann Doane has argued that melodramas of the post–World War II period tend to express a female protagonist's anxieties regarding the limitations of small-town life in middle America through depiction of claustrophobic domestic settings, *The Best Years of Our Lives* reveals subtle pessimism regarding the postwar dream by showing that, following World War II, male veterans met similar anxieties regarding feelings of passivity after returning from war and rejoining the families they left behind.[17]

In "Masculinity as Spectacle: Reflections on Men in Mainstream Cinema," Steve Neale argues that male figures undergo an entirely different process than female figures when subjected to the cinematic gaze due to the different erotic registers of male bodies in cinema and because the male protagonist's subject position is often defined in opposition to the passivity that defines the female figure in traditional cinema. Neale writes that in films focusing on heteronormative male relationships, the erotic nature of the gaze must be repressed in order to allay homophobic anxieties resulting from the display of a male body to another man, but this repression of eroticism "seems structurally linked to a narrative content marked by sado-masochistic phantasies and scenes . . . especially evident in those moments of contest and combat . . . at which a narrative becomes pure spectacle." Here, male bodies are "stylized and fragmented [and] heavily mediated by the looks of the characters involved" much like female characters subjected to cinema's traditional male gaze, but unlike women rendered passive by the cinematic apparatus, male figures subjected to the same process are characterized by "bodies unmarked as objects of erotic display," looked on "not by desire, but rather by fear, or hatred, or revulsion." Homer Parrish anticipates—and sometimes receives—just such a gaze from those he interacts with, but, unlike Parrish, most able-bodied specularized masculine figures in film retain the perceived potency associated with the traditional male hero in narrative cinema.[18] These notions of American masculinity emerged in part out of a postwar experience that differed greatly from countries that experienced wartime violence on their own soil for the duration of the conflict.

Tony Judt argues that World War II, by considerably reducing the male population of many European countries and Europe's presence on the world stage, allowed the United States to rise as a world power while producing a European continent feminized by wartime violence. The aftermath of World War II caused countries that had experienced violence directly to reassess their future roles as players on the world stage; this was particularly true in Europe. Under fascism, national myths depended on heteronormative notions of masculinity for coherence. After the war, the diminished status of the post-fascist male subject rendered fascist ideology untenable, while the devastated landscape of postwar Europe served as an ever-present reminder for those living in European countries of the war's unprecedented levels of violence and destruction.[19] The physical landscape of the United States, left largely untouched by war, stood in stark opposition to the disorder of postwar Europe. Returning from war, disabled American GIs learned to live with damaged bodies that presented a constant reminder of the lasting impact of wartime violence otherwise absent in America's pristine postwar landscape; these men faced pronounced difficulties reintegrating into American society, largely due to the destabilizing effect of physical disability on traditional, heteronormative notions of masculinity. Moreover, cultural narratives elided deep uncertainties regarding the fate of the traditionally gendered equation of wife and family despite the United States' increased role as a world power. As Hayward notes, male unease surrounding the newfound economic independence of women who had entered the American workforce during wartime, as well as more general dissolution resulting from "the failure of the post-war American ideology to deliver promises," led to anxiety that—though not always directly expressed within the dominant culture—was certainly present during the period. This anxiety often found expression in texts produced by an influx of foreign-born directors who, like Wyler, came to Hollywood during the 1930s and 1940s and could view "the contemporary United States and American masculinity in crisis . . . from a distance."[20] Central to this crisis was the contradiction between a masculinity defined through action and dominance and a more complex reality that undermined straightforward narratives of America's place of dominance in the postwar world.

FRAUGHT MASCULINITIES, MARKED BODIES: THE POSTWAR LANDSCAPE AND THE POSTWAR MAN

In *Postwar: A History of Europe Since 1945*, Judt considers at length the uncertainties faced by Europe in the aftermath of World War II and the way these forces influence global politics to this day, arguing that the cumulative effect of World Wars I and II was the dissolution of coherent myths by which people and nations of Europe made sense of themselves and their place in the world. Yet because the discrediting of European illusions that began in the aftermath of World War I did not reach full realization until the end of World War II, the postwar period that came to define the modern age followed the second "great war," not the first.[21] If we are to use World War II as a demarcation point for understanding the present, however, we must view the war and what followed it not teleologically but through the eyes of Walter Benjamin's Angel of History: "Where we perceive a chain of events, he sees one single catastrophe which keeps piling wreckage upon wreckage and hurls it in front of his feet."[22] Notions of masculinity are clearly implicated in this wreckage, as Judt notes when discussing the diminished status of European males—in number and stature—following the war: "Much has been made of [the] over-representation of women in postwar Germany especially. The humiliated, diminished status of German males—reduced from the supermen of Hitler's burnished armies to a ragged troupe of belatedly returning prisoners, bemusedly encountering a generation of hardened women who had perforce learned to survive and manage without them—is not a fiction."[23]

Films produced by Americans and Europeans alike after the war express concern and fascination with the situation described by Judt in the above passage. Billy Wilder's *A Foreign Affair* (1948) captures scenes of a bombed-out Berlin with a documentarian's eye while its plot uses the upheaval of gender roles as material for a screwball comedy, only hinting at deeper implications of the instability of sexual categories in the postwar context. Through its reliance on Hollywood formulas mandating the closure of all narrative threads to satisfy the audience, *A Foreign Affair* demonstrates the impulse "to make whole what has been smashed" in the aftermath of war and uses humor to comment on the tenuous place of the postwar man in gendered relationships.[24] Throughout the narrative, the film's male protagonist, Captain John Pringle, demonstrates American mastery of a feminized postwar Berlin by flouting army regulations, participating in the black market, and maintaining an illicit relationship with Erica Von Schlutow, a cabaret singer and former Nazi hiding from the authorities in Berlin. Siobhan S. Craig argues that in *Foreign Affair*, "American masculinity—newly refurbished in military supremacy—collapses, its vacuity as an epistemological category undermined by the chronic inability of an American soldier to maintain gender stability as he crosses and recrosses its ruptured boundaries."[25] *A Foreign Affair* thus demonstrates the way in which, in the postwar context, destruction of the European landscape further serves to feminize the continent, much like a disabled body can implicitly feminize the masculine subject.

Wilder made *A Foreign Affair* just three years after he was commissioned by the United States Department of War to direct *Death Mills*, the first film to document the Allies' discovery of Nazi atrocities during the liberation of Europe. *Death Mills* is a harrowing but relatively straightforward example of the documentaries produced by the US government during and after World War II in support of the war effort; *A Foreign Affair* uses documentary footage of postwar Berlin shot by Wilder with the aid of the War Department, intercut with scenes shot on a soundstage, to reinforce the fictional film's illusion of verisimilitude. As Craig notes, Wilder's fictional account of postwar Berlin begins with a clear revision of Riefenstahl's *Triumph of the Will* (1935) as a lone American military aircraft descends from the sky over the ruins of postwar Berlin. Where Riefenstahl's film depicts a godlike Hitler descending over a natural landscape that gradually gives way to the orderly urban space of Nuremberg, Wilder's film begins with shots that mirror Riefenstahl's in point of view but show an urban Germany reduced to rubble by Allied bombs. The implied relationship between the opening sequences of these two films is clear: the illusion of order imposed by fascism has been destroyed by American military might, conferring on the Allied forces the mastery of land and air once forcibly maintained by Hitler's Third Reich. This sequence (and its correspondence to its fascist antecedent), Craig argues, "foregrounds the intense ambivalence that suffuses this film about the aftermath of Nazism."[26] Inside the American aircraft, a team sent to Berlin to aid in reconstruction efforts discusses the wreckage visible from its privileged vantage point. Though most of the talk focuses on the specifics of bombing campaigns, one member of the team notes that Berlin now "looks like chicken innards at frying time."[27] Through this simile, rendered in the stereotypical American vernacular of Hollywood, one sees subtle linkage between a landscape ravaged by war and an abject, mutilated body.

Tropes linking landscape and the body are almost always gendered. Yet where this trope traditionally genders the landscape as a feminine entity acted on by masculine forces, the broken landscapes of Europe in the postwar context come to be associated with the abject bodies of male subjects renegotiating their relationship to masculinity. In *Postwar*, Judt notes the parallel between the disruption of masculinity as a stable epistemological category and the disruption of cityscapes as a result of wartime destruction of European cities. His book opens with a descriptive passage evoking scenes of destruction that, for him, offer "a prospect for utter misery and desolation." Judt writes, "Photographs and documentary films of the [postwar period] show pitiful streams of helpless civilians trekking through a blasted landscape of broken cities and barren fields. Orphaned children wander forlornly past groups of worn out women picking over heaps of masonry. Shaven-headed deportees and concentration camp inmates in striped pajamas stare listlessly at the camera, starving and diseased. Even the trams, propelled uncertainly along damaged tracks by intermittently available electric current, appear shell-shocked. Everyone and everything—with the notable exception of well-fed Allied occupation forces—seems worn out, without resources, exhausted." Judt's description none too subtly emphasizes the spectacle of postwar destruction captured by American and European filmmakers in documentary and fiction films. Of note in this description of recently liberated Europe is the conspicuous absence of men, or at least of specific reference to them, until the very end of the passage. Postwar Europe is a landscape of "pitiful and barren fields" and "heaps of masonry" populated by "orphaned children" and "worn out women," placed in opposition to "well-fed liberators," implicitly male.[28] Although Judt notes the limitations of understanding the reality of postwar Europe solely through received images like these, his language nonetheless demonstrates the extent to which gender is implicated in depictions of postwar wreckage. The landscape has been feminized by wartime trauma, but this feminization is shown to demonstrate *male* lack. Moreover, Judt describes the postwar landscape using metaphors of bodily injury: French coastal towns "eviscerated by the U.S. air force" are only one example in an exhaustive catalog of destroyed cities that "serve as a universal shorthand for the pity of war." While Judt argues that World War II and its aftermath ultimately produced the birth of a new Europe, the author frames his argument by highlighting markers not of birth but of death and dismemberment, absence and loss; these images serve as metonymic signifiers linking abject bodies and fraught masculinities to a landscape likewise violently altered by war.[29]

Germany Year Zero, the final—and bleakest—film in Roberto Rossellini's war trilogy, explores the dark side of gender relations in postwar Germany, focusing directly on the effects of the dissolution of fascism on the psyche of German males. The film details the last days in the life of Edmund, a thirteen-year-old German boy forced to shoulder the full weight of manhood while his brother, Karl-Heinz, hides to avoid prosecution as a war criminal and his father wastes away from the effects of an unnamed, consumption-like illness. Edmund spends most of his time wandering aimlessly through the rubble of Berlin, not only in a desperate attempt to find work to help feed his family but also to avoid the bombed-out apartment he, his father, brother, and sister share with five other families. In his narrative, Rossellini explores at length the diminished nature of German males in postwar Germany—in fact, male characters in the film repeatedly comment on just this fact. Men still sympathetic to Nazism, like Edmund's former teacher Herr Enning, continue to equate masculinity with the ideology plainly seen crumbling around him: "A fine situation we're in. Before, we were still men, National Socialists. Now we're just Nazis." Under the dominant fiction of National Socialism, masculinity was synonymous with status as a soldier or membership in the Nazi Party. Now that these terms have been decoupled, masculinity is set adrift in a sea of uncertainty, and the word *Nazi* is a synonym for *criminal*, or worse. Edmund's family and those around him note his father's illness as a burden ("All that fuss with their father—tea, hot water bottles, hot compresses. This can't go on."); this literal sickness also functions metaphorically for the state of all post-fascist German men. "Sick! We're all sick!" comments the nameless patriarch of Edmund's shared household when one of his daughters defends Edmund's family's use of limited shared resources to care for their ailing father. He tells his daughters, "No one has it any better," implying that his statement "We're all sick" refers all Germans, yet all the figures explicitly associated with illness in the film are male.[30]

Illness, Susan Sontag notes, often figured in Nazi rhetoric for all "that corrupts morally and debilitates physically"—anything violently excluded from the fascist dominant fiction.[31] Of note in *Germany Year Zero* is the way metaphorical illness destabilizes the masculine subject. For Silverman, "'male' and 'female' constitute our dominant fiction's most fundamental binary opposition"; the dominant fiction influences all aspects of personhood for subjects seeking recognition within its narrative, and its "many other ideological elements . . . all exist in metaphoric relation to these terms [and] they derive their conceptual and affective value from [the] relation" of a male/female binary opposition.[32] This binarism more fundamentally structures the ideological makeup of fascist states and, as such, renders their dominant fictions particularly unsustainable. In his study of the German Freikorps, volunteer armies organized by officers returning from World War I to quell populist uprisings among the German working class, Klaus Theweleit argues that fascist ideology is built on the violent exclusion of the feminine from the psyche of the male subject. Theweleit argues that although this exclusionary impulse structures the construction of all masculine subjectivities under fascism, it operates most explicitly in soldiers. The Freikorps in particular interests Theweleit because its members later became the core of Hitler's SA and, in some cases, key figures in the Third Reich.[33] In her forward to volume I of Theweleit's *Male Fantasies*, Barbara Ehrenreich notes that, while it would be an oversimplification cite this organization as the sole source of fascism's rise in Germany, it is clear that the "organizational strength . . . of the Freikorps" played a key early role in shaping the relationship between German fascism and masculinity.[34] Theweleit argues that in documents recording how these soldiers related to women—largely the men's own letters—one sees the formation of masculinity through an exclusionary matrix producing a binarism associating women with fluid elements of the physical landscape (bodies of water) and males, both physically and psychologically, with rigid elements of the landscape: "a body with fixed boundaries." For Theweleit, recurrent images of floods in the soldiers' letters represent the threat femininity exerts on the soldier-male's body, and the author points to examples from letters showing "the way in which soldier males freeze up, become icicles in the face of erotic femininity." This erotic femininity can be literal or figurative. Theweleit writes, "By reacting in that way, in fact, the man holds himself together as an entity, a body with fixed boundaries. . . . Now when we ask how that man keeps the threat of the Red flood of revolution away from his body, we find the same movement of stiffening, of closing himself off to form a 'discrete entity.' He defends himself with a kind of sustained erection of his whole body, of whole cities, of whole troop units. Junger: 'Only steely individuality could hold out there without slipping into

the whirlpool."[35] This process of masculinity emerging through materialization resonates with Foucault's understanding of the soldier's malleable,
docile body militarized over time as "he [learns] the profession of arms little
by little." The machine-like body of the soldier emerges from a process of
materialization, maintained through an ongoing, internalized self-policing
of the body itself. Foucault writes that "the soldier has become something
that can be made; out of a formless clay, an inapt body, the machine required
can be constructed; posture is gradually corrected; a calculated constraint
runs slowly through each part of the body, mastering it, making it pliable,
ready at all times." Yet through the obsessive (if largely unconscious) focus on individual body parts necessitated by this process, the soldier-male
implicitly acknowledges that his body is not "an indissociable unity" but a
construction that must constantly be re-produced through a reiterative process.[36] The body of the soldier-male, then, comes to "matter," as all gendered
bodies do.[37] Hence, the soldier-male is constantly aware of literal and figurative threats to his bodily continuity and, implicitly, his masculinity: "The
flood is close at hand, then, either in oneself or on the outside. The men seem
to relate every actual or imminent flood directly to themselves, each one
to his own body. The terrain of their rage is always at the same time their
own body; this feeling is found in every single utterance associated with the
'Red flood.'"[38] The flood imagery through which the men of the Freikorps
imagined threats to the stability of their masculine bodies clearly resembles
a metaphorical understanding of illness as "a ruthless, secret invasion" to be
countered by aggressive treatments in military terms. For this reason, illness
is a particularly effective metaphor as used by Rossellini in *Germany Year
Zero* to signify the dissolution of fascist masculinity in postwar Germany.[39]

Moreover, Rossellini's film dramatizes the implications of fascism's collapse on a German understanding of family predicated on fascist notions
of heteronormative masculinity. In *Germany Year Zero*, Edmund's status
as child limits his ability to help his family survive the harsh conditions of
postwar Berlin. The film's opening shots evoke Judt's description of a postwar European landscape in which everything, from spatial codes to gender
norms, seems irrevocably disrupted. Early in the film, in the context of these
images, Edmund is denied work digging graves because he is too young and
begins to wander aimlessly through the literal and figurative rubble surrounding him. Unsupervised, he comes under the influence of his former
teacher, who continues to espouse Nazi ideology. Edmund discusses his family's dire situation and his father's ill health with Herr Enning, who advises
him that "life is a cruel struggle for survival where one must deal mercilessly

with the weaklings [who] are just a burden to us." Edmund takes this advice literally, poisoning and killing his father. Although Enning recoils in horror when he learns what Edmund has done, Slavoj Žižek notes that Edmund's response—"You just talked about it, I did it!"—"in no way suggests a shift of responsibility to the teacher." Edmund's statement is merely "a cold, impassionate ascertaining of the . . . absolute *gap* that separates words and deeds." Žižek's argument that the film does not represent "a story of how the morally corrupted Nazi ideology can spoil even a child's innocence and induce him to accomplish patricide" but rather that Edmund's "act . . . cannot be properly located [and] is therefore somehow interminable" demonstrates the near complete collapse of ideology in this postwar context. Yet this indeterminacy is what makes the film so unsettling: for Žižek, Edmund's patricide is "at the same time an act of supreme cruelty and cold distance *and* an act of boundless love and tenderness, attesting that he is prepared to go to extremes to comply with his father's wishes." Rossellini underscores the instability of the Nazi dominant fiction in the events leading up to the film's finale. Edmund, trying to sell a recording of one of Hitler's speeches, plays it on a portable phonograph for two British soldiers: "all of a sudden, Hitler's voice resounds through the debris-filled hallways; the accidental passersby grow stiff marveling at the sudden appearance of this uncannily familiar voice." This scene, which juxtaposes images of ruin irreconcilable with Hitler's statements regarding the grandeur of the Third Reich, emphasizes not just, as Žižek argues, "the invisible pervasiveness of the corrupt Nazi ideology" but also its now obvious falseness. The juxtaposition between sound and image lays bare the untenability of the fascist "will to totality" by which "the dominant fiction neutralizes the contradictions which organize [its] social formation [through] the non-recognition of the infinite play of differences," as described by Silverman.[40]

For Edmund, who had previously fully taken up fascist ideology, Nazism's dissolution is also his own. In the film's haunting final minutes, the child wanders alone through the rubble of Berlin, and somehow, we know he is headed toward his death. As Žižek notes, "A group of children refuse to let him join their game . . . so he awkwardly plays hopscotch alone for a few moments, but he is unable to let himself go into the game—childhood is lost for him."[41] He begins a long, slow climb into a deserted building and the heart of the rubble of postwar Berlin. He stops periodically, peering through the large holes in the broken walls at the rubble below, foreshadowing his suicide. Picking up a discarded piece of metal that is uncannily pistol shaped, he ponders it, placing its barrel-shaped end to his forehead. Reaching the building's top floor, he is strangely isolated even in his solitude. He seems not to hear as his family members, who have been searching for him, call to him from the street, and he leaps to his death in the rubble below an open widow; Edmund, a sacrificial witness to the ideological dissolution of the postwar world, ends his own life, engulfed by the postwar rubble.

The Problem of Recognition: The Disabled Veteran and Masculinity as Spectacle

The uncertain postwar realities faced by America following World War II, though less obviously visible than those of Europe, similarly challenged notions of American masculinity based on mastery of one's environment. Scenes early in Wyler's film foreshadow the struggles its protagonists will face in returning home from war, as the trio of veterans views the American landscape from the vantage point of an airplane, much like the protagonists of *A Foreign Affair*. In this case, however, the plane carries American veterans returning home from the Pacific and European theaters, and the landscape in question is not war-torn like Japan's or Germany's; here, Wyler's images and dialogue underscore the difference between the overseas and American postwar experience in comparison to Wilder's film. As the men sit in the nose of the plane and watch the midwestern countryside— divided into even sections of farmland—pass, their conversation turns to the markers of postwar prosperity they see below them: roads and automobiles. Parrish, who served in the navy on a flattop aircraft carrier before his injury, comments on the surprise he feels witnessing the beauty passing beneath him during this, his first ride in an airplane, remarking that he "never knew things looked so pretty" from above. Derry, a former bombardier, replies, "I never thought so. This used to be my office." In the scenes that follow, there is subtle foreshadowing of the separation each of the film's protagonists will feel from the American postwar dream. Here, through glass and from above—what was once, during the war, a position of dominance—postwar America is something these men can see but not touch; the distance between them and home is already palpable. Subsequent shots in the sequence reinforce Derry's comparison between this "nice view of the good old USA" and the vantage point he previously occupied when dropping bombs over Germany as Wyler presents viewers with images evoking newsreel footage of bombing runs.[42]

While discussing the American landscape passing below, the protagonists pointedly reference what will serve to prevent their reintegration into American society—most notably for Homer Parrish, the loss of his hands and the prosthetic hooks the navy gave him as a replacement. Although his family already knows of his injury, he worries that Wilma, his high school sweetheart, will no longer love him because of his disability: "Wilma's only a kid. She's never seen anything like these hooks," he states. Following this reference to his injury, Parrish recalls his career as a celebrated high school football player just before the three men see a new airport full of decommissioned warplanes waiting for the scrap yard, destined to be "stripped of their engines and propellers . . . like Homer, disabled and unwanted."[43] This scene, and its pointed comment on the perceived value of surviving soldiers who sacrificed their bodies for their nation, serves to connect Parrish's disability to broader uncertainties facing the American man in postwar America. Additionally, Wyler refers back to these images in the film's climax, as Fred Derry recalls his own psychological war trauma before overcoming his posttraumatic stress.

Unlike Homer Parrish, Fred Derry reintegrates comparatively easily into postwar life, in part because his trauma is psychological and not physical and, as such, is not subject to the same stigmatization physical disability is shown in the film to elicit. His primary obstacles to reintegrating into home life are his class and the recurrent flashbacks he suffers, as he is unable to process the wartime trauma he experienced when his plane caught fire and crashed during his final bombing run. His poor job prospects, however, do not prevent him from attracting the eye of a fellow veteran's daughter, and his vulnerability—revealed to his sweetheart when she discovers him having a nightmare about his plane crashing—only increases her attraction to him; nevertheless, his posttraumatic stress is shown to be the central obstacle to his happiness. After being fired from his drugstore job for punching a customer who was harassing Homer, Derry walks to the local junkyard where old military aircraft are turned to scrap metal for building prefabricated houses and wanders among rows of planes in various stages of disassembly. Shots of twin-prop planes missing both engines, which appear to have been sawed off, visually recall Homer's severed hands: these planes, used up by war and discarded when no longer useful, clearly stand in for soldiers who sacrificed their bodies for their nation. Derry approaches a bomber like the one in which he used to fly and climbs into his "old office," the bombardier's perch in the nose of the plane. Here he relives his trauma one last time, coming out of his reverie when the junkyard owner demands to know what he is doing. Sympathizing with Derry, the owner offers him a job. This moment coincides with Derry's ability to get his memories "out of his system," as he says: the cure for Derry's trauma is his reintegration into the world of work, and his recovery follows almost miraculously.[44]

Thus, *The Best Years of Our Lives* connects issues of space, place, and postwar trauma in ways that parallel European cinema of the time, further underscoring differences between the European and American postwar experience. For Gilles Deleuze, Italian neorealist films like *Germany Year Zero* demonstrate a postwar collapse of both "the sensory-motor schema which constituted the action-image" of prewar cinema and the sensory-motor coherence of human bodies. Deleuze argues that the traumas of World War II specific to Europe propelled European film into the future—like Benjamin's Angel of History—leaving American films behind, at least in terms of formal innovation. Deleuze notes that the postwar innovations of European films are inseparable from their thematic interest in bodies and landscapes irrecoverably altered by the violence of war. He characterizes the protagonist of the neorealist films made following the war as a person experiencing metaphorical paralysis in the context of a disrupted physical landscape like the one Judt describes in *Postwar*. The postwar masculine subject is *defined* as passive rather than active in the context of spaces that retain traces of wartime destruction: "these were 'any spaces whatever,' deserted but inhabited, disused warehouses, waste ground, cities in the course of demolition or reconstruction. And in these any-spaces-whatever a new race of characters was stirring, a kind of mutant: they saw rather than acted, they were seers." In Italian neorealist films in particular, Deleuze observes the emergence of a new type of sight, unfettered by tired Hollywood clichés, tied to the impaired mobility and sensory disruption many individuals experienced in the context of World War II's destruction of Europe. This new vision plays out as time is represented in film directly through long static shots rather than the aestheticized camera movements of classical Hollywood continuity editing. Thus, Deleuze writes, in neorealism "the character has become a kind of viewer. He shifts, runs, and becomes animated in vain, the situation he is in outstrips his motor capacities on all sides, and makes him see and hear what is no longer subject to the rules of a response or an action. He records rather than reacts. He is prey to a vision, pursued by it or pursuing it, rather than engaged in action."[45] The disruption of film's sensory-motor schema identified by Deleuze in the context of Europe's fractured postwar landscape necessarily undermines traditional notions of cinematic masculinity. Laura Mulvey argues that the masculine spectator's identification with the male protagonist is contingent on identification with notions of mastery associated with masculine subjectivities, which become spectacle when subjected to the mediation of the cinematic apparatus. The male protagonist of classical cinema defines himself through superior command not only of the situations he must by necessity overcome but also of his own body: he is "a figure in the landscape [who] can make things happen and control events better than the subject/spectator, just as the image in the mirror was more in control of motor co-ordination" during the Lacanian mirror stage of childhood.[46] In *The Best Years of Our Lives*, Homer Parrish is prey to vision precisely because his altered physicality stands apart from his surroundings, the unmarred landscape of America surrounding him on his return from war. Yet the junkyard scene of *The Best Years of Our Lives*, by depicting the space wherein the debris of war (whether human or purely material) can be successfully reintegrated into the postwar economy, presents us with a uniquely American any-space-whatever. It shows the interaction between the workings of capital and the postwar dominant fiction of the United States while elucidating the difference between Derry's and Parrish's postwar experiences, despite the clear associations between them presented in the film. Derry, who is able bodied and whose psychological disability is assumed to be temporary, can, unlike Parrish, take on a new masculine role at the film's conclusion by realizing his value in the economy as a worker, even if his new job lacks the glamour and status he enjoyed as a pilot and military officer. Parrish, who now defines himself mainly through his visible physical difference from other men, is not offered the same opportunity in Wyler's narrative.

The emphasis placed on Parrish's highly visible disability in the film illustrates the impact of the character's altered physicality on both himself and others. Wyler's camera repeatedly focuses on Homer's prosthetics, linking his sense of social dislocation to the visual markers of his perceived difference from other men around him. The film's first scene introduces not Parrish but Fred Derry, highlighting how Derry's working-class status limits his reintegration into postwar America following his honorable discharge from the air force. He is forced to wait several days for a plane to take him home to Boone City after arriving in the States, while a wealthy man receives preferential treatment from the airline and is allowed to board a plane with the same destination immediately after offering to pay for his sixteen pounds of excess baggage. Likewise, Parrish's introduction scene foregrounds how his disability—like Derry's class—informs the response he receives when interacting with others, yet unlike the economic subtext subtly present in Derry's introduction scene, the scene introducing Homer focuses entirely on the struggles he faces as an amputee. When Fred Derry meets Parrish while waiting for the military transport that will take them home, onlookers pause uneasily as Parrish takes a pencil from a desk clerk to sign his name after the clerk offers to do it, assuming Homer's prosthetics prevent him from doing so. Here, the film establishes how Parrish's disability often impacts him socially more than physically, as he exceeds the expectations placed on him by others and eagerly demonstrates the ease with which he can accomplish tasks requiring complex motor skills with the aid of the hooks the navy has trained him to use as hands. Later, when Parrish refuses help lighting a cigarette, his disability becomes spectacle as the viewer wonders at the fluidity of motion with which Parrish lights cigarettes for himself, Derry, and Stevenson.[47] As the three men smoke, he lists off the activities his prosthetics allow him to perform: "I can dial telephones, I can drive a car, I can even put nickels in a jukebox. I'm all right."[48]

Yet despite his apparent confidence within the predominantly male environment of the navy, Parrish clearly remains anxious about his reunion with his family and, in particular, with Wilma. As the cab taking the three men home after they land in Boone City, Iowa, pulls up in front of Parrish's childhood home, Wyler frames the three men in the car's rearview mirror, sitting lined up in the backseat. Homer nervously suggests they stop at a bar rather than drop him off: clearly, all three men share anxieties regarding their homecoming reunions. However, subsequent scenes further demonstrate how Homer's disability pointedly excludes him from the postwar life he desires as, at times, the loss of his hands places him in a passive position irreconcilable with normative notions of masculinity. Central to Silverman's thesis in *Male Subjectivity at the Margins* is that "our dominant fiction calls upon the male subject to see himself, and the female to recognize and desire him, only through the mediation of images of an unimpaired masculinity." In her reading of *The Best Years of Our Lives*, Silverman argues that "Homer's lack positions him in the relational position usually reserved for the female subject within classic cinema" specifically because of his disability: "He has lost his hands—and with them his power to be sexually aggressive. . . . Every night, his wife will have to put him to bed, and it will be her hands that will be used in making love."[49] Yet by defining Homer's position exclusively through his lack, Silverman's argument elides a more complex reading of his disability. In *Disability Theory*, Tobin Siebers argues that a theory of "complex embodiment" is necessary to understand disability, postulating a reciprocal relationship between social representations and the body wherein "the body and its representations [must be seen as] mutually transformative." Complex embodiment theories seek to modulate constructivist theories of the body by raising "awareness of the effects of disabling environments on people's lived experience of the body [while emphasizing] that some factors affecting disability . . . derive from the body."[50] *The Best Years of Our Lives* uniquely underscores the reciprocal relationship between bodies that differ physically from what is considered normal and social structures that constitute these understandings of embodiment; this presentation of disability pushes against the framework of traditional psychoanalytic film theory.

Although the film shows Homer at his most vulnerable when he allows Wilma to see him without his prosthetics as she helps him undress before bed, an earlier scene shows with more complexity how disability influences the negotiation of masculine subjectivities when a group of neighborhood children—including Homer's sister—witness one of Homer and Wilma's tentative early interactions. Looking for Homer, Wilma finds him practice shooting in the shed behind his parents' house. As Homer finishes shooting and cleans his gun, their conversation broaches the subject of his injury and what it means for their relationship, but only subtextually. Homer says his marksmanship is now "only fair," and Wilma responds, "You did fine," attempting to persuade him that he still has mastery of his masculinity. When they discuss the status of their relationship explicitly, Homer looks into the gun barrel to clean it, and Wilma asks anxiously if the gun is loaded. Homer rebuffs her question, saying, "Of course it isn't. Don't you think I know how to handle a gun?" As they talk, the children gathered outside watch through a window. Homer, noticing them, shouts, "You want to see how the hooks work? You want to see the freak?" and shoves his hooks through the window, shattering his reflection and terrifying the children on the other side.[51] This is the most notable in a series of scenes in which reflections in mirrors and windows figure prominently to demonstrate the three main characters' feelings of dislocation from the postwar world they have rejoined but from which they remain distant. Although it is tempting to read the aforementioned exchange as a scene in which Parrish confronts the illusory nature of bodily coherence established during the Lacanian mirror stage in childhood, this formulation alone does account for the destabilizing influence of the presence of the neighborhood children on Homer and Wilma's private attempt to negotiate the terrain of their newly altered relationship. What we see instead in this scene is evidence of the intersubjective nature of the body as understood by Jean-Paul Sartre: the body not only exists in relation to the self but "exists also *for-others*."[52] Prior to coming home, Homer seems more or less comfortable with his new appendages; it is not until his disability forces him to renegotiate his relationships with friends and loved ones that he begins to see himself, through their eyes, as a "freak."

Parrish's sense of embodied self is emphasized here as a social location—but a very complex one. This scene, in which Homer struggles as a disabled man to take up the mantle of masculinity, shows the difficulties inherent in parsing disability identity. Disabled bodies clearly destabilize the "exclusionary matrix by which [gendered] subjects are formed, [which] requires the simultaneous production of a domain of abject beings, those who are not yet 'subjects,' but who form the constitutive outside of the domain of the subject," as described by Judith Butler in *Bodies That Matter*.[53] Thus, disabled bodies, excluded as they are by dominant ideologies, offer a cogent critique of the forces producing normative notions of sex and gender. Yet while it is clearly a culturally located position, disability also uniquely clarifies Butler's often debated position on corporeality. Even if we think of the body itself as a construction, doing so in no way undermines the felt reality of the body for anyone, whether they consider themselves disabled or not. Moreover, it is Parrish's *perceived* lack that places him outside the traditional masculine position within classic cinema, which "impose[s] masculinity as a 'point of view.'"[54] Just as Homer struggles with his own passivity, his visual presentation acts as a stumbling block to the viewer seeking to identify with a masculine protagonist. The heightened realism achieved through Parrish's portrayal by a visibly disabled actor defamiliarizes the character's body, undermining the process of identification central to how cinema makes meaning. Cinematic vision itself rests on a denial of passivity: "film must at all costs conceal from the viewing subject the passivity of that subject's position" through the suturing of the viewer's gaze to that of the cinematic apparatus, which Silverman refers to explicitly as the metaphorical "suturing over of a wound." Suture is successful, Silverman writes, "at the moment when the viewing subject says, 'yes, that's me' or 'yes, that's what I see.'"[55]

For Silverman, "Harold Russell's double amputation does not 'make the movie spill over into the real world,' but it does situate the image of Homer Parrish's arms on a different level of representation than the rest of the film." Silverman writes, "At every other point, there is a dimension of performance or simulation to which the stumps and hooks cannot be subsumed. Russell's injury is no more 'present' than any other profilmic event; it too is recorded, and its 'unfolding' is purely 'fictive.' However, in this instance the filmic representation exercises a strong referential pull, seeming to point beyond the text and Russell's acting to his body and the traces left there by the war." Here again, Silverman resorts to the trope of male lack to explain even the realism of Russell's portrayal of Parrish in the film. Russell's lived physical body and the lack experienced by the character he plays become nearly inseparable in Silverman's analysis. Because of the reality of Russell's amputation, she explains:

> Homer's stumps and compensatory hooks constitute a crisis not only of vision but of representation—a crisis which is the result of combining documentary detail with the spectacle of male castration. . . . There is a sort of doubling up of belief, a reinforcement of the disavowal Metz and Comolli identify in the cinematic experience [that] *negates the cinematic signifier* [my emphasis], inclining the spectacle even more precipitously than usual towards the referent or object. Yet at the same time what most passes for "the real thing" in *The Best Years of Our Lives*—what provokes the representational "lurch" toward the profilmic event—is precisely what classic cinema is generally at most pains to deny, and against which it marshals such protective measures as projection, disavowal, and fetishism: male lack.[56]

Notably, Silverman uses the language of physical experience to describe the representational effect Russell's disabled body evinces in its signification of a fictional character's embodiment: you do not "lurch" with your eyes—you lurch with your body.[57] It is clear from the above passage that despite the privileging of the visual throughout Silverman's argument, there remains some representational excess of signification directly related to Wyler's use in *The Best Years of Our Lives* of a disabled nonprofessional actor in the role of Homer Parrish. Silverman's language—slipping from the visual to corporeal—seems to indicate that scenes that focus directly on the visual evidence of Parrish's amputation evince in the critic a response that cannot be fully accounted for within the paradigm of visual signification.

"Fleshing Out" the Visual

In disability studies, analyses of the stigmatization of disabled people often focus on how visible disabilities elicit cultural stigma. Disability identity might thus be understood as the experience of an intersubjective relationship wherein it is almost always a nondisabled viewing subject whose vision others the disabled individual according to a perceived visual difference from cultural versions of normalcy. This understanding of the intersection between disability identity and the forces of an ableist culture squares well with both constructivist understandings of the body and psychoanalytic theories of film that liken cinematic signification to a linguistic system as understood by poststructuralists. Film foregrounds visual signifiers in its production of meaning and, as such, provides an ideal text through which to understand the modalities of physical disability as culturally understood.

Film theories that focus on the role of visual perception and the spectator provide important insight into this understanding of disability, but disability—as specific cultural formation—necessarily alters accounts of film as system of signification that focus primarily on visual aspects. As this chapter has already shown, the formulation of the gaze as understood by feminist psychoanalytic apparatus theory can be productively applied to the depiction of disability in a film like *The Best Years of Our Lives* to understand how the stigma attached to visible physical disability destabilizes the position traditionally occupied by the masculine subject in mainstream American cinema. Yet film clearly does not read gender and disability identically, partially because gender and disability are distinct identity categories and partially because meanings attached to gendered bodies by the male gaze are distinct from meanings attached to visual signifiers of disability by the same gazing subject. Garland-Thomson notes, "If the male gaze makes the normative female a sexual spectacle, then the stare [elicited by disabled bodies] sculpts the disabled subject into a grotesque spectacle. The stare is the gaze intensified, framing [the disabled] body as an icon of deviance. . . . The stare is the gesture that creates disability as an oppressive social relationship. And as every person with a *visible disability* [my emphasis] knows intimately, managing, deflecting, resisting, or renouncing that stare is a part of the daily business of life."[58] Disabled people are described as being *seen* as different and, as a result, are often understood as *feeling* this difference as a feature of their embodiment. An attempt to account for the felt reality of disability, and a tendency to privilege this subjective aspect of disability experience, has led many scholars in disability studies to criticize purely constructivist formulations of embodiment exemplified in particular by Butler but also by Foucault. In a polemical move that exhibits a common complaint with constructivist understandings of the body as well as poststructuralism more generally, Siebers criticizes Butler's account of embodied subjectivity, which privileges "the pain of *guilt* [my emphasis] to produce conformity with what she calls the 'morphology' of the heterosexual body," arguing that "pain in current body theory is rarely physical."[59] For Siebers, poststructuralist theorizations of the body do not "feel" disability and, as such, cannot take full account of disability identity. This view reduces the implications of Butler's insights into the materialization of embodied gender and sex norms to feelings of exclusion from those norms through a rejection of the basic insights of their reformulation of embodiment. In a similar vein, academic film theory has taken a "bodily turn" in an effort to more fully account for the subject position of the film viewer than the primarily visual paradigm of psychoanalytic film theory affords.

Theorists like Vivian Sobchack argue that "more often than not, the body, however privileged, has been regarded as an object among other objects—most often like a text and sometimes like a machine" in the visual paradigm currently dominant in film theory.[60] Phenomenological film theorists posit that the visual paradigm of psychoanalytic film theory overprivileges the eye and constructs an ontology of film that ignores the input of other sensory organs in its understanding of how cinema makes meaning. For these theorists, vision alone cannot fully account for film's impact on the viewing subject because "the perceiving subject is itself defined dialectically as being *neither* (pure) consciousness *nor* (physical, in itself) body." Phenomenological accounts of the experience of film foreground aspects of this experience mediated in the body—tactilely rather than visually—because consciousness itself cannot be understood as "a pure self-presence"; as such, "the subject is present and knows itself only through the *mediation* of the body, which is to say that this presence is always mediated, i.e., is indirect and incomplete."[61] Sobchack reformulates the cinematic viewer as traditionally understood as a *cinesthetic subject* that "both touches and is touched by the screen—able to commute seeing to touching and back again *without a thought* and through sensual and cross modal activity."[62]

This bodily turn in film theory presents a potentially productive moment for disability scholars seeking to engage with film studies beyond discussions of social stigmatization because disability studies and embodiment film theory both tend to see the physical body and its representations as mutually constitutive. Moreover, disability theory and theories of the embodied spectator often make similar rhetorical moves in their reconsideration of the relationship between the body and image culture. Yet it is crucial to note that Sobchack's formulation of a cinesthetic subject also represents an inward turn for film theory, focusing (by her own admission) on intensely subjective individual responses to the tactility of the film viewing experience. In her view, we feel what is projected on the screen through an identificatory process that inscribes on-screen experiences onto our own physical bodies such that "my body's intentional trajectory, seeking a sensible object to fulfill this sensual solicitation, will *reverse its direction* to locate its partially frustrated sensual grasp on something more literally accessible. That more literally accessible sensual object is *my own subjectively felt lived body*."[63] The scene in which Homer Parrish breaks the window of his father's shed as his fiancée and the neighborhood children watch seems a natural site to apply a cinesthetic perspective, given the scene's intense combination of visual and tactile elements. In this scene, Parrish's response to the voyeuristic eyes of the neighborhood children represents a rare moment of actual violence in the film. Here, by "show[ing] . . . how the hooks work," Parrish performs his own abjection; yet, somewhat counterintuitively, it is in this performance that abjection undoes itself as a subject position.[64] For Kristeva, an encounter with the abject at its "most elemental" provokes a bodily response regardless of whether the stimulus provoking the response is visual or tactile. She explains that "when the eyes see or the lips touch that skin on the surface of milk—harmless, thin as a sheet of cigarette paper, pitiful as a nail paring—[she] experience[s] a gagging sensation and still, farther down, spasms in the stomach; and all the organs shrivel up the body, provoke tears and bile, increase heartbeat, cause forehead and hands to perspire."[65] Even purely visual experiences often elicit bodily responses; more importantly, even involuntary bodily responses to encounters with the abject are always already informed by the cultural forces that structure subject formation.

It is in this moment, when Parrish is most at prey to vision, that the tactile erupts violently from the scene in a sudden crystalizing moment through the literal shattering of the glass in which Parrish has only previously been reflected. This is both a visual and a tactile shock—a sensory overload implicitly connected to the unseen trauma that happened to Parrish's hands prior to the film. We are given vicarious access to the experience of trauma at the center of the film, but only for a moment: we not only see the violence that was done to Parrish's hands but also, in a limited sense, feel it as violence done to us. The crucial question, however, is, What is actually accomplished filmically by this shattering of glass? It is tempting to say that, here, the able-bodied viewing subject no longer just sees Parrish's disability—they *feel* it as well. As Parrish's hooks crash through glass, the cinesthetic subject vicariously inscribes the corresponding pain onto their own fleshy hands (pain, crucially, that Parrish's metal appendages do not themselves feel). Sobchack argues that "the cinema, while encouraging a certain bodily knowing, also, and in that very process, opens up the recognition of a peculiar kind of non-knowing, a sort of bodily aphasia, a gap which sometimes may register as a sense of dread in the pit of the stomach, or in a soaring, euphoric sensation. . . . Out of these tensions are generated a series of differences, gaps or discontinuities between knowing and feeling that sometimes sharpen into a sense of the uncanny."[66] Thus, the imperfect match between the cinesthetic subject's vicarious bodily experience and the fictional experience projected on-screen is actually a productive disjuncture, a gap that produces meaning. It is crucial to note, however, that the tactile elements of this particular scene in no way overturn the primacy of the visual in the film; they merely present a way of undoing, for a moment, the oft-criticized, seemingly inscrutable hierarchical relations of the visual regime of psychoanalytic film theory. The stigmatization Parrish faces in the film remains primarily visual. It is the tactile, working in conjunction with the visual—not in opposition to it—that opens a space in the regime of vision demonstrated by the film, yielding a potential moment of radical empathy with the disabled subject on screen and briefly destabilizing the "social relationship between people that is mediated by images" described by Guy Debord in *The Society of the Spectacle*, which produces among its subjects perceived unity but actual separation.[67]

Although the vulnerability present in Wyler's depiction of all three veterans prevents easy identification with any of the three protagonists throughout his film, it is Homer Parrish's remasculinization that remains most pointedly unresolved at the film's conclusion. The final scenes of *The Best Years of Our Lives*, by once again creating spectacle from Parrish's disability, prove so unsettling to notions of normative masculinity as to undercut the apparent reclamation of masculinity the other two protagonists have undergone and even the narrative closure of the film itself. Silverman notes that "the contact of flesh and steel" as Homer and Wilma recite their vows belies the anxiety still surrounding their marriage, crystallizing the "crisis of vision" that structures Homer's intersubjective relationships.[68] Similar visuals used by Wyler connecting all three protagonists throughout the film take on a broader resonance in this final scene as Parrish's disability comes to signify a dislocation from society for all three men. Although the focus has returned to the visual in the film's denouement, the final image of hooks touching hands is made more haunting and resonant through its evocation of the previously discussed moment of "tactile" perception and the partial, vicarious identification this offers the able-bodied spectator. The visual disjuncture of "the contact of flesh and steel" retains a trace of tactile signification, broadening the resonance of the film's conclusion. Ultimately, in *The Best Years of Our Lives*, Parrish's impairment stages a sudden loss of masculinity not because of the physical limitations his character faces but due to the disruption of specular masculinity the character's highly visible disability presents, demonstrating the extent to which masculinity itself cannot be understood apart from the symbolic network of an ableist culture.

Notes

1. Pryor, "William Wyler and His Screen Philosophy," 1.
2. Tod Browning's 1932 feature film *Freaks* is a clear predecessor to Wyler's film in its casting of nonprofessional disabled actors in prominent roles. Nancy Bombaci argues that the

film "pushes to the limit the public's tolerance for grotesque spectacles." Bombaci, *Freaks in Late Modernist American Culture*, 97. While *The Best Years of Our Lives* certainly departs from these aims in its presentation of Homer Parish, the inclusion of a visibly disabled serviceman in a mainstream Hollywood film in 1946 did push against the norms of the time for the representation of injured servicemen returning from combat.

3. Newman, *Diary of a Sergeant.*

4. Ibid.

5. Garland-Thomson, *Extraordinary Bodies*, 10.

6. Newman, *Diary of a Sergeant.*

7. Ibid.

8. Garland-Thomson, *Extraordinary Bodies*, 7.

9. Newman, *Diary of a Sergeant.*

10. *Diary of a Sergeant* contains no references to Russell's father, whose presence is not depicted in the film. As discussed later in chapter 3, in *The Best Years of Our Lives*, Homer Parrish's father takes on a caretaking role for his adult son until Homer is married. The elision of the presence of a father figure in *Diary of a Sargent* allows for a more straightforward narrative of heteronormative masculinity reclaimed, as we are not shown any renegotiation of a father and son relationship for the fictionalized version of Russell depicted in the documentary film. Newman, *Diary of a Sergeant.*

11. Pryor, "William Wyler and His Screen Philosophy," 1.

12. Wyler, quoted in Silverman, *Male Subjectivity at the Margins*, 66.

13. As noted in this book's second chapter, posttraumatic stress disorder (PTSD) was called *war neurosis, combat fatigue* or *combat exhaustion* after World War II, euphemistic terms representing a shift in tone from earlier descriptors of combat-related psychological ailments like *shell shock.* This shift in discourse was often addressed specifically in documentary films made by the US War Department in response to postwar anxieties regarding the mental stability of returning veterans (see, for example, the 1945 film *Combat Exhaustion.*) As Macor notes, "the term 'post-traumatic stress disorder' (PTSD) was coined after the Vietnam War." Macor, *Making "The Best Years of Our Lives,"* 5. I use this more contemporary term to describe Fred Derry's mental state throughout this chapter.

14. Silverman defines the term *dominant fiction* in the context of her argument as follows: "'Dominant fiction' is opposed here neither to an ultimately recoverable reality nor to the condition of 'true' consciousness. 'Fiction' underscores the *imaginary* rather than the delusory nature of ideology, while 'dominant' isolates from the whole repertoire of a culture's images, sounds and narrative elaborations those through which the conventional subject is psychically aligned with the symbolic order." Silverman, *Male Subjectivity*, 15–16, 54. Although Lacanian psychoanalysis provides much of the framework for Silverman's argument in *Male Subjectivity at the Margins*, her notion of the dominant fiction clearly references "a social relationship between people that is mediated by images" and results in perceived unity but actual separation, as described by Guy Debord in *The Society of the Spectacle.* Debord, *The Society of the Spectacle*, 12.

15. Silverman defines *historical trauma* as follows: "A historically precipitated but psychoanalytically specific disruption, with ramifications extending beyond the individual psyche," or "any historical event, whether socially engineered or of natural occurrence, which brings a large group of male subjects into such intimate relation with lack that they are at least for the moment unable to sustain an imaginary relation with the phallus, and so withdraw their belief in the dominant fiction." Silverman, *Male Subjectivity*, 55.

16. Gledhill, "The Melodramatic Field," 34, 14; Hayward, "Melodrama," 203.

17. Doane, "The Moving Image," 285. Wyler's film certainly belongs to a body of post–World War II texts intended to assuage public fears regarding the reintegration of veterans into postwar American society, as Chopra-Gant and Gerber foreground in their readings.

Both authors, however, acknowledge a cynical undercurrent fairly unique within the canon of postwar reintegration narratives running counter to the film's more positive surface message. Chopra-Gant, "Reinvigorating the Nation," 551; Gerber, "Heroes and Misfits," 31–37.

18. Neale, "Masculinity as Spectacle," 12, 14, 12.

19. Judt, *Postwar*, 13, 9, 13, 19.

20. Hayward, "Melodrama," 206.

21. Judt, *Postwar*, 2.

22. Benjamin, "Theses on the Philosophy of History," 257.

23. Judt, *Postwar*, 19.

24. Benjamin, "Theses on the Philosophy of History," 257.

25. Craig, "The Ghost in the Rubble," 72.

26. Ibid., 71.

27. Wilder, *A Foreign Affair*.

28. Judt, *Postwar*, 13.

29. Ibid., 16, 1.

30. Rossellini, *Germany Year Zero*.

31. In *Illness as Metaphor*, Sontag notes that "syphilis was to become a standard trope in anti-Semitic polemics. In 1933 Wilhelm Reich argued that 'the irrational fear of syphilis was one of the major sources of National Socialism's political views and its anti-Semitism.'" Sontag, *Illness as Metaphor*, 59.

32. Silverman, *Male Subjectivity*, 35.

33. The Sturm Abteilung, or SA, was a paramilitary organization that developed out of the Freikorps, the "volunteer armies . . . organized by German officers returing from [World War 1]," and was a crucial early element of the Nazi Party. For more information on the SA and its relationship to Nazism, see Theweleit, "Men and Women," in *Male Fantasies*, 20–23.

34. Ehrenreich, "Foreword," in Theweleit, *Male Fantasies*, x.

35. Theweleit, *Male Fantasies*, 244–45.

36. Foucault, "Docile Bodies," 135, 137. Notably, notions of the docile body critiqued by Foucault subtly inform language used to describe the rehabilitative project of military medicine: in *Diary of a Sergeant*, soldiers undergo large portions of their physical rehab in a wing of the hospital devoted to orthopedic occupational therapy nicknamed "The Workshop." Newman, *Diary of a Sergeant*.

37. As Judith Butler reminds us, sex "is a regulatory ideal whose materialization is compelled, and this materialization takes place (or fails to take place) through certain highly regulated practices" as "an idealized construct which is forcibly materialized through time." Butler, *Bodies That Matter*, 1.

38. Theweleit, *Male Fantasies*, 233.

39. Sontag, *Illness as Metaphor*, 5. Although Theweleit takes care to note that *Male Fantasies* is not concerned with homosexuality, latent or otherwise, the author's formulation of a threat to masculinity as a covert invasion "close at hand . . . either in oneself or on the outside" resonates not only with metaphorical understandings of illness but also with the operation of the closet as understood by Eve Kosofsky Sedgwick. The closet produces a binarism so unstable that "*every* impulse of *every* person . . . could be called homosexual desire." Sedgwick, *Epistemology of the Closet*, 92. This correspondence does not imply the simplistic understanding of fascism as repressed homosexuality criticized by Ehrenreich but rather demonstrates a complex interrelationship between heteronormative understandings of the body, wellness, masculinity, and sexuality. Ehrenreich, "Foreword," in Theweleit, *Male Fantasies*, xi.

40. Žižek, "Why Is Woman a Symptom of Man?," 39, 42, 40, 42; Silverman, *Male Subjectivity*, 54.

41. Žižek, "Why Is Woman a Symptom of Man?," 39.

42. Wyler, *The Best Years of Our Lives*.

43. Silverman, *Male Subjectivity*, 80.

44. Wlyer, *The Best Years of Our Lives*.

45. Of note in Deleuze's description of postwar sensory-motor impairment is its correspondence to the motor impairment characteristic of childhood, a time when one "shifts and runs" while trying keep up with surrounding adults, figures who "outstrip" the child's still-developing motor capacities. Often seen a few steps behind an adult, struggling to keep up, the neorealist child is a seer witnessing the postwar world from a unique vantage point, simultaneously privileged and fraught. Deleuze, *Cinema 2*, xi, 3. In *Germany Year Zero*, Edmund certainly qualifies as a "seer" in the neorealist sense, an individual whose unique relationship to Deleuze's any-space-whatever enables a dangerous understanding of postwar realities.

46. Mulvey, "Visual Pleasure and Narrative Cinema," 21.

47. Robert Eberwine notes that "the sharing and exchange of cigarettes serves as a significant way of demonstrating bonding among men in combat films. Virtually every new recruit into the armed services had to watch John Ford's *Sex Hygiene* (1944), a training film about venereal disease. Included in that film is a warning about sharing cigarettes. Later training films did not include this caveat, but, to the extent that sharing had at some point been presented as a potential risk, it is interesting to see how often the exchange of cigarettes signals the depth of a bond and trust among soldiers." Eberwine, "As a Mother Cuddles a Child," 157.

48. Wyler, *The Best Years of Our Lives*.

49. Silverman, *Male Subjectivity*, 42; Warshaw, quoted in Silverman, *Male Subjectivity*, 71.

50. Siebers, *Disability Theory*, 25.

51. Wyler, *The Best Years of Our Lives*.

52. Sartre, "The Body," 445.

53. Butler, *Bodies That Matter*, 3.

54. Mulvey, "Visual Pleasure and Narrative Cinema," 29.

55. Silverman, "Suture," 205.

56. Silverman, *Male Subjectivity*, 72–74.

57. "Lurch, n: A sudden leaning over to one side, as of a ship, a person staggering, etc. Also, a gait characterized by such movements. Lurch, v: To make a lurch; to lean suddenly over to one side; to move with lurches." *OED Online*.

58. Garland-Thomson, *Extraordinary Bodies*, 26.

59. Siebers, *Disability Theory*, 61, 63.

60. Sobchack, "What My Fingers Knew," 3.

61. Gary Madison, quoted in Sobchack, "What My Fingers Knew," 4.

62. Sobchack, "What My Fingers Knew," 71.

63. Ibid., 76–77.

64. Wyler, *The Best Years of Our Lives*.

65. Kristeva, *Powers of Horror*, 2–3.

66. Ibid., 75.

67. Debord, *The Society of the Spectacle*, 12.

68. Silverman, *Male Subjectivity*, 87.

4

RETURNS AND REPRESSIONS

Economies of Violence and Anxieties on the Home Front

IN HIS ESSAY "OF OTHER Spaces: Utopias and Heterotopias," Michel Foucault discusses spaces that, for various reasons, function nonhegemonically, presenting for those who visit or reside there an experience that departs from standard ways of being in the world. Heterotopias are localized and distinct from their surroundings, often set off by boundaries whose permeability functions as part of what defines the specialness of the space they delimit but do not quite contain. "Think of a ship," Foucault writes. "It is a floating part of space, a placeless place, that lives by itself, closed in on itself and at the same time poised on the infinite ocean, and yet, from port to port, tack by tack, from brothel to brothel, it goes as far as the colonies, looking for the most precious things hidden in their gardens." The ship, for Foucault, is "the heterotopia par excellence" due to its ability, as a "floating part of space," to function as a finitely delimited locality that remains distinct from its surrounding area, which exists continually in flux. Fixed and yet forever in motion, the ship delimits and contains while remaining part of an infinite field constituted by the ocean. Although this unique type of space has likely always existed for humans in some form, Foucault nevertheless considers heterotopic spaces to be defining of twentieth-century experience.[1] As such, it is perhaps odd that Foucault neglects to identify the heterotopic qualities of the airplane or the automobile in his account of other spaces. Though the heterotopia constitutes a type of space that—for him—typifies post-nineteenth-century experience, Foucault foregrounds in his discussion of heterotopia's space-delineating modes of transport that signify pre-twentieth-century modernity: boats, trains, and other technologies that form "closed or partly open" sites most directly associated with either the Industrial Revolution or eras that preceded it.

The airplane cockpit—a heterotopia unique to the twentieth century and later—is a central image of Dorothy B. Hughes's *In a Lonely Place*, her 1947 hard-boiled detective novel that tells the story of the dark homecoming of Dixon Steele, a former fighter pilot who stalks and kills women in an attempt to recapture the exhilaration he felt while aloft in a warplane: "that feeling of power and exhilaration that came with the loneliness of the sky."[2] Other spaces of the sort described by Foucault proliferate in Hughes's text and are sought out by her narrator as he moves about the nocturnal landscape of postwar Los Angeles searching for victims. *In a Lonely Place* is one of many texts set in the period in which it was written that tell stories of the America beneath the surface of the midcentury normalcy thought to characterize the lives of newly upwardly mobile Americans who benefited from the GI Bill and other state programs put in place following World War II that played a large part in the creation of the American middle class. Though stories like that of Dix Steele—veteran turned strangler of women—tended, as noted earlier in this book, to be sensationalized accounts with little correspondence to the actual lives of soldiers returning to the United States from Europe, hard-boiled detective fiction and noir films of the postwar period nevertheless belied cultural anxieties regarding the place of men in the postwar world. *In a Lonely Place* remains fairly unique in the canon of midcentury American pulp fiction in that the narrative features, instead of a femme fatale, a violent male figure who murders his first victim while serving abroad in England, the darkness inside him brought out during a foreign conflict and carried home on his return to America.

Hughes's novel is an American fiction haunted by European realities. Mary Louse Roberts has argued, for example, that the US military intentionally eroticized its presentation of the coming American liberation of Europe in order to motivate soldiers prior to the invasion of Normandy and that this sexualized rhetoric influenced how GIs treated the European women they encountered overseas. Billing military service as an "erotic adventure" for American GIs, who would be greeted as liberators by a grateful French citizenry—most notably, French women—these fantasies met with a reality that at times played out as sexual violence. The notion of twentieth-century Europe as an "other space" presenting, for American men in particular, an environment free of social mores functioning as a forum for self-actualization dates at least to the post–World War I years. The United

States' new global role following World War II as liberator and key player in the rebuilding of postwar Europe produced new valences in a narrative that otherwise presented an old story. Roberts writes that France's national body had begun to be eroticized in American discourse (and in the minds of GIs) in the years since World War I; at the conclusion of World War II, erotic fantasies of sexually available French women became suffused with the emerging power dynamics of the postwar period, played out between American soldiers and the European women with whom many GIs had sexual relationships during overseas deployments. France, as both an ally of the United States and a "conquered state" that had collaborated with its fascist occupiers, proved in the immediate postwar years to be a place where female citizens were particularly vulnerable to exploitation and sexual violence, a reality exacerbated by a visual rhetoric of American photojournalism and propaganda that participated in the "mapping of sexual relations onto American war aims."[3]

Roberts's focus on sexual relations between American GIs and French women highlights both how the eroticization of liberated France was part and parcel of broader War Department rhetoric and how the sexualization of wartime aims was emphasized differently in France than in other parts of the European theater. Roberts notes, for example, that the phrases "Kein Zigaretten! [No Cigarettes!]" and "Waffen niederlegen! [Throw down your arms!]" were considered "essential German" for all GIs likely to interact with German-speaking people as part of the war effort, whereas "crucial French phrases included 'Vous êtes très jolie. [You are very pretty.],' 'Vous avez les yeux charmants. [You have charming eyes.],' 'Je suis un general [I am a general.],' 'Je ne suis pas marié. [I am not married.],' and 'Vos parents sont-ils chez eux? [Are your parents at home?].'"[4] Though both translation guides mediated an American dominance of liberated Europe via conversational language translated for use by soldiers involved in the liberation, this domination played out differently in the two contexts. Conversational German taught to the American GI emphasized dominance in an explicitly wartime context, while conversational French phrases mapped this dominance onto sexual relations between American soldiers and the French women they would encounter during the liberation. *In a Lonely Place* presents a character like many male figures in postwar noir narratives, who feel isolated, disenfranchised, and excluded from promises the American Dream offered to men in the years following World War II. Hughes's novel, however, also examines masculine violence as a function of the misogyny often present in but not always critiqued by male-authored noir texts.

The first three chapters of *The Illegible Man* trace different modalities of disability as they interact with formulations of masculinity that emerged in response to historical and cultural crises of the mid-twentieth century. While these initial chapters touch on masculine violence as an aspect of male identity, this fourth chapter confronts more directly the way masculine subjectivity is constituted through the violent exclusion of terms seen to destabilize the identity of the masculine subject by association with otherness or alterity. In part, this chapter delves into repressed histories of the World War II era that played out on the American home front, exploring how these narratives intersect with normative and nonnormative formations of masculinity in different ways. It engages with genre texts like pulp and noir—those texts Paula Rabinowitz has argued express "the foundation for the masochistic fantasy" symptomatic of "mid-twentieth-century American culture."[5] To elucidate the violence inherent in the formation of heteronormative masculine subjectivity, I devote the first half of this chapter to a discussion of three texts that explore the policing of masculine identity through aggressively violent acts. This chapter begins with a discussion of Ann Petry's 1947 novel *Country Place*, which tells the story of the homecoming of Johnny Roane from the war in Europe as he questions his masculinity and acts out violently when he comes to suspect that his wife was unfaithful during the time they spent separated by the war. Set against the backdrop of small-town rural America, Petry's novel depicts an undercurrent of violence in American culture similar to the harsh realities explored in her debut novel *The Street* in 1946, substituting her first book's urban setting of 1940s Harlem for an idealized vision of postwar America she depicts as existing largely in the minds of *Country Place*'s white, middle-class characters. The chapter continues with a discussion of Richard Brooks's novel *The Brick Foxhole*, published in 1945, which details the lives of male soldiers deployed stateside during World War II and the emasculation they experience as a result of exclusion from overseas combat. The novel, set on the American home front near the conclusion of the war, explores the economy of violence that develops out of central characters' anxieties regarding the direction of male sexual desire into socially acceptable channels. Deprived of both the combat experience they believe would invest them with masculine potency and a socially acceptable outlet for sexual desire (as their deployment separates them from available women despite remaining in the United States while serving their wartime assignments), the men depicted in *The Brick Foxhole* express their perceived emasculation through eruptions of violence seemingly at odds with their surroundings far removed from a foreign war. Though both *Country Place* and *The Brick Foxhole* deal in part with soldiers' fears regarding infidelity on the part of their spouses during the war, these texts also grapple with the broad social effects of World War II on postwar American society, examining the intersection of class, gender, physical ability, and racial identity in narratives of returning veterans.

This chapter also touches on Ted Allenby's narrative from Studs Terkel's *"The Good War": An Oral History of World War II*, which details Allenby's experiences serving as a closeted marine at a time when the sexual identities of American soldiers were becoming increasingly policed. It shows the workings of the violence of signification in a subject whose internalized and often self-directed homophobia demonstrates the exclusionary impulse traced in the chapter's first sections. Allenby's sexual identity represents both something he views as the essential, defining feature of his being and something he might be able to exclude from his life through the practice of ritualized violence he hopes to find in military service. Taken together, the Terkel, Brooks, and Petry texts demonstrate the constitution of masculine subjectivity through violent exclusion of any term or impulse not permitted within the narrowly constituted nexus of ableist heteronormative masculinity in the late 1940s and early 1950s.

This chapter concludes with an extended reading of John Sturges's 1955 film *Bad Day at Black Rock*, which concerns events that unfold when a disabled American veteran returns to America and begins searching for the father of a Japanese American soldier who died saving his life during the Italian campaign, only to uncover that the man's father was the victim of a racially motivated murder while his son was away at war. *Bad Day at Black Rock* has been read by Philip F. Norden as a straightforward story of a disabled American soldier's remasculinization through further violent heroism following the war as he avenges the murder of his friend's father despite his disability. Norden's analysis, however, elides the subtle yet pervasive destabilization of heteronormative masculinity presented by the addition of the protagonist's disability to an action story published in *American Magazine* in 1947. *Bad Day at Black Rock*'s use of a disabled male figure as the protagonist in an action-oriented Western film complicates the equation of masculine sufficiency operating in this period to the extent that it largely disrupts the film's symbolic content in its conclusion, illustrating a fundamental breakdown of masculinity as a stable epistemological category in the postwar period and, ultimately, the futility of violence as both a literal act and a means of signification.

This chapter thus examines texts in which violence erupts, recurs, and returns as a symptom of a culture's attempts to repress or cast off male subjects whose presence is not easily reconciled with masculine subjectivity as constituted in postwar America, placing the previous chapters' readings of texts produced either during wartime or immediately following it in a broader historical and cultural context.[6] While the potential for masculine violence has been an undercurrent in many of the texts discussed in this book up to this point, this chapter turns to texts that meditate directly on the role of masculine violence in homecoming narratives produced in the late 1940s and early 1950s. While fears that returning veterans might act out violently if they failed to properly reintegrate into American society following World War II were certainly overstated in the immediate aftermath of the conflict, capacity for violence nevertheless remains one of the defining features of American masculine subjectivity as hegemonically constructed and understood.[7] The remaining two chapters of this book, therefore, grapple with the increasingly prevalent role masculine violence plays in American postwar narratives of social reintegration and rehabilitation from disabling injuries incurred during combat.

American Homecomings and Postwar Economies of Violence

Where William Wyler sets *The Best Years of Our Lives* in a romanticized, Hollywood version of small-town Iowa to emphasize his protagonists' displacement from idealized visions of postwar American prosperity on their return to the States, Ann Petry's *Country Place* deals with similar themes regarding the limitations of small-town life in the postwar context through focus on characters who lament the passing of simpler times as a fast-paced, urban lifestyle gains primacy. Against this backdrop, Petry explores undercurrents of masculine violence in postwar America through a narrative that draws heavily on hard-boiled fiction and noir films of the postwar period. In "Pulping Ann Petry: The Case of *Country Place*," an anthology chapter later expanded and included in her book-length project *American Pulp: How Paperbacks Brought Modernism to Main Street*, Rabinowitz details the harsh reviews Petry received for the novel following its publication in 1947, a departure from the critical acclaim the author had received for *The Street*. Rabinowitz argues that Petry's novels are best read as part of a pulp tradition—for insights that contrast dominant cultural narratives emphasizing an optimistic outlook for the United States following the war with the darker depiction of postwar America represented by noir fiction and film. In presenting an uneasy contrast between the "social chaos [that] appeared openly visible on the teeming city streets" of the postwar United States and "rural America, with its drowsy small towns and mid-sized cities built around a single industry [that] masked class and ethnic and racial tensions within mostly impenetrable homes and isolated landscapes," novels like *Country Place* explore contradictions structuring postwar American society often elided by more mainstream texts.[8] Petry presents *Country Place*'s narrative in the voice of Doc—the man who runs the town drugstore—to emphasize the novel's small-town atmosphere, draw contrasts between the attitudes of the town's white, mostly middle-class residents and those of the author herself, and lend a sense of voyeurism to a story mediated largely through small-town gossip. In this way, the novel depicts a pervasive discontent with small-town life on the part of many of its characters as the promise of postwar prosperity seems to have missed the town. Socioeconomic stagnation and cultural isolation thus serve as the backdrop for Johnny Roane's feelings of emasculation on his return to his hometown, as he and his wife must live with his parents in Roane's childhood home and sleep in a bed his mother purchased for his bedroom when "he was fifteen and growing fast and she said he needed a man-sized bed." It is here that Roane commits his first violent acts after returning from deployment overseas, raping his wife when she refuses his sexual advances and then attacking her again, convinced her reluctance to sleep with him is evidence of her infidelity.[9]

Country Place comments on the conflation of heteronormative masculinity and the able body in the postwar context when Roane's wife, Glory, notes the limitations placed on her by life in a small town devoid of able-bodied men during wartime. When Roane accuses her of being unfaithful in his absence the morning after he assaults her, Glory replies, "How could there be [anyone else]? There aren't any young single men left in Lennox. The ones who went off to war got married before they left. There's nobody around but old men and wrecks of young ones—the ones who came back without arms or legs."[10] Glory defends herself from her husband's accusations of infidelity by impugning men who remained stateside *and* men whose war experiences resulted in physical injuries as similarly undesirable sexual partners, doing so because she understands it will only exacerbate her husband's own feelings of inadequacy. Johnny's inability to live with his wife outside of his parents' home due to financial strictures undermines his ability to conform to cultural narratives of remasculinization from the period, which foregrounded the soldier's reintegration into postwar society through work and the promise of class mobility. The marriage bed Roane shares with his wife—ironically "man-sized" and provided by his mother—fails as a site for

Roane to enact remasculinization according to his understanding of masculine sufficiency. Johnny Roane's response when he encounters challenges to his narrowly defined version of masculinity is violence, and Petry undermines the efficacy of his acts throughout her narrative.

In this way, Petry's text demonstrates that even veterans who had escaped physical injury could be viewed as potential sources of social unrest and became figures embodying public concerns regarding sexual deviance following the war. Vets were seen, in the words of Glory, as having "gone queer in the head."[11] Rabinowitz notes that "by the mid-1930s, queer had come to mean both odd or crazy and homosexual or effeminate in American slang"; when Glory finally does sleep with local gas station owner Ed Barrel and Johnny finds out about it, Glory "defiantly declares she 'slept with Ed [because] he's a man and you're not.'"[12] Thus, pulp texts like *Country Place* demonstrate that public concerns over issues like the "veteran problem" were inseparable from broader cultural anxieties related to gender and sexuality and the racial and class tensions many mainstream narratives elided in their depictions of postwar America. Concerns among the American public surrounding disabled veterans could not be neatly separated from a broader crisis of American identity during the period.[13] Anxieties surrounding the sexual identities of returning soldiers were in fact often related directly to their status as veterans. Jennifer E. Langdon writes:

> As the war drew to a close and Americans contemplated the demobilization of millions of G.I.s, these competing representations of masculinity raised profound doubts about the very possibility of a "return to normalcy," both for civilians and the G.I.s themselves. Much of the postwar discourse on demobilization was dominated by the political concern that the returning veterans, damaged by their wartime experiences with violence, death, and military discipline, might be vulnerable to the lure of fascist demagogues. However, experts were also deeply concerned that the war had unleashed an aggressive and dangerous male sexuality. Of particular concern were the intense homosocial (and potentially homoerotic) bonds created by the war experience.

Langdon notes that World War II "marked a critical turning point in the creation of gay communities throughout the United States," as overseas deployment provided closeted soldiers the opportunity to explore desires they may have been less likely to express in their stateside lives.[14] Though Sedgwick foregrounds the Stonewall Riots of June 1969 as a turning point in gay self-definition—while acknowledging that "the reign of the telling secret was scarcely overturned by Stonewall"—Langdon and other scholars have more recently highlighted the role of earlier, less dramatic moments as central to the development of gay community and gay identity in America. Langdon argues that "truly, World War Two was something of a national 'coming out' experience" for the United States.[15] Yet as many minority groups became an increasingly acknowledged presence in the United States during this time, cultural acceptance of minority identities in the mainstream often lagged behind their increased visibility.

The Brick Foxhole: Homosexual Panic and the Epistemology of the Closet

Set prior to the end of the war, *The Brick Foxhole* focuses primarily on the insecurities of Corporal Jeff Mitchell, a young man who, after enlisting in the armed forces, is employed as an illustrator making animated propaganda films for the military as part of the stateside, bureaucratic arm of the emerging military-industrial complex. In his author's note introducing the novel's first edition, published in 1945 by Sun Dial Press, Richard Brooks describes the lot of enlisted men serving in *brick foxholes*, a term denoting "a barracks somewhere, anywhere in America." Brooks's preface contrasts the lives of stateside soldiers to those of men whose active duty was spent overseas in combat. As Brooks explains, brick foxholes

> house millions of men, men of all kinds, who have been suddenly wrenched from the normal pursuits of civilian life and thrown together under abnormal conditions of preparation for war. Almost everything about their new life is unnatural: the discipline, and tedium of standing in lines and waiting around, the drilling, the fatigue, the excess of animal spirits they finally know as their bodies are toughened up and they become more physically fit than they ever have been before, the lack of privacy, the dearth of feminine companionship, and the sharpening of every male tendency of the daily impact of a thousand factors and incidents that go into the making of a soldier's world.

In this description of stateside military life during World War II, Brooks juxtaposes the banal day-to-day existence of soldiers awaiting deployment with the masculine potency figuratively embodied by the soldier, thought to emerge as military training shapes body and mind into an idealized but ultimately accessible formulation of masculinity. The passage describes men whose natures, though not essentially altered, have been fine-tuned so that every impulse becomes directed toward military aims and combat objectives; the novel concerns the effect this process has on soldiers excluded from direct military action due to noncombat deployments. Jeff Mitchell feels particularly lacking because, as an artist producing propaganda, "he kills Japs with pictures" rather than bullets. The novel's perspective reinforces this distinction between fighting men of the army and soldiers not selected for combat duty. In the opening scene, the narrator states, "A soldier went overseas and he forgot how to talk. A soldier stayed in the United States, cooped up in a brick coffin, and all he did was talk," setting up contrast between enlisted men not selected for overseas duty and the stoic and taciturn nature of a "real soldier," valorized during the period, who learns to "keep things in," as one soldier treated for posttraumatic stress disorder (PTSD) in *Let There Be Light* is told to do by the staff of Mason General.[16]

Mitchell's scrutiny of masculine identity becomes explicitly epistemological when directed outward at other men rather than inward toward himself. This is most clear when he first meets Mr. Edwards, the novel's only explicitly homosexual character, whose violent death—though not depicted directly—serves as the text's central event. As Jeff attempts to define the man through the differential system of language, his interest in Mr. Edwards seems almost phrenological, focusing on the man's facial features as potential markers of difference the protagonist consciously struggles to interpret. Brooks writes:

> Jeff looked at the man's face in the rear-view mirror. The first thing that struck him was that Mr. Edwards was pale. The sun had not touched his face. He had a thin nose and deeply set eyes. They were pale eyes. The brow was good. The cheekbones high. The face was hungry. Jeff didn't know what the hunger was. He knew, however, that it wasn't for food. The man's clothes told him that, and the high-priced car. Mr. Edwards had full, red lips and his teeth were almost too white. Jeff made a mental sketch of him. He saw that the outstanding feature in the man's face was his eyes. Yes, and something else. The heavy lines that started at the nose and formed a deep parenthesis around the mouth. Jeff looked at the hands on the wheel. They were graceful hands. Too graceful. The fingers were thin and long, the wrists slender and flexible. There was something familiar about the man and yet Jeff knew he had never seen Mr. Edwards before.

Jeff others Mr. Edwards primarily through his attempt to locate the difference he perceives in the man specifically in his physical characteristics, yet the passage is most notable for the process of misrecognition it depicts: despite the protagonist's intense scrutiny of Mr. Edwards's physicality, Jeff's conclusions about him remain indistinct. The protagonist insists there is "something familiar about the man," but it is only after he hears another soldier mock Edwards for his sexuality that "Jeff knew from Monty's tone that Mr. Edwards was a fairy." Through Monty's speech act, the violence of signification transforms Edwards from someone who is "familiar" to someone who, for these men, embodies otherness and abjection on an essential level.[17] The process of willful misrecognition depicted here is similar to the act of othering Baldwin's protagonist performs in *Giovanni's Room* when he explains that the patrons of Guillaume's bar repulse him precisely because of his inability to successfully construct them as other, despite going to lengths to dehumanize the men through animal-like descriptions.[18] Where Baldwin uses a Parisian setting to explore the epistemological instability inherent in sexual identity formation, Brooks's text demonstrates the extent to which homophobic violence is a physical manifestation of the violence of signification, as the soldiers force Edwards into a position of abjection first with their words and then with their fists.

Mitchell's focus on Mr. Edwards's physiognomy is notable for what it tells us about how epistemologies come to be constructed. Sedgwick argues that the understanding of same-sex desire has been problematically linked to "two contradictory tropes of gender" since approximately the end of the nineteenth century. Homosexuality has been understood either through a "trope of inversion" that constructs the homosexual as "'a woman's soul trapped in a man's body'—and vice versa" or through a "trope of gender separatism," which inverts the previous formulation, postulating that "far from its being of the essence of desire to cross boundaries of gender, it is instead the most natural thing in the world that people of the same gender, people grouped together under the single most determinative diacritical mark of social organization . . . should bond together also on the axis of sexual desire." As she explains, "gender-separatist models would thus place the woman-loving woman and the man-loving man each at the 'natural' defining center of their own gender, again in contrast to inversion models that locate gay people—whether biologically or culturally—at the threshold between genders."[19] Ultimately, Brooks's novel remains invested in an essentialist view of homosexuality, despite the sympathy Jeff Mitchell clearly shows toward the character of Mr. Edwards.[20] Jeff's own understanding of Mr. Edwards's identity, however, is pinned between the two tropes of gender identification Sedgwick lays out in her discussion of the construction of homosexual identity. Though Brooks differentiates Jeff from the other soldiers in this scene through Jeff's feelings of guilt regarding what he understands is about to happen to the man they have just met, much of the dramatic tension in the scene derives from the fact that the reader is meant to recognize Edwards as homosexual—as other—before Jeff himself does. The recognition of homosexuality Brooks attempts to elicit from his reader depends on Jeff's description of Mr. Edwards's physical characteristics, drawn in a manner evocative of the exaggerated scrutiny of a cartoonist's illustration. Yet despite Jeff's attempt to locate Mr. Edwards's alterity in his individual physical characteristics, the description fails to cohere into a stable depiction, instead remaining fragmentary and indeterminate. The concreteness with which Jeff tries to depict Edwards comes undone in the indistinct construction of phrases like "His teeth were almost too white" and "They were graceful hands. Too graceful." Jeff seizes on these characteristics as markers of alterity he insists can be perceived in Edwards's *body*, but he ultimately fails to localize this excess in any of the specific physical markers he utilizes in his description. The passage demonstrates the extent to which Jeff is unable to parse his conscious attempt at othering Mr. Edwards (by insisting on elements of Edwards's physicality as visible markers of sexual deviance) from the familiarity of the indeterminacy he *identifies with* in Mr. Edwards. The passage illustrates misrecognition and recognition as occurring simultaneously and, perhaps, as two parts of the same intersubjective identificatory process. Jeff identifies with his vision of Mr. Edwards not (necessarily) because he himself is or fears that he might be homosexual; rather, he seems—on some level—to recognize indeterminacy *itself*, and it is perhaps this recognition of indeterminacy and its demonstration of the instability of epistemological knowledge that elicits violence as a response from the other soldiers.

The desire to violently separate oneself from associations of otherness and alterity attached to gay identity in the postwar period can, of course, also result in self-directed violence. The section of Studs Terkel's *"The Good War": An Oral History of World War Two* entitled "Reflections on Machismo" includes the narrative of Ted Allenby, who enlisted in the marines in December 1942 and received a dishonorable discharge from the navy in 1963 when his superiors discovered that he, then a naval chaplain, had been having an affair with another serviceman, his male assistant. Allenby enlisted in the marines, he tells the author, as soon as he turned eighteen due at least in part to his belief that military service might deflect others' suspicions about his sexual identity and because he felt military training would help him discipline sexual impulses he viewed as deviant. In his interview with Terkel, Allenby states:

> I enlisted in the Marine Corps. This had a good deal to do with my being homosexual. In my middle teens, I made a discovery. My dad was a

pharmacist. In his drugstore they had a lot of bottles, some which had a skull and crossbones. That's how I perceived the label "homosexual." I'll wear a skull and crossbones, and I'm not gonna let anybody see this. It's bad, it's a disease, it's a poison. This is my dirty little secret. . . . How do you deal with it? You deal with it by trying to prove how rugged you are. After all, homosexuals are sissies and pansies. You're not a man. You're not a male, you're not female, you're nothing. I chose the Marines for that reason. It's the toughest outfit. This business about the Marine Corps builds men became a slogan. It was something we believed.

In his testimonial, Allenby speaks of himself as marked—visually—by what he sees as his essential and immutable difference from other men; as he tells Terkel, his desire to identify with an exclusionary version of masculinity through military service comes to be expressed in his life as violence that is both self-directed and projected onto those around him.[21] Thus far, this book has examined cultural valences of disability in postwar America by focusing on men whose experiences of injury and trauma rendered untenable the cultural narratives of masculinity foundational to American identity in the mid-twentieth century, but its broader concern has always been to trace different ways nonnormative masculinities were marked in the postwar era. The passage above encapsulates particularly well the violence inherent in the ableist narrative of masculine sufficiency on which the American male identity rests. Yet Allenby's story is also about a side of American military experience that is, even today, at times suppressed or contested within military culture. Allenby comments that despite his fears about being outed during his military service, he nevertheless found solace in feelings of connection with other closeted soldiers, even when they did not speak explicitly of their shared experiences of difference.[22] Although Allenby was initially drawn to military service as a way to prove his masculinity in a heteronormative sense, his life in the military also played a part in his eventual self-acceptance.

In his interview with Terkel, Allenby speaks frankly of the ways in which, early in his life, internalized homophobia led him to attempt to violently police how others perceived his sexual identity. The once-closeted marine describes various ways his sexual identity has been constructed specifically as a process of signification. In the passage quoted in the previous paragraph, Allenby explains his fear from an early age that homosexuality marks him visibly as other. In his terms, it is an identity from which he can separate himself—it is a skull and crossbones he wears—but homosexuality also becomes something akin to a foreign body that has invaded his own, "a disease" or "a poison" he fears has become an immutable, essential part of his being. Allenby's discussion of the violence he enacts to assuage his internalized homophobia follows the same logic as the violence enacted by Jeff Mitchell's fellow soldiers, but Allenby's story—that of a gay man who uses violence to police the reception of his sexual identity by those around him—adds another layer to the equation discussed in this chapter. In his account of his time spent in two branches of the armed forces from 1942 to 1963, Allenby details the nature of military service for closeted soldiers during that time. Allenby acknowledges the likelihood that, day to day, he interacted with more gay servicemen than he consciously realized at the time, despite the prevalence of antigay sentiment expressed by most servicemen, himself included. Asked to speak about his feelings regarding such "banter," Allenby states that he participated in exchanges out of fear that if he did not, his fellow soldiers would become suspicious of his sexual identity. Allenby tells Terkel, "You develop quite a repertory of tricks to prevent detection. Be even more vociferous than everybody else." Yet Allenby's interview complicates this narrative of closeted service when he expands on the place of homosexual identity in the armed forces during World War II. He tells Terkel, "I think the Marine Corps is a kind of sadomasochistic outfit," explaining:

> A great deal of sexual feeling is expressed. In those days we marines wore leather belts. They got rid of them because marines were using them as weapons in fights with swabbies or each other. You'd take that leather belt and wrap it around your fist and it became something like brass knuckles. I remember we'd slap each other with 'em, back and forth. It was a game of skill, to see how quickly you could dodge and duck and how hard you could hit the other guy. We'd have these welts on our back. . . . There's an old axiom. If you can't love, you gotta hate. If you can't show affection show aggression. A great deal of homosexuality was shown in the barracks. . . . It was never done with real meanness. Instead of a pillow fight, we'd fight with these leather belts.

Terkel's questions structure the interview in a way that juxtaposes the indeterminacy of the acts' violence—interpretable as both homophobic and homoerotic—with seemingly clear-cut examples of more traditional machismo to undermine stereotypical depictions of either straight or gay masculinity that could potentially emerge from Allenby's narrative. Immediately following this passage, for example, Terkel asks Allenby, "Do you know if you killed anybody at Iwo Jima?" Allenby replies, "Of course I did. I was a machine gunner." In this instance, the spareness of Allenby's reply and its lack of emotional affect contrast immediately with the excess that characterizes his description of the marines' homosocial locker-room behavior at the barracks. Yet Allenby also details more positive experiences from his time as a soldier, including the companionship he found with other closeted recruits and the romantic relationships he had during both of his enlistments. The inclusion of these experiences in Allenby's narrative further complicates traditional cultural narratives about the role of the military in forming men: "You have good buddies. It is something subconscious. I had one in San Diego. We were lovers, but we never had a sexual encounter. There was the intimacy, the closeness, deep, deep feelings, little subtle things that you reserve just for that special person. He was a deeply religious kid, Baptist. We were both homosexuals, but neither of us would dare use that word with each other. He didn't go to Iwo Jima with me. War brings people together very quickly and separates them just as quickly. It was a traumatic experience when I said goodbye to him."[23] As Rabinowitz notes, "men can be together in America only by dying together [in war] or through the triangle of the third, the other woman, who dies instead," but Allenby's narrative gives voice to realities often expressed only in a coded fashion in American culture during this period.[24] In his interview, Allenby discusses the military's surprising amount of unofficial permissiveness toward same-sex relationships during World War II and the subsequent tightening of regulations regarding the private lives of enlisted men following the war's conclusion. Allenby notes that "by [the mid-1950s,] trapping homosexuals had become quite a hobby, especially for military intelligence. Unlike [during] World War Two, the military had considerable preoccupation with homosexuality."[25] Although it is an oversimplification to assert that the military was unconcerned with issues like homosexuality during wartime, it is clear that from the late 1940s into the 1950s, an increasingly invasive culture of scrutiny became codified in the United States, characterized by government-sponsored reports like the *Senate Report on the Employment of Homosexuals and Other Sex Perverts in Government* in 1950 and the conduct of the House Committee on Un-American Activities that followed on that legislation's heels early in the decade.[26] This decade also saw the introduction across all four branches of the military of the Uniform Code of Military Justice, which specifically forbade homosexual activity, considered grounds for expulsion from military service. At the close of his interview with Terkel, Allenby recalls his discharge from the military after twenty years of service following the discovery of his year-and-a-half-long love affair with another naval chaplain. "One day I was placed under arrest," Allenby states, explaining, "The charge was violating Article 125, Uniform Code of Military Justice. That's sodomy. The UCMJ came in in the early fifties."[27]

The changing modalities of visibility vis-à-vis queerness and disability as overlapping and interconnected identity categories in the postwar years are explored by David Serlin in his essay "Disability, Masculinity, and the Prosthetics of War, 1945–2005." The essay discusses the "Amputettes," a group of disabled servicemen who performed campy musical routines at Walter Reed Medical Hospital in the spring of 1945, dressed in drag outfits that prominently displayed the new prosthetic limbs they were learning to utilize as a part of their rehabilitation following wartime injuries. As Serlin notes, "newspaper descriptions [of the Amputettes' performances] are refreshingly cheeky and lack disapprobation, running counter to the claims of most historians and cultural critics who have interpreted the 1940s as an era of heightened insecurities about appropriate gender roles and normative sexual behaviors, especially among soldiers." He importantly adds, however, that "the popular appeal of [these] drag performances 'lined up' neatly with the patriotic fervor of rehabilitation culture during World War II, thereby allowing soldiers and rehabilitation therapists to diffuse their putatively queer content."[28] The Amputettes' performances displayed a visible marker of disability in the context of a drag performance, diffusing potential anxieties surrounding both terms. By framing the use of prosthesis specifically as part of a performance, the Amputettes allayed fears that either queerness or disability marked a constituent part of their identities. As I have shown throughout this work (and particularly in the first chapter), narrowly defined formulations of ability and heterosexual masculinity similarly disrupt the matrix of heteronormative identity formation such that, in certain contexts, to be queer or disabled positions one as the constitutive outside of the masculine subject. The Amputettes' performances realigned association between queerness and disability in a way that largely deflected anxieties attached to both terms, but only within the context of postwar rehabilitative culture.

MASCULINITY, MYTH, AND THE CRISIS OF THE ACTION-IMAGE

Early in John Sturges's 1955 film *Bad Day at Black Rock*, sexual tension for the most part absent in the rest of the film erupts between the protagonist, John J. Macreedy (Spencer Tracy), and Hector David (Lee Marvin) when Macreedy finds the man—a henchman for local tough Reno Smith (Robert Ryan)—waiting in the hotel room he has procured for his stay in Black Rock, Arizona. Tracy's character, a World War II veteran unable to use his left arm due to an unspecified wartime injury, has just arrived in Black Rock and will soon learn that Smith and his henchmen have murdered the father of the soldier who saved his life during the war. Macreedy rents a room in the local hotel and proceeds upstairs. Shortly after, Hector David instructs the desk clerk to find out all he can about the stranger and heads upstairs to "crowd him a little." Macreedy enters his room after freshening up in the hotel's shared washroom and finds David stretched out on the bed. Their subsequent verbal exchange is loaded with homoerotic subtext, which Lee Marvin's character means to use to intimidate the protagonist:

MACREEDY: Guess maybe you're in the wrong room.
DAVID: You think so? What else you got on your mind?
MACREEDY: Why, nothing else, I guess.
DAVID: If you had half a mind, boy, you would have paid attention to what Pete, downstairs, said. He said this room here's for us cowboys—for our every wish and comfort.
MACREEDY: And this one is yours, I guess?
DAVID: When I'm in town. And I'm in town, as any fool can see. You can see that can't you, boy?

When Macreedy offers to gather his belongings and find another room—refusing to acknowledge the game of intimidation playing out in this scene—David replies, "If you really wanted this room, we could maybe settle your claim without all this talk. I believe a man's nothing unless he stands up for what's rightfully his."[29] David's response conflates the unmistakable eroticism of his previous statements with masculine violence as he attempts (in the first of many such exchanges in the film) to provoke Tracy's character into a fight that would justify the use of force against a person the townspeople view as an outsider and a threat. Notably, however, this exchange is the one place where such homoerotic tension erupts in the narrative directly. The Coen Brothers use a similar scene in their 2001 throwback to classic noir, *The Man Who Wasn't There*, to make a postmodern comment on the practice of depicting same-sex desire in a coded fashion in noir films of the postwar period. Ed Crane (Billy Bob Thornton) meets Creighton Trolliver (John Pallotta) in a seedy hotel room to discuss a business partnership, and Crane spurns a thinly veiled sexual advance on Trolliver's part, asking him outright, "Is that a pass?" and responding, "You're out of line, mister."[30] The Coen scene decodes the presence of same-sex desire in classic noirs; in Sturges's 1955 version of the same exchange, this depiction—though not represented directly—is so straightforward as to be nearly undisguised. Despite its placement early in the narrative and its apparent innocuousness in comparison to the direct threats of bodily violence the protagonist later faces, the scene is one of the most profoundly violent moments the film.

From the beginning, Macreedy's unexpected presence in the town elicits from most inhabitants the subtly loaded resistance characteristic of racial or sexual prejudice, and the coded innuendos in this scene in particular—directed to a wounded veteran—evoke concerns among the American public regarding the gender identity of soldiers returning from foreign deployment. In a sense, the scene begins the film by replicating for Macreedy the position in the town experienced by Komoko, the murdered man, who was a racial outsider in Black Rock. It allows the film, as several critics have noted, to function—like Fred Zinnemann's *High Noon* (1952)—as an allegorical representation of Hollywood blacklisting during the Red Scare.[31] Viewing Macreedy's disability as a signifier for either racial or political stigma, however, does not fully account for the implications of the inclusion of a disabled protagonist in the film. Issues of gender and sexuality tend to be at play where disability is concerned, yet none of the available scholarship on *Bad Day at Black Rock* fully addresses this concern as present in Sturges's film. One might argue that the previously discussed scene sets up an equation in the film linking violence and homosexual sex acts, wherein physical violence substitutes for sexual violence for the remainder of the film; the conspicuous absence of similarly coded exchanges from the rest of the film complicates such an equation, but the clear homoeroticism of the hotel room scene nevertheless colors the film's subsequent depictions of violence such that heteronormative masculine sufficiency always remains at stake in the violent altercations that unfold between Macreedy and the cowboys.

Bad Day at Black Rock thus belongs to a group of postwar American films that explore the nature of American masculine identity as it relates to violence, a thematic precursor to films like Arthur Penn's *Bonnie and Clyde* (1968) and Sam Peckinpah's *Straw Dogs* (1971). Like David Sumner (Dustin Hoffman), Peckinpah's protagonist in *Straw Dogs*, Macreedy faces subtle and then blatant harassment from the male inhabitants of an insular, rural community until he is provoked to respond to their hostility with acts of force. Moreover, *Bad Day at Black Rock* is rich and complex in its depiction of racism in the United States and its evocation of the increasingly insular character of postwar American society during the Cold War. Although the film is set in 1945, immediately following World War II, it is steeped in the visual iconography of Western films set in the late 1800s and follows the conventions of the Western genre. John J. Macreedy arrives Black Rock, Arizona, and discovers a town-wide cover-up of a racially motivated murder that occurred during the Japanese American internment ordered by President Roosevelt during World War II. Marita Sturken has noted *Bad Day at*

Black Rock for its depiction of the absent presence of the Japanese American internment in both the visual record of World War II and national historical narratives of the period. US government propaganda presented the camps as a "benevolent exercise in civil obedience," and American citizens held at the camps were prohibited from possessing cameras to limit the potential creation of images that might contradict this depiction. "This limited cultural representation of the camps," Sturken notes, "was compounded by the protracted silence of many of the former internees."[32] A notable exception to this silence on the part of Japanese Americans who experienced internment is Miné Okubo's *Citizen 13660*, which consists of hand-drawn illustrations done by Okubo during internment to document her daily experiences in two different camps, combined with text she later wrote for the book's publication by Columbia University Press in 1946.[33] Where *Citizen 13660* represents "the first personal documentation of the evacuation story," the 1992 documentary *History and Memory: For Akiko and Takashige* explores the internment's ongoing legacy by combining the remembrances of director Rea Tajiri's mother with images related to the internment from various sources, including *Bad Day at Black Rock*.[34] Sturken argues that "in *History and Memory*, Tajiri notes that the 1954 film *Bad Day at Black Rock*, directed by John Sturges, perhaps most powerfully reenacts the absent presence of the Japanese American internment" in our collective understanding of World War II, telling "its story through presenting absence."[35] While certainly of interest for its depiction of an underrepresented aspect of World War II American history, *Bad Day at Black Rock* is no less notable for its inclusion of a disabled protagonist in a film that blends elements of film noir with the Western genre. Though the film is set immediately following the end of World War II, Sturges's depiction of Black Rock, Arizona, is steeped in anachronistic visual iconography of the West, and the town itself is populated by characters drawn as self-conscious Western archetypes: men who refer to themselves as *cowboys* and enact hypermasculine identities through blatant intimidation and then outright violence when faced with the appearance of a mysterious stranger they fear has arrived to investigate a murder most of the town conspired to cover up four years prior to the film's beginning. Though various critics have addressed the film's depiction of an often-repressed element of twentieth-century United States history, the significance of Macreedy's disability has been undertheorized in discussions of the film.

Like William Wyler's *The Best Years of Our Lives*, *Bad Day at Black Rock* is instructive in demonstrating the cultural valences of physical disability in film by placing a once able-bodied masculine figure in the position of male protagonist in a specific genre of film. This book's previous chapter discussed Wyler's use of melodrama to examine how assumptions of feminized passivity often attach to the social stigma surrounding physical disability, showing the struggles of male protagonists through the lens of what was at the time generally understood to be a genre used to depict women's issues. Here, I am interested in examining the effect of "disabling" the protagonist of what Steve Neale and others have identified as the quintessentially masculine genre of American film, particularly in the postwar period. Like Sturken, John Streamas has discussed Sturges's use of the Western to explore the repressed history of Japanese American internment in the American narrative of World War II, discussing the way in which the film's pervasive whiteness comments, through pointed absence of Asian American characters on-screen, on the absence of Japanese American narratives in national understanding of the World War II period. As Streamas notes, "all the characters are white, and the protagonist Macreedy is an unlikely champion of racial justice, a luckless veteran so badly injured in combat that he has lost the use of an arm," arguing that "Sturges seems to say that, even in a remote and desolate place such as Black Rock, to render a people absent is the surest way to write them out of history."[36] In his analysis, Streamas connects Sturges's method of depicting racism in *Bad Day at Black Rock* to the director's use of the Western genre to tell a story that takes place in the late 1940s rather than the late 1890s, deconstructing the relationship between the white male privilege expressed by the film's cowboy characters and their belief in cultural narratives self-consciously internalized from Hollywood cinema.[37]

John J. Macreedy's dramatic arrival by train at the film's beginning is, of course, a stock device of the Western, but Macreedy himself, dressed in a rumpled black suit and matching fedora for the duration of the film and thus visually emphasized as an outsider, has more in common with the hard-boiled detective exemplified by Dashiell Hammett's Continental OP than he does with the conventional Western hero. It is particularly noteworthy that Macreedy's disability, a paralyzed arm resulting from a war injury, is an addition specific to Millard Kaufman's screen adaptation of the original source material, Howard Breslin's 1947 story "Bad Time at Honda." Kaufman stated that he made John J. Macreedy a disabled veteran in his adaptation of Breslin's story to increase audience sympathy with the film's central figure and because he felt the added complexity would entice Spencer Tracy to accept the role, which he had previously turned down due to lack of interest.[38] This understanding of Macreedy's character in *Bad Day at Black Rock* and the protagonist's relationship to his disability is more or less reproduced in the few critical discussions that exist of Sturges's film. In *Cinema of Isolation*, Norden asserts that the protagonist's disability in *Bad Day at Black Rock* functions mainly as a device used by the screenwriter and filmmaker "to stress Macreedy's difference from the other characters or to enhance his vulnerability." The addition of a physical disability to the character, along with the actor's age (Tracy was a veteran of World War I and in his mid-fifties at the time of filming), was used by the makers of *Bad Day at Black Rock* "to increase the movie's tensions by stacking what they perceived as near-insurmountable odds against their courageous lead character, who in effect becomes 'remasculinized' through his heroic deeds."[39] Norden thus reads the addition of Macreedy's stiff arm to the film version of Breslin's story in much the same way Mitchell and Snyder discuss disability as a trope in *Narrative Prosthesis*: as a device used to heighten narrative tension and as shorthand for the uniqueness of the disabled character.[40] Such a reading reduces Macreedy's disability to a motivation for his character's pursuit of justice and an obstacle he must overcome in achieving his goals. While Norden does acknowledge the centrality of the protagonist's masculinity to the film's narrative, his analysis elides the extent to which the addition of a disability to the protagonist's character alters, on a fundamental level, how masculinity functions in the film versus the original version of the story.

Breslin's story emphasizes protagonist Peter Macreedy's intimidating physicality, depicting the mysterious outsider largely from the point of view of the town (a device similar to the narrative technique used by Petry in *Country Place*). Often referred to by the omniscient narrator simply as "the big man," Peter Macreedy is an imposing figure who moves with grace despite his bulk, and his arrival is enough to break the town's silence regarding its role in the death of his friend's father. In Breslin's version, Macreedy cracks the case just by showing up and looking tough; the story's protagonist does not resort to actual physical violence at any time during the narrative. In fact, he hardly does anything other than make himself visible as he moves about the town asking questions of the guilty parties, who turn against each other when they find out that, before the war, "the big man had been a cop. Very much a cop. A boss one, they said." Despite this background information, which the townspeople obtain through a phone call to the protagonist's native Chicago, Peter Macreedy remains largely a cipher in the text: he simply *is* masculine sufficiency, a materialization of nothing more than masculinity as a rhetorical effect absent any actual content. Unsurprisingly, Breslin's story enacts heteronormative gender roles in a more or less straightforward fashion. In the single instance of violence depicted directly rather than recounted for the reader after the fact, one of the toughs responsible for the murder attempts to intimidate the protagonist by ambushing and firing on him when Macreedy visits the crime scene accompanied by Liz Brooks, a young woman who has reluctantly agreed to assist in his investigation:

> The loud twang of metal on metal startled them. There was the high whine of a ricochet, and then, from the hills the flat slap of a rifle. . . . Macreedy moved fast. He took one step, hooked a leg behind Liz's knees, deftly shouldered her over, and fell on top of her. They were on the ground before the station wagon's bullet-scarred fender stopped quivering. . . . "Stay down," said Macreedy. The girl twisted beneath him, and he pushed her flat, holding her there with a hand on her shoulder, his arm rigid. . . . He rolled away from Liz, and rose to a crouch, balancing on one fist like a football player. Macreedy's other hand held a gun, a square black automatic, compact and heavy.

The manner in which Macreedy handles this situation is explicitly gendered. The protagonist responds almost instinctively to protect the woman accompanying him with a gesture filled with sexual tension and containing the unmistakable hint of sexual violence. Yet even the story's only action scene ultimately emphasizes the essentially specular nature of Macreedy's authority when, after saving Liz's life by manhandling her to the ground and holding her beneath him, he tells her, "That gun of mine . . . It's a Beretta. Italian make. You might want to mention it around Honda. I'm not fond of people shooting at me." Here, Peter Macreedy operates under the assumption that structures all his interactions in the story: his performance of masculinity is itself so potent that the assertion of its presence, even indirectly, is enough of a threat that actual violence remains unnecessary for him to retain a position of mastery. Yet this performance, as Macreedy tacitly acknowledges in this instance, operates almost purely on the level of abstraction in the story; as such, it is notable that the protagonist's most direct invocation of masculine authority is mediated symbolically, in the image of his gun, through the female figure of Liz Brooks.[41]

The substitution of a disabled protagonist in Sturges's film version complicates the above-described equation of masculine sufficiency, disrupting the spectacle of masculinity carefully maintained by Peter Macreedy throughout Breslin's story in ways neither Kaufman nor Norden accounts for in their statements regarding the film. Though John J. Macreedy's impairment in *Bad Day at Black Rock* does serve an othering purpose in the narrative by subjecting the protagonist to the stigma often associated with visible physical disability, his paralyzed arm in no significant way affects his ability to function as the protagonist in a violent action film. Macreedy's disability instead causes the film's numerous antagonists to repeatedly underestimate the mysterious stranger's ability to handle himself in violent situations. One key difference between Breslin's story and the film version made nearly ten years later is the addition of several violent action scenes in which Macreedy incapacitates assailants in hand-to-hand combat with ease despite his injury. In this way, *Bad Day at Black Rock* places its protagonist in a position similar to that of Homer Parrish in *The Best Years of Our Lives*, with the disabled protagonist repeatedly exceeding the physical limitations assumed of him by other characters in the narrative. *Bad Day at Black Rock* thus provides a useful counterpart to *Best Years* in that it includes a similarly impaired protagonist, in this instance portrayed by an ostensibly able-bodied actor: Tracy holds his left arm stiff and hides it beneath his suit coat for the duration of *Bad Day* to simulate his character's disability, whereas Russell's metal prosthetics become the visual focus of nearly every scene of Wyler's film in which he is included. *Best Years* foregrounds the extent to which Parrish has had to adapt to his disability, as the character (and thus the disabled actor playing him) is required to repeatedly demonstrate the workings of his prosthetics—in *Bad Day at Black Rock*, Tracy plays Macreedy's disability very differently. Although the cowboys repeatedly reference the protagonist's injury, Macreedy's disability rarely seems to function as an actual physical shortcoming for which the character must compensate. Where much of Harold Russell's acting in Wyler's film constitutes the performance of his disability for able-bodied characters (and presumably a largely able-bodied film audience), Macreedy's paralyzed left arm is only acknowledged through Tracy's performance as a physical hindrance in one instance, when he fumbles with a phone receiver while attempting to make a phone call to the state police to inform them of an attempt on his life.

Moreover, *Bad Day at Black Rock* places its disabled protagonist in an explicitly masculine environment, an anachronistic version of the American West transposed into the post–World War II period and placed into conflict with its historical context, thereby increasing the valances of the crisis of masculinity the film depicts. The film frequently contrasts its historical and thematic aspects not only through visual elements but also through the voices of characters themselves, as in an early scene when the desk clerk at Black Rock's hotel (the set design of which references the visual iconography of the Western) tells Macreedy, "This is 1945, mister: there's been a war on," in an attempt to dissuade the protagonist from staying in town by telling him all the rooms are unavailable.[42] The film's antagonists consistently underestimate Macreedy precisely because he does not project the sort of masculinity the cowboys attempt, unsuccessfully, to perform. Yet the film does not allow for a simple, dichotomous reading of the cowboys' excessive masculinity and Macreedy's even, measured composure in the face of their resistance to his investigation and eventual attempts to kill him before he uncovers their secret. Although Macreedy initially resists responding to the cowboys' intimidation tactics in kind—with force—the film leaves open the question of whether or not the specific violent acts eventually committed by the protagonist are justified within the circumstances. The first notable example of the film's subtle ambivalence to its own violence occurs after Macreedy is run off the road and nearly killed by Reno Smith's henchmen and then followed by them to the local saloon, where he orders food as the toughs pursuing him enter and continue to harass him. It is unclear at this point in the film whether Smith and his gang intend to kill Macreedy or to scare him off with increasingly dangerous methods of intimidation, yet the protagonist (in a reluctant show of force) easily incapacitates Coley Trimble (Ernest Borgnine) with repeated chops to the neck with his right arm after Trimble finally provokes Macreedy to violence by implying the protagonist's disability would make him helpless in a fight. Though the film consistently attempts to distinguish Macreedy's skillful and measured use of force when provoked from the cowboys' violent masculine excess, it is the protagonist who hits first in this instance, blurring the distinction between the two modes of masculine authority depicted in the film. In fact, Macreedy's reaction is both precisely what Hollywood logic demands in response to a belligerent show of masculine force *and* a skillful deflection of masculine excess. What results is one of several displays of cinematic action in the film that do not make traditional sense because they subtly contradict the sensory-motor coherence of the action-image as described by Deleuze. The violence in the bar fight scene inevitably escalates, but not in the expected way, as Macreedy attempts to deflect the cowboys' assaults for as long as possible rather than meet them head-on. Deleuze describes a "crisis of the action-image" in postwar cinema, wherein "the sensory-motor links tend to disappear, a whole sensory-motor continuity which forms the essential nature of the action-image vanishes [as] clumsy fights, badly aimed shots, a whole out-of-phase of action and speech replace the too perfect duels of American Realism." Here, Deleuze writes primarily of the formal innovations that distinguished postwar European cinema such as Italy's neorealism, which he views as the birth of a "new image . . . that can attempt to identify in the post-war American cinema, outside Hollywood." What *Bad Day at Black Rock* demonstrates is a similar breakdown of coherence within formalist American cinema itself, inseparable from a breakdown in the violently constituted equation of traditional masculine sufficiency.[43]

The film ratchets up the depicted violence as its narrative progresses, carefully maintaining a balance between Macreedy's reluctance to use force and the other men's clearly violent intentions so that each time the protagonist acts violently, his response registers as largely justifiable but also completely excessive in its resulting human damage. Macreedy's responses to the cowboys' threats of violence seem to operate on the level of pure reaction—they do not quite fit in the logic of the scenes in which they are included, the protagonist himself often strangely detached from his actions and their results. Macreedy responds in the way demanded by the situations in which he finds himself, but his reactions feel a bit out of sync—as though he responds just before or just after the moment violence would logically erupt from the protagonist in such a scene. Deleuze notes that, in postwar film, "the first things compromised everywhere are the linkages of situation-action, action-reaction, excitation, response, in short, the sensory-motor links which produced the action-image. Realism, despite all its violence—or rather with all its violence that remains sensory-motor—is oblivious to where the synsigns disperse and the indices become confused."[44] The film's climactic scene is a case in point. After revealing to Macreedy the circumstances surrounding Komoko's murder, Doc Velie and Pete Wirth agree to get Macreedy out of town at nightfall, with Liz's help. Liz pretends to help Macreedy but instead drives him to the desert, where Reno Smith is waiting. Here, the film extensively revises the shoot-out scene from Breslin's story. As in the original version, Smith ambushes Macreedy, leaving the protagonist and Liz pinned behind the young woman's jeep. At this point, the filmed scene departs significantly from the scene in Breslin's story. Unafraid, Liz steps forward, expecting thanks from the gang leader for her assistance in setting up Macreedy, and Smith shoots her, leaving no witnesses to the murder he intends to commit. Still crouched behind Liz's jeep, the unarmed Macreedy fashions a Molotov cocktail, filling a discarded bottle on the ground with gasoline from the jeep's gas tank as Smith repositions himself for a clearer shot. As in the bar fight scene, Macreedy acts decisively, throwing the bottle at Smith before the villain can take his shot, and Smith is engulfed in flames from the explosion, an image that anticipates the climactic violence depicted at the end of Peckinpah's *Straw Dogs*. Smith screams and writhes in pain on the ground until the flames burning his body go out while Macreedy watches with a strange detachment, an emotionless performance of excessive violence that complicates the film's apparently clear-cut moralism and foreshadows the ambivalence of the conclusion. *Bad Day at Black Rock* lays bare the radical incoherence Deleuze argues is depicted most frequently in postwar European film, placed here in a specifically American context. The film's depictions of physical violence ultimately demonstrate not Macreedy's reclamation of his masculinity in any clear-cut sense but instead his navigation of a landscape in which masculinity as a rhetorical effect—the libidinal currency of the Western genre—has lost its potency.

Narratives of masculine sufficiency become the film's explicit concern in its denouement. We learn that the town's hostility to Komoko was instigated by the fact that the Japanese American's cultural knowledge allowed him to draw water from the arid landscape of Adobe Flats (making Komoko's previously undesirable land an unexpected source of jealousy for the town's other men) and that Komoko's murder occurred after cowboy ringleader Reno Smith was denied entry in the US military following Pearl Harbor because of his inability to pass the physical examination required for enlistment. Sore over his rejection from the service and denied an outlet for his anger at the Japanese (now perceived as a threat), Smith persuades his drinking buddies to accompany him to Adobe Flats and force Komoko to give up his land by burning down his home; Komoko, inside, dies as a result of the fire. That Smith suffers a similar fate at the hands of Macreedy at the film's climax lends a harshness and cruelty to the justice meted out in the film, despite the protagonist's clear moral superiority to every other figure who appears in the narrative. In "The Western," André Bazin writes:

> If it is to be effective . . . justice must be dispensed [in the Western] by men who are just as strong and just as daring as the criminals. These virtues, as we have said, are in no way compatible with virtue in the absolute sense. The sheriff is not always a better person than the man he hangs. This begets and establishes an inevitable and necessary contradiction. There is often little moral difference between the outlaw and the man who operates within the law. Still the sheriff's star must be seen as constituting a sacrament of justice, whose worth does not depend on the worthiness of the man who administers it.

Bazin adds that the mythic structure of the Western necessitates "the administration of justice, which, if it is to be effective, must be drastic and speedy—short of lynching, however—and thus must ignore extenuating circumstances, such as alibis that would take too long to verify."[45] As previously discussed, *Bad Day at Black Rock* carefully walks this line, consciously concerned with the problem of distinguishing necessary and just uses of violence from violent acts of mob rule. Scenes throughout Sturges's film comment on the emptiness of Western authority by demonstrating the powerlessness of the town sheriff. When Macreedy first finds Sheriff Tim Horn (Dean Jagger) dozing in the bed of an unused jail cell, Sturges positions the camera so that the sheriff's badge is repeatedly framed between the cell's bars; later, the badge is further shown to be an empty signifier of authority as it is passed from man to man after Horn fails to prove his loyalty to Reno Smith and Smith summarily strips Horn of his title as sheriff.

Yet *Bad Day at Black Rock*'s final scene depicts a fundamental rejection of myth itself. As Doc Velie walks Macreedy back to the train that brought him to town at the start of the film, he asks the protagonist to give Komoko's son's Medal of Honor *to the town*, offering the vague explanation that he hopes the medal will help the town's citizens by giving them "something to build on." Macreedy wordlessly hands over the medal to Doc Velie, and Velie tells him, "Thanks Mr. Macreedy—thanks for everything."[46] Macreedy's gesture ironically reverses the final scene from *High Noon*, released just three years prior. An allegorical representation of Hollywood blacklisting during the Red Scare, *High Noon*'s narrative is similar to *Black Rock*'s in that a lone protagonist is forced to defend himself in the face of a town's indifference to law and justice. In the film, Marshall Will Kane (Gary Cooper) defends the New Mexico town of Hadleyville from outlaws he learns are coming to kill him in retribution for his running them out of town years earlier, bringing law, order, and prosperity to a once lawless territory. Kane kills the outlaws without the town's assistance after he proves unable to raise a posse to meet the outlaws because the townspeople believe that the outlaws' vendetta is against Kane himself rather than the town and that, as such, it is not their concern. When Kane throws his badge into the dirt at his feet before leaving the town he has once again saved, his gesture is an expression of disgust with the town rather than a loss of faith in what the badge represents. *Bad Day at Black Rock*'s revision of the earlier film's conclusion is more cynical. Will Kane's rejection of Hadleyville works as it does precisely because Kane himself has just reinvested the object he discards with symbolic potency; that Macreedy wordlessly ascents to give the doctor Komoko's Medal of Honor despite the ludicrousness of the request underscores the extent to which symbolic markers of masculinity are empty of meaning in Sturges's film. Both scenes demonstrate that in mythic structure, "any material can arbitrarily be endowed with meaning." Key to Roland Barthes's understanding of mythic structures outlined in his essay "Myth Today" is that "mythical speech is made of material which has *already* been worked on so as to make it suitable for communication: it is because all the materials of myth (whether pictorial or written) presuppose a signifying consciousness, that one can reason about them while discounting their sustenance."[47] In *High Noon*, Will Kane discarding his badge is a meaningful act—at once an insult to and a rejection of the town he has rescued—precisely because the badge itself remains an object that means something within the mythic structure of the film. *Bad Day at Black Rock*'s revision of this exchange retains the message of the original scene by showing that the town is unworthy of the symbolic masculinity it has come to reify. The difference is that Macreedy (unlike Cooper's Kane) understands what the town does not: the symbol itself has been rendered empty of meaning, the mythic structure it represents remaining mere form, void of content.

Like *Bad Day at Black Rock*, Chester Himes's 1945 noir novel *If He Hollers Let Him Go* also comments with some ambivalence on intersection of various identity categories associated with otherness in the postwar period, using a crime story to focus more directly on racial exclusion and violence in World War II–era America. The novel begins with the narrator's description of a series of dreams that blur the distinction between the interior landscape of the protagonist's psyche and the wartime landscape of the United States, obliquely foreshadowing key events in the book while connecting issues of race, class, and disability in a World War II era context. Robert (Bob) Jones, the protagonist of Himes's first novel, is introduced to the reader as he narrates waking from a fitful sleep, punctuated by surreal images structured by dream logic that foreshadows the anger at white America that propels the book's loosely plotted structure. Jones struggles to suppress violent responses to "the whole structure of American thought," which Rabinowitz argues "is aimed at diminishing him and other racial minorities through violence and expropriation."[48] Like Richard Wright's *Native Son* did almost a decade earlier, Himes's novel presents violent Black anger as a response to both subtle and overt incidences of daily racism enabled by white supremacy and the social structures it produces and through which it is expressed. The brief dream episodes, which punctuate Jones's narration throughout Himes's novel and express the character's fear and anxiety as a Black man living in mid-to-late 1940s America, present these feelings in an explicitly racial context near the novel's end. Bob dreams of "a white boy and a colored boy . . . fighting on the sidewalk" for control of a knife that the white figure eventually uses to kill the Black figure, "just chasing the colored boy and stabbing him to death with a quarter-inch blade and laughing like it was funny as hell."[49] When the novel opens, however, the narrator's fear-suffused dreams evoke the novel's themes a bit more indirectly. The narrator first dreams he is given a dog to care for he does not want and then that "a white fellow named Frankie Childs had been killed" in the war plant where he works and that the police are seeking "a big tall man with strong arms, big hands, and a crippled leg" as their primary suspect. Though the race of the killer is not explicitly stated, the police begin interrogating the plant's Black employees, and, in the dream, they exonerate their suspects by asking each man called in for interrogation to run up a set of stairs to the plant's third floor to "look the dead body of Frankie Childs in the face." In exposition following the narration of dreams that opens the novel, Jones directly links his own experience of America as a person of color with the experiences of Japanese Americans interred during the war, explaining how his consciousness of his precarious position in American society became particularly acute after he had "seen them send the Japanese away" following the attack on Pearl Harbor.[50] Over the course of Himes's book, Jones struggles to choke back his anger at white America, resisting the urge to respond to the racism he experiences with violence. Near the conclusion of the book, he is accused of rape by a white female coworker whose sexual advances he had previously rejected when they are subsequently found together after a chance encounter. Though Madge, Jones's accuser, eventually drops her charges against him, the novel's narrator is forced to enlist in the army at the novel's conclusion. Jones enlists to avoid a weapons charge resulting from being caught with a gun on the floor of the war plant after Madge's accusation leads to the protagonist's rash decision to act on violent fantasies he has entertained throughout the novel of killing a white male coworker who, like Madge, has subjected him to racial slurs throughout the narrative. Though Bob Jones does not ultimately commit the murder as he initially intends, being caught with a weapon leads to his enlistment in the army to avoid a jail sentence.[51]

The imprecise parallels between Bob's initial dream of police seeking a disabled suspect for a violent crime and the conclusion of the book, in which he himself runs afoul of the law despite not having committed a crime beyond the possession of a weapon, make *If He Hollers Let Him Go* a particularly fraught example of how, in the postwar context, noir texts function as forums for the examination of anxieties suppressed by mainstream texts. These anxieties, which nevertheless could not be entirely contained within postwar American culture, were expressed by "the mediated space of American pulp during and immediately after World War II . . . designed to engage the reader in a familiar yet bizarre world—a world of murder and rape; a world of dreams that invade waking and make it impossible to differentiate reality from fantasy—for the characters in the books and their readers." Similar to novels by Black authors written during and after the war "where whiteness codes black rage and alienation through ethnic or queer characters" like Baldwin's *Giovanni's Room* or Zora Neale Hurston's *Seraph on the Suwanee*, Himes's reference to physical disability in conjunction with perceived criminality—a common trope in the noir canon—does not equate Blackness and disability but helps create the dense web of uneasy and unspecified parallels between markers of ability, gender, class, and race the author pointedly references at the start of his novel.[52]

Noir texts like those discussed in this chapter explore places in the literal and psychic landscape of the postwar United States often unacknowledged by mainstream cultural narratives produced during the time: other spaces populated by marginalized figures and repressed currents of anger and fear that increasingly structured how American citizens interacted with each other and how America itself interacted with the broader world as the Cold War intensified. In many of the texts discussed in this chapter, references to disability or the presence of a disabled character serve to crystallize and bring to the surface thematic elements that tend to be repressed or left unaddressed by more mainstream postwar cultural productions. This chapter has sought to account for disability's fraught relation to the dense web of anxieties projected on figures of otherness in an increasingly insular America in the years following World War II. Because disability functions as a lasting reminder of the repressed violence of foreign conflict, its presence in texts that explore the anxieties of the home front can serve as a locus for the expression of the diffuse concerns that haunted American shores in at the beginning of the second half of the twentieth century. That masculine violence became an increasingly prevalent concern in American narratives of masculine sufficiency in the second half of the twentieth century is not incidental. As long-held cultural narratives of American identity came into greater conflict with the changing nature of the postwar world over the course of the twentieth century, violence increasingly came to be seen as the last recourse of men who felt themselves to be forgotten or discarded by a society that had moved on without them.

Notes

1. Foucault, "Of Other Spaces," 336, 330.
2. Hughes, *In a Lonely Place*, 5.

3. Roberts, *What Soldiers Do*, 8, 1–5, 62.

4. Ibid., 66.

5. Rabinowitz, *Black & White & Noir*, 11, 14.

6. Laplanche and Pontalis define the return of the repressed as "the third and last phase" of repression, wherein the repressed element of the psyche returns in the guise of symptoms, dreams, parapraxes, etc." Laplanche and Pontalis, *The Language of Psychoanalysis*, 351.

7. For a more in-depth discussion of this phenomenon, please see chapter 2 of this book.

8. Rabinowitz, "Pulping Ann Petry," 50.

9. Petry, *Country Place*, 23, 26.

10. Ibid., 29.

11. Rabinowitz, "Pulping Ann Petry," 53, 149.

12. Petry, *Country Place*, 142.

13. Rabinowitz, "Pulping Ann Petry," 54.

14. Langdon, *Caught in the Crossfire*, 126–27, 130. See also John D'Emilio and Estelle B. Freedman's book *Intimate Matters: A History of Sexuality in America* (New York: Harper and Row, 1988), which provides much of the historical context for Langdon's own argument and further discusses the role played by World War II in the development of gay communities in the United States.

15. Sedgwick, *Epistemology of the Closet*, 63, 67; Langdon, *Caught in the Crossfire*, 127.

16. Brooks, *The Brick Foxhole*, vii, 19, 1.

17. Ibid., 86.

18. See chapter 1 for my analysis of this specific scene in Baldwin's novel.

19. Sedgwick, *Epistemology of the Closet*, 87, 88.

20. As Langdon notes, "Brooks's juxtaposition of Mr. Edwards and Max Brock—the novel's despised Others—is also significant. In sharp contrast to Max's performance of manly heroism and Universalist Americanism, Mr. Edwards's performance of womanliness—from his good manners to his pathetic tears—mark him as weak and pitiable. Brooks is clearly contemptuous of the 'hunger' that drives Mr. Edwards, and his constant iteration of the man's anxious, desirous responses to the G.I.s' come-ons—grateful glances, blushes, nervously licked lips, and hard swallows—implies that Mr. Edwards 'asked for it.'" Langdon, *Caught in the Crossfire*, 132.

21. Terkel, "Reflections on Machismo," 179.

22. Ibid., 181–82.

23. Ibid., 180.

24. Rabinowitz, *Black & White & Noir*, 9.

25. Terkel, "Reflections on Machismo," 184.

26. Serlin, "Disability, Masculinity, and the Prosthetics of War," 176.

27. Terkel, "Reflections on Machismo," 185.

28. Serlin, "Disability, Masculinity, and the Prosthetics of War," 157, 160.

29. Sturges, *Bad Day at Black Rock*.

30. Coen, *The Man Who Wasn't There*.

31. Streamas, "Patriotic Drunk," 108.

32. Sturken, "Absent Images of Memory," 36.

33. Reissued by Washington University Press in 1983.

34. Okubo, *Citizen 13660*, ix.

35. Sturken, "Absent Images of Memory," 40. Explaining the importance of works like *Citizen 13660* and *History and Memory* as corrective narratives, Sturken writes that "in many ways, the [official] historical narrative of the internment remains intact," as "the internment continues to be narrativized as a regrettable step that appeared necessary in its time—not as bad as what other countries did." For Sturken, this mediated depiction of the internment meshes seamlessly with larger cultural narratives of the World War II period in troubling

ways. "Even though the term 'concentration camps' was used by government officials and Presidents Roosevelt and Truman," Sturken argues, "the image of prison camps where people were peaceably assembled screens out the image of prison camps where people became ill and died and where residents were shot. The historical claim of the internment as benevolent remains fixed through its alliance with the claim of the use of the atomic bomb as inevitable, an act that was appropriate in its time. To question one of these narratives would be to question them all, hence they remain fundamentally unexamined." Sturken, "Absent Images of Memory," 36.

36. Streamas, "Patriotic Drunk," 99, 104.

37. Ibid., 104.

38. Kaufman, "A Vehicle for Tracy," 76.

39. Norden, *Cinema of Isolation*, 197, 189.

40. David T. Mitchell and Sharon L. Snyder have, in works of scholarship both cowritten and published independently, advanced their thesis of *narrative prosthesis*: the notion that disability tends to function in cultural texts either as "a stock feature of characterization" or "as an opportunistic metaphorical device." In this formulation, "disability lends a distinctive idiosyncrasy to any characters that differentiate themselves from the anonymous background of the norm." Mitchell, "Narrative Prosthesis and the Materiality of Metaphor," 15, 16.

41. Breslin, "Bad Time at Honda," 19, 20, 26, 22, 23.

42. Sturges, *Bad Day at Black Rock*.

43. Deleuze, *Cinema 1*, 213, 214.

44. Ibid., 210.

45. Bazin, "The Western," 146.

46. Sturges, *Bad Day at Black Rock*.

47. Barthes, "Myth Today," 110.

48. Himes, *If He Hollers Let Him Go*, 129; Rabinowitz, *American Pulp*, 52.

49. Himes, *If He Hollers Let Him Go*, 150

50. Ibid., 2, 3.

51. Ibid., 203.

52. Rabinowitz, *American Pulp*, 53, 144.

5

LANDSCAPES OF LOSS

Disability, the American Wilderness, and the Remasculinization of the Vietnam Veteran

RON KOVIC DESCRIBES EXPERIENCING A powerful moment of recognition on first reading Dalton Trumbo's protest novel *Johnny Got His Gun*, a work with a clear intertextual relationship to his own disability memoir. Trumbo's book, written in response to World War I but not published until 1939, tells the story of a young soldier who awakens in a hospital to find his arms and legs amputated, his face mutilated, and his sense of sight and hearing lost. These grave injuries, sustained from a German artillery shell, plunge protagonist Joe Bonham into a world of limited sensation, leaving him almost completely unable to communicate and without access to most of the experiences through which individuals understand themselves in relation to the world around them. Cut off from human contact for most of the novel—save for periodic visits from the nurses and doctors with whom he can only interact in a limited fashion—Bonham spends days, months, perhaps years in a world consisting entirely of his memories and limited perceptions of a hospital room located somewhere in Europe. In the introduction to *Johnny Got His Gun* he wrote in 1990, Kovic describes his immediate identification with Trumbo's protagonist: "'That's me!,' I kept thinking, 'that's what I went through.'" Kovic details the following anecdote about meeting Trumbo in 1971 at a premiere party for the film version of the novel: "The night we met, Trumbo seemed very moved by my tribute to his book, and I remember asking him for his autograph. 'Would you sign my wheelchair?' I asked. And he complied, bending down and carefully writing on the back of my wheelchair the words 'Nothing more can be said—it can only be done' and then signing it, 'Dalton Trumbo.' I remember carrying that back-piece long after the wheel chair wore out, carrying it with me wherever I went and eventually losing it." Kovic describes being confused by the meaning of the inscription, but the words evoke the dilemma faced by Trumbo's own protagonist at the end of his novel. Though Bonham has by the end of the book devised a means to communicate with his doctors using Morse code, they reject his pleas to be "let out"—to be taken out of the hospital and allowed to interact with other people. This denial of his desire for human contact catalyzes Bonham's intent to spread an antiwar message throughout the world even though he has no agency to do so, dependent as he is on an unsympathetic medical establishment for nearly everything. Kovic's antiwar memoir *Born on the Fourth of July* shares many similarities with the narrative presented in Trumbo's book, and both works became important texts in the canon that inspired the antiwar movement of the Vietnam era. In his own account of postwar disability, Kovic seems to borrow structural devices from Trumbo's book, alternating chapters between first and third person in a manner that evokes the instability of voice present in *Johnny Got His Gun* when the third person narrator shifts abruptly into first person or jumps from a flashback to the present without warning. Stylistically idiosyncratic in similar ways, the two texts foreground the horrifying nature of the physical experience of disability for their respective protagonists. In both texts, the men disassociate profoundly from their newfound embodiment while remaining fixated on the imprisoning nature of their dramatically altered bodies as they understand them.[1]

This chapter builds on the book's preceding section to discuss the role of violence in narratives of masculine sufficiency in the second half of the twentieth century by looking at texts drawn from the Vietnam era and its aftermath. Where the previous chapter focused on texts from the period following World War II into the 1950s and dealt with violent responses elicited by external threats to the masculinities of individual men as heteronormatively understood, this chapter examines later texts that demonstrate more clearly the deep structures informing and at times constituting narratives of American masculinity that likewise rely on violence to police and maintain masculine sufficiency. This chapter concludes *The Illegible Man* by reading late twentieth-century accounts of masculinities that react to the crises examined in this project not by reimagining maleness in a new context or deconstructing canonical representations of male figures that are limiting and exclusionary but by responding to the increasingly fraught nature of American identity for men during the Vietnam era with narratives that attempt to reconstitute American masculinity as previously imagined in some of the country's foundational myths.

The Vietnam-era texts examined in this chapter try to reconcile the instability of the twentieth-century masculine subject by looking back to early American narratives of rugged masculine identity for a way of being in the world that might successfully resist feminizing influences understood as a threat to individualized masculinity and American culture during this time. Scholarship on the Vietnam War tends to frame the conflict (and the cultural responses to it) as a departure from previous periods of foreign conflict for the United States. In *The Remasculinization of America: Gender and the Vietnam War*, Susan Jeffords notes ideological tendencies shared by key figures in the United States government and American establishment culture who believed that feelings of guilt and shame about American power and influence had pervaded American society and were preventing the United States from exercising its will and adequately protecting its interests at home and abroad.[2] This so-called *Vietnam Syndrome*, a term coined by Richard Nixon to indicate a cultural paralysis believed to inhibit the decisive action necessary for America to win the war in Vietnam, was just one aspect of an American society that had, in this view, become feminized in the decades following the end of World War II. Through an analysis of texts taken from print and visual culture, Jeffords identifies a corresponding tendency in Vietnam War narratives to attempt, through various structural and representation devices and certain narrative patterns, to exert a corrective influence on an emasculated American society. Jeffords writes, "Because the war in Vietnam is interpreted in U.S. culture differently from other wars, it can provide insight into the ways in which the structure of gender is both maintained as a general frame and altered in relation to specific cultural circumstances. In particular, it has been altered to produce, validate, and secure what I call here a 'remasculinization'—a regeneration of the concepts, constructions, and definitions of masculinity in American culture and a restabilization of the gender system within which it is formulated."[3] Jeffords's book presents the Vietnam era and its responses to masculinity in crisis as a historically specific departure from traditional depictions of American masculinity in the context of war, tracking with nuance a remasculinization of America mediated textually via narrative structures that exclude the feminine and excise any narrative elements that would complicate this exclusion. In this way, Jeffords argues, "America's collective unconscious" is presented as "a masculine consciousness" through narratives of war that portray a collective masculine experience through absolute exclusion of feminine subjectivities.[4] More recent film studies scholarship on the Vietnam era by Sylvia Shin Huey Chong does important work to productively recenter the discussion of the Vietnam War on depictions of Vietnamese figures, often neglected in analyses of texts pertaining to the conflict, and likewise foregrounds aspects of this period of American history that are, for the most part, unique to it. While the representational strategies of Vietnam-era texts presenting men's experiences with war and bodily damage may show a new, different, historically specific response to wartime violence and its effect on the masculine subject, the narratives presented by these texts themselves are nevertheless deeply familiar and draw from constructions of American masculinity foundational to American identity in earlier periods. These constructions of identity, while historically specific, depend on particularly resilient American cultural narratives that resurface during times of profound cultural crisis.

The aim of this chapter, therefore, is to build on previous discussions of key Vietnam-era texts portraying masculinity and/or disability produced in the United States by locating them in a specifically American literary and cultural tradition. To this end, this section looks at Michael Cimino's film *The Deer Hunter* (1978), Ted Kotcheff's film version of David Morell's popular novel *First Blood* (1972), and Morell's novel itself, examining parallels between the formulation of masculinity presented in these texts and foundational ideas regarding American masculine sufficiency that originate in frontier narratives of the United States, typified by but not exclusive to the works of writers like James Fenimore Cooper. The chapter also discusses Ron Kovic's antiwar disability memoir *Born on the Fourth of July* (1976) in the context of this formulation of masculine subjectivity to examine how disability and masculinity in the Vietnam era interacted in ways ultimately in line with conventional historical conceptions of American masculinity. Unsurprisingly, disability pervades cultural texts produced in the United States during the Vietnam era. This chapter thus approaches the texts it discusses from a disability studies perspective and, in doing so, provides an account of the role of disability in American culture during this period by placing late twentieth-century texts in context with broader, long-standing patterns structuring understandings of masculine subjectivity and its relationship to national identity in the United States. The chapter argues that these texts' interest in disability and masculinity presents a continuation of the general representational trends discussed in this work's earlier chapters, serving as evidence of an increasingly pronounced effort to elide the contradictions at the heart of American masculine identity through a resurgence of formulations of masculinity that predate the twentieth century.

When the texts discussed in this chapter stage a reclamation of heteronormative masculinity, they often do so in a setting reminiscent of the rugged landscape of the North American continent imagined by authors like Cooper as the archetypal forum for forging a uniquely American masculine subjectivity. This chapter argues that in both versions of *First Blood* and in *The Deer Hunter*, the trauma of war comes to be mapped onto the physical landscape of the postwar United States; the American wilderness functions as an external site for an attempted regeneration of American masculinity for subjects experiencing physical and/or psychological injuries as a result of the war through a conflation of Vietnamese and United States landscapes, both physically and symbolically. Ultimately, these Vietnam-era texts undermine and at times call into question distinctions between war zone and home front through inability or unwillingness to construct the war and home as distinct physical and ethical spaces. In *Frames of War: When Is Life Grievable?*, Judith Butler argues that different populations are produced as either recognizable or unrecognizable as fully human subjects in the context of war based on how a conflict is framed via various forms of technological mediation. Although the process of framing in some sense remains abstract, the force of Butler's argument is that these discursive frames result in very real, material effects on human bodies and, as such, ought to be considered instruments of warfare. Such framing also designates certain spaces as locations of "grievability," wherein casualties that occur to certain populations in those spaces are mourned or not mourned based on the value assigned to these populations according to the meanings produced by the framing discourses to which they are subjected. Both films discussed at length in this chapter are ambivalent about their dramatization of masculine violence but nonetheless reflect an increasing preoccupation in American culture regarding the nature of American masculine identity as it relates to violence: a simultaneous idealization of violence as a necessary cost of military supremacy in the postwar world and a self-conscious reflection on a uniquely American fascination with violence itself. By presenting their versions of American wilderness as new iterations of a mythologized space haunted by anxieties about American masculinity in an uncertain postwar world, both *First Blood* and *The Deer Hunter* collapse the distance from war and its consequences afforded to certain populations and localities by dominant frames of war. Returning soldiers pass from the war zone to the home front carrying with them traces of war and its violence back to a space previously constructed and understood as untouchable by the lasting effects of war. The body of the soldier-male, in passing between the boundaries of national borders, carries with him traces of foreign conflict that undermine constructed boundaries the masculine subject as normatively constituted is compelled to produce and police, often violently.

WOUNDED VISIONS: NARRATIVES OF MASCULINE VICTIMIZATION

By the mid-1980s, narratives about the victimization of men and the denigration of masculinity in the wake of cultural upheaval, represented for some by the 1960s and 1970s, had become commonplace in American culture. These narratives held that the gains of the women's movement of the 1970s in particular had been made at the expense of men, traditional conceptions of masculinity, and values through which many males sought to identify. Men in general were often seen to be the target of criticism, but male veterans at times felt themselves to be particularly denigrated by progressive cultural forces like second-wave feminism, which they felt had redefined American culture.[5] Men who held these views also felt that it fell to them to conform to new, uncertain standards for male behavior at the expense of their own well-being, forced to repress natural aspects of their masculinity to conform to revised gender expectations.[6] The late 1970s and 1980s saw the rise of various reactions to this perceived disenfranchisement: social phenomena like the mythopoeic men's movement associated with American poet Robert Bly and an assortment of cultural texts that valorized the resurgence of rugged masculinity in opposition to effeminizing forces that often included official institutions of authority such as the American government.[7]

Bly's *Iron John: A Book about Men*, a highly anecdotal pastiche of sources drawn from various mythological and theoretical traditions and published by Bly in 1990, bears discussion here not because of any insight of its own into masculine subjectivity in the late twentieth century. Its attempt at synthesizing various sources into a coherent account of an American masculinity diminished by the feminizing influences of the women's movement offers a particularly clear example of masculinist backlash against social changes of the 1960s and 1970s, thinly disguised as a progressive theory for rescuing men by putting them back in touch with the lost, essential maleness Bly believed was key to reinvigorating American masculinity. In the book, Bly treats the cultural narratives of masculinity he discusses not as constructions arising within culturally and historically specific conditions (like the mythic structures Roland Barthes explicates in his book *Mythologies*) but as archetypal examples of maleness taken for granted as universal in form and value. Bly's theoretical apparatus draws heavily on Sigmund Freud, Carl Jung, and Wilhelm Reich but is fleshed out with anecdotal and often unattributed examples of masculinity devalued and diminished by contemporary American society in the decades following World War II.[8] Bly laments the phenomenon of what he calls the "soft male," a man characterized by "isolation and depravation" and, above all, "passivity."[9] Bly writes, "There's something wonderful about this development—I mean the practice of men welcoming their own 'feminine' consciousness and nurturing it—this is important—and yet I have the sense that there is something wrong. The male in the past twenty years has become more thoughtful, more gentle. But by this process he has not become more free. He's a nice boy who pleases not only his mother but the young woman he is living with." In the preface to *Iron John*, Bly states dramatically that the book will help contemporary American men "[follow] the tracks of one's own wound through the forest and [find] that it resembles the tracks of a god," allowing men to access mythic narratives that "are meant to be taken slowly into the body" and "continue to unfold, once taken in." Bly offers these stories as a quasi-mystical cure-all for effeminized masculinity that men can access deep in their psyches once these narratives are relearned and internalized in specific forms accessed via external cultural sources. He insists on the importance of reviving and regaining access to myths of masculinity unbound, which, according to Bly, "popular culture constantly declares [do] not exist."[10] Despite the author's statement to the contrary, many cultural texts of the Vietnam era and its aftermath feature just the sort of male figure Bly valorizes in his book. In fact, American popular culture of the late 1970s and 1980s was awash in depictions of victimized men resorting to hypermasculine excess in response to social forces they perceived as restricting them from behaving like "real" men. So widespread were narratives of masculine disenfranchisement linked to the Vietnam conflict during this time that in 1989, social scientist Jean Bethke Elshtain concluded that the Vietnam War had been "reconstructed as a story of universal victimization" in which all parties involved—combatants on both sides, Vietnamese civilians, and those on the American home front (but "in particular white men")—had been exploited by each other and fallen victim to forces that seemed beyond their control.[11]

A darker side of this backlash was the role it played in the rise of the modern white power movement, which, though elements had existed prior to the Vietnam era, consolidated itself into what would become its current form during this time. In her work, Kathleen Belew details how some male veterans who felt they had been betrayed by their country and, in particular, its government during and after the war returned from Vietnam and became involved in various white supremacist organizations.[12] The military training these veterans had received through participation in the war was seen as valuable by extremist groups, and narratives of a lost war resulting in white male disenfranchisement helped unify disparate factions and cohere them into a larger movement.[13] During this period, the American white power movement began to construct a story of disenfranchised white masculinity and its revitalization. Drawing symbolic power from iconography from the American War in Vietnam combined with narrative elements from American frontier mythology, "white power activists adopted and recognized the weapons and uniforms of the U.S. military as a part of both their tactics and public presentation," while "invocation of the 'cowboy and the woman pioneer' reinscribed gender expectations for women into the white power movement [and] fit into a longer narrative of a romanticism of the [American] West."[14]

The historical phenomenon of white male backlash against second-wave feminism and the civil rights movement has been widely discussed in both trade and academic publications. While this chapter examines texts in the context of this historical moment, it also seeks to show that the perception of masculine disenfranchisement that occurred following the Vietnam War was deeply related to the broader crisis of masculinity this project identifies, a crisis that only intensified as the twentieth century progressed. Although the texts discussed in this chapter concern precisely the type of disenfranchised male figures Jeffords identifies in her work, they also represent a nostalgic regression to a much earlier formulation of masculinity drawn generally from nineteenth-century narratives of manifest destiny and, in particular, from James Fenimore Cooper's *Leatherstocking* novels. In his *Studies in Classic American Literature*, D. H. Lawrence argues that two seemingly contradictory impulses structure American masculine identity, which Jon Thompson describes as "a tension that becomes definitive of American culture: wanting to be both 'savage' and 'American,' wanting, that is, to be both primitive and modern, instinctual and rational, native and European." For Lawrence, the best examples of the relationship between the American landscape and this bifurcated formulation of American masculine identity are Cooper's Leatherstocking Tales and their protagonist, Natty Bumppo. Lawrence views Bumppo, who lives on the edge of the frontier and derives his identity from a unique position that gives form to civilization by defining its limits, as a figure of wish fulfillment for Cooper.[15] An ascetic whose rugged life precludes romantic entanglements that might civilize him, Bumppo's masculinity is defined simultaneously by violent excess and carnal restraint, and his function in the Leatherstocking Tales is to police and maintain essentially permeable racial and gender boundaries. He kills to protect the purity of white womanhood and frequently refers to his own racial identity as unmixed. Throughout *The Last of the Mohicans* in particular, Bumppo repeatedly declares he is "a white man without a cross," indicating with an almost obsessive fervor that his lineage is free from miscegenation.[16] References to the character's whiteness are often made in conjunction with a demonstration of his inherent physical superiority to the novel's nonwhite male characters, conflating whiteness with the able body. By the end of his life, however, as Cooper writes in his 1849 introduction to *The Prairie*, Bumppo finds that "the sound of the axe has driven him from his beloved forests to seek refuge, by a species of desperate resignation, on the denuded plains that stretch to the Rocky Mountains," the very forces of manifest destiny that propelled him now depriving him of agency.[17] Where those who remain sympathetic to Cooper tend to frame the Leatherstocking novels as ideological precursors to the modern environmentalist movement, Lawrence focuses on Bumppo as an archetypal figure of rugged American sufficiency whose violent exclusion of both feminine and racial alterity is foundational to traditionally constructed American masculinity.[18] Jeffords's astute diagnosis of the tendencies in narratives of American masculinity and the policing of its boundaries in the Vietnam era identifies elements structuring masculine accounts of the Vietnam War from an American perspective specific to this particular body of narratives. The ultimate ideological purpose of these techniques—the violent exclusion of the feminine in service of the preservation of an exclusively male experience and point of view—can be just as accurately applied to Cooper's tales of Bumppo's exploits.[19] In fact, the underlying mechanisms by which these exclusionary representational techniques function are nearly identical to the matrix of exclusionary forces present in Cooper's work as elucidated by Lawrence.

The novel *First Blood*, its subsequent film version, and *The Deer Hunter* all present similar depictions of rugged masculine individualism inhabiting a boundary between civilization and wilderness. Where Special Forces veteran John Rambo (Sylvester Stallone) returns to the United States following his internment in a Viet Cong prisoner of war (POW) camp only to be pushed from civilization by representatives of local law enforcement whose abuses of power quickly become vigilantism, protagonist Michael Vronsky (Robert De Niro) in *The Deer Hunter* presents a similar asceticism that is largely self-imposed. From the start of the film, Vronsky's character—who serves in Vietnam as an Army Green Beret—demonstrates familiarity with various folkloric knowledge traditions that sets him apart from the other men in his immediate peer group. As the film begins, the five principal male characters, three of whom leave their small, industrial town in rural Pennsylvania to fight in the war, depart work at a local steel mill to prepare for a hunting trip meant to celebrate the wedding of Steven Pushkov (John Savage) to Angela Ludhjduravic (Rutanya Alda), the event around which the first third of the film centers. Though the film presents Michael's knowledge system as fairly ad hoc (he references sun dogs and their significance as "an old Indian thing"), he nevertheless follows what he believes to be a rigorous, if self-devised, belief system seemingly derived from hierarchies of the natural world.[20]

That Vronsky's asceticism seems to preclude romantic relationships is not incidental. While the character Stanley (John Cazale) and various critics read Vronsky's reticence to form romantic attachments with women as evidence of homosexuality, Jeffords argues that the masculine bonds depicted in the film are exclusively heterosexual and that the conflict in the film between Michael and his close friend Nick Chevotarevich (Christopher Walken) is not sexual in nature, deriving instead from Nick's perception that Michael broke his promise early in the film not to leave him behind in Vietnam.[21] For Jeffords, Morrell's *First Blood* and the series of films it inspired are paradigmatic of the cultural politics of mainstream Hollywood depictions that present Vietnam veterans "as emblems of an unjustly discriminated masculinity" whose "manhood is revived, regenerated principally by a rejection of the feminine and sexuality." Jeffords argues that war narratives of the Vietnam era present "a revived and restructured myth of America that reevaluates everything except the very framework within which that myth resides—the construction of gender."[22] In the character of Michael Vronsky in particular, one can see a clear recurrence of one of the oldest and most enduring archetypes of American masculinity: the Leatherstocking of James Fenimore Cooper's frontier novels. *The Deer Hunter* transposes the psyche of the Leatherstocking onto the figure of the Vietnam veteran via Vronsky's character, inflecting Cooper's archetype of American masculine sufficiency with a new historical specificity through the character's experience of post-traumatic stress as a result of his time spent as a POW. Vronsky's aversion to physical and emotional intimacy at times registers less outright as a symptom of wartime trauma than the displays of emotion and violence present in Steven's outbursts in the Veterans Administration hospital or Nick's reenactment of his torture at the hands of the Viet Cong as manifested in his

Russian roulette compulsion. Yet the character's resistance to romantic companionship is part of a more general asceticism that aligns Vronsky with the protagonist of Cooper's Leatherstocking novels such that *The Deer Hunter* can be seen as enacting the civilization/savage dichotomy Lawrence traces in his *Studies in Classic American Literature*. Of Bumppo, Lawrence writes, "Rather than be dragged into a false heat of deliberate sensuality, he will remain alone. His soul is alone. So he will preserve his integrity, and remain alone in the flesh. It is a stoicism that is honest and fearless, and from which Deerslayer never lapses, except when, approaching middle age, he proposes to the buxom Mabel."[23] The indeterminacy present in Vronsky's character— his trauma recognizable simultaneously as a result of his war experience and as a response to a more general dissolution of masculinist categories that structure his understanding of self—is of a piece with the film's structure, which forgoes standard narrative closure and presents a loosely organized story. The narrative of *The Deer Hunter* is bound not by the cause-and-effect relationships of the classical Hollywood plot but by a symbolic structure that preexists the film and pervades American culture; the film's unconventional narrative structure allows it to comment on many tropes of the veteran's homecoming depicted in a more straightforward manner in the films of earlier eras. Though *The Deer Hunter*, a quintessential New Hollywood text, might seem to have little in common with the postwar films of the 1940s, Cimino's film restages most of the familiar beats of traditional homecoming narratives like *The Best Years of Our Lives*, defamiliarizing what would otherwise be a melodramatic plot through a manipulation of traditional narrative structure. The film begins with a marriage—the type of device used to provide closure at the end of Wyler's film—and the plot that unfolds in *The Deer Hunter* undercuts the traditional resonances of a marriage in a Hollywood film. Cimino's film, though it unfolds chronologically, defies narrative conventions in that the episodes it depicts remain somewhat disconnected.

PRECARIOUS LIFE AND THE CRISIS OF THE ACTION-IMAGE IN *THE DEER HUNTER*

The Deer Hunter's story of three young men who depart a working-class Russian immigrant enclave in Pennsylvania to fight in Vietnam, leaving their tight-knit community behind, is organized loosely by a three-act structure and begins stateside, with Steven Pushkov's wedding to his pregnant girlfriend, Angela. The fact that the marriage celebration also serves as a going away party for Steven, Nick, and Michael undercuts the happiness of the event and the traditional narrative function of a wedding to mark a protagonist's reintegration into their community (as in the conclusion of Wyler's World War II film). Knowledge that Steven is not the father of Angela's unborn child further undercuts the traditional resonance of the wedding scene, and masculine violence pervades the first section of the film, well before Vietnam is introduced as a setting. Shortly after we meet Linda (Meryl Streep), the woman whose presence forms a triangulated relationship linking Nick and Michael, her eye is blackened by her father in an incoherent, drunken rage as she prepares for her role as a member of the wedding party. This act of violence, unlike the later events in the film, is presented as tragically ordinary in the life of Linda, and the early scenes establish that women's position in the film tends to be to manage and contain instances of violent masculine excess.

After the wedding, the men hunt deer in the Pennsylvania wilderness and then return to town for a night of drunken revelry. Only the deep sense of foreboding that pervades these opening scenes provides a semblance of continuity when the film abruptly cuts to images of the war-torn Vietnamese countryside; competing forces destroy a rural village, and the three men are captured and become POWs. Their capture occurs off screen, as the film generally elides moments that might serve as narrative connective tissue between the events it depicts. The men, forced to play Russian roulette at the hands of their captors, eventually escape when Michael convinces the guards to up the stakes of the game by loading the gun with extra bullets, giving him enough ammunition to kill the Viet Cong soldiers when their guard is down. The men travel downriver until spotted by a rescue helicopter. After pulling himself into the ascending chopper, Nick watches helplessly as Steven loses his grip and falls into the water below, breaking his legs, and Michael lets himself fall after him. Michael carries Steven through the jungle past enemy lines and delivers him safely into the hands of a passing South Vietnamese convoy. Nick, unaware of the fate of his friends and now under the care of military doctors in Saigon, starts to experience symptoms of posttraumatic stress and eventually begins playing Russian roulette for money in various clandestine locations throughout the city.

The scene in Saigon foreshadows Steven's loss of his legs, as Nick finds himself one of the few physically uninjured American soldiers recuperating in a crowded hospital. Nick responds hesitantly when the doctor who checks him in for treatment asks his name. When asked if Chevotarevich is a Russian name, Nick responds, "No. It's American." When asked whether the wallet containing his identification and a picture of Angela belongs to him, he defiantly says, "It's his," gesturing to a Black American soldier lying on nearby gurney with bandaged arms that have both been amputated at the elbow.[24] In light of Chevotarevich's later act of disassociation, the character's reluctance to respond to fairly clear-cut questions meant to confirm his identity reads simultaneously as an uneasy (and unreciprocated) identification with a physically injured fellow soldier and the beginning of loss of a coherent sense of self. Chevotarevich begins to sob softly, unable to look away from the disabled man as the attending physician asks Nick to verify the birthdates of his parents. Familial, racial, national, and bodily identities become contested sites for Nick in a moment when he might otherwise begin recovering from the trauma he has experienced.

Jeffords writes that "the first half of *The Deer Hunter* revolves around the promise of reproduction, and the second is motivated by that which denies reproduction, the promise of the masculine bond. The structure of the film revolves around Nick, the figure who links these two experiences."[25] Nick's absence for much of the film's third act provides an organizing function in that it motivates Michael's eventual return to Vietnam in search of him near the film's conclusion, but the narrative itself exhibits the deliberately weak linkages Deleuze identifies as a central feature of the crisis of the action-image in postwar American cinema.[26] It is this loose structure that somewhat counterintuitively allows for continuity between the sections of the narrative that occur stateside and those that take place on foreign soil, subtly undermining spatial distinctions between the film's two primary settings and the apparent disjuncture between different narrative threads of the film. In *First Blood*, a similar reinscription of foreign trauma onto an American setting is rendered quite literally when, early in the film, John Rambo relives his torture at the hands of the Viet Cong while interrogated by the police in Hope, Washington; images of his previous torture and confinement are intercut with and superimposed on shots of the interior of the police station before he escapes and flees into the wilderness of the Pacific Northwest. This spatial conflation is indicated even more directly in the novel that provides the film's source material. Set in Kentucky rather than Washington, David Morrell's *First Blood* is told by an omniscient narrator who describes the mountainous setting into which John Rambo escapes as "high and wild, thickly wooded, slashed by ravines and draws and pocked with hollows. Just like the North Carolina hills in which he had been trained. Much like the hills he had escaped through in the war."[27] A focus on topography rather than vegetation allows for the conflation of a Vietnamese jungle landscape with an archetypal American setting: a vast, primeval forest, the rugged landscape common to many foundational accounts of American masculine identity. *The Deer Hunter*, more loosely structured than the film version of Morrell's book, undermines the distinction between foreign and domestic spaces less didactically, as the significance of Michael's return to the woods once he is back in the States is kept ambiguous by his decision not to shoot the deer in the film's second hunting sequence, hinting at a moment of possible healing through rejection of violence.

The trope of spatial conflation presented in these texts can be seen as a literalization of the effects of posttraumatic stress disorder (PTSD) noted by Cathy Caruth, one of the theorists who developed the central tenets of trauma theory in the 1990s. Caruth notes that the inherent latency of the traumatic experience is part of what defines it: "the impact of the traumatic event lies precisely in its belatedness, its refusal to be simply located, in its insistent appearance outside of the boundaries of any single place or time."[28] Yet in these texts, the American wilderness also serves as a forum for potential reclamation of masculinity for the protagonists, wherein the wartime landscape of Vietnam and the peaceful landscape of the United States are conflated such that a foreign conflict comes to be inscribed on the home front. Despite Michael's choice to forgo killing the deer in *The Deer Hunter*'s second hunting sequence as necessitated by his philosophy, which valorizes acts of violence only if exercised with the utmost control and restraint, the film's narrative ultimately does not allow the character to leave the violence of the war behind him.

Judith Butler's work in the last decade on issues of exposure and survivability is helpful in clarifying some of their previous statements about the nature of the body as an entity with boundaries that materialize as an effect of power and, as such, remain essentially indeterminate—and also in explicating elements of *The Deer Hunter* that have caused disagreement for critics since its release. In *Frames of War*, Butler notes that following 9/11, national security analyses tended to focus on the permeability of US borders as a threat to safety and national identity, and yet they argue that both personal and national "identity is not thinkable without the permeable border, or else without the possibility of relinquishing a boundary." Intersubjective identity formation by necessity entails risks such as potential loss of perceived autonomy: in the case of persons and nations, "a boundary is given up precisely in order to establish a certain connection." Butler builds on and revises the work of Viennese psychoanalyst Melanie Klein in their analysis of the intersubjective nature of identity formation and the precarity it entails. Precarity is a necessary and, in fact, central part of human existence: "according to Melanie Klein," Butler writes, "we develop moral responses in reaction to questions of survivability." Butler agrees with this basic insight but argues that Klein's understanding of the source of individual morality is limited precisely because it overemphasizes the individual. For Klein, moral responses grow out of the subject's desire to protect *itself*. In Klein's terms, Butler states, "it is the ego's survivability that is finally at issue." Butler's break with Klein foregrounds a materialization of self that is constitutively intersubjective. They expound on their objections to an egocentric understanding of morality in the following passage:

> Why the ego? After all, if my survivability depends on a relation to others, to a "you" or a set of "yous" without whom I cannot exist, then my existence is not mine alone, but to be found outside myself, in this set of relationships that precede and exceed the boundaries of who I am. If I have a boundary at all, or if a boundary can be said to belong to me, it is only because I have become separated from others, and it is only on condition of this separation that I can relate to them at all. So the boundary is a function of relation, a brokering of difference, a negotiation in which I am bound to you in my separateness. If I seek to preserve your life, it is not only because I seek to preserve my own, but because who "I" am is nothing without your life, and life itself has to be rethought as this complex, passionate, antagonistic, and necessary set of relations to others. I may lose this "you" and any number of particular others, and I may well survive those losses. But that can only happen if I do not lose the possibility of any "you" at all. If I survive, it is only because my life is nothing without the life that exceeds me, that refers to some indexical you, without whom I cannot be.[29]

Butler has been criticized by scholars in disability studies and other disciplines based on the perception that their work, *Bodies That Matter* in particular, overemphasizes the socially constructed nature of the body to the extent that it ignores the material experience of embodiment.[30] Butler's reference to an indexical body in the passage above grounds their analysis of precarity in the material vulnerability of the body without undermining their understanding of bodies as socially constructed, contingent entities. Precarity (and moral questions surrounding the vulnerability of bodies), in Butler's analysis, depends largely on factors that are socially located and play out *between* individuals. "It is not as an isolated and bounded being that I survive," Butler writes, "but as one whose boundary exposes me to others in ways that are voluntary and involuntary (sometimes at once) [and] survival depends less on the established boundary to the self than on the constitutive sociality of the body."[31] Though Butler's earlier work may seem to deemphasize the somatic experiences of a body in the world, a constructivist view need not preclude an understanding of the potential material consequences of the vulnerability of the physical body as experienced somatically.

The material precarity of the body—a central feature of embodied experience as foregrounded and explicated in *Frames of War*—is central to *The Deer Hunter*'s understanding of violence. Butler writes, "War is precisely an effort to minimize precariousness for some and maximize it for others." As captives of the Viet Cong, Nick, Steven, and Michael are hyperaware of their vulnerability in a way that their captors are not aware of their own: the power imbalance in the scene results in part from the extent to which the Viet Cong continually work to keep captives' awareness of their abject, threatened status foremost in their minds. The POWs outnumber their captors, but a constant state of fear and continued dehumanization prevents them from taking action to escape even when not confined in the bamboo cages in which they are held. The logic of Michael's plan to escape the POW camp, however, derives from understanding the nature of precarity in a more nuanced manner than his captors. On the surface, the reasoning behind Michael's request for more bullets in the revolver is simple: if chance allows the Americans to avoid dying from self-inflicted gunshot wounds (made more likely by the increased number of bullets in the gun) and if they are able to catch the Viet Cong by surprise, they will have more ammunition to use against their captors in an escape attempt. In the economy of the forced game of Russian roulette, the protagonists of *The Deer Hunter* can only increase their chances of survival by increasing their risk. The position of power occupied by the Viet Cong in the scene is more tenuous than they as captors realize because the narrative they impose on their captives blinds them to their own reciprocal vulnerability. Yet Vronsky's logic is inescapably nihilistic: in killing to save itself, the subject ultimately brings itself closer to its own annihilation, but this is simply a necessity in a cruel world where all relationships are structured by dominance. Vronsky's later attempt to save his friend by appealing to a shared humanity fails because it departs from the logic of domination that structures and makes legible all relationships in the film and characterizes most attempts at communication between its characters.

Sylvia Shin Huey Chong's reading of *The Deer Hunter* from a psychoanalytic perspective, first in her article "Restaging the War: *The Deer Hunter* and the Primal Scene of Violence" and later in her book *The Oriental Obscene: Violence and Racial Fantasies in the Vietnam Era*, argues that violence in *The Deer Hunter* generally functions through a logic of transference: American soldiers enact self-inflicted violence that substitutes within the symbolic system of the film for acts of violence experienced by the Vietnamese at American hands.[32] This logic of transference, which in Chong's view blurs distinctions between American and Vietnamese subject positions in the film, results in scenes of violence that are difficult to parse. Cimino disrupts standard cinematic language through a camera that undermines the creation of stable relationships within its frame by avoiding standard shot/reverse shot scene constructions. As a result, "the American soldier is not diametrically opposed to the Vietnamese (as represented by the VC in charge of the game), but is also taking the place of the Vietnamese (as prisoner of war)" even during scenes that depict Americans tortured at the hands of the Viet Cong.[33] This destabilization of the camera's vantage point as a position of control and authority creates a fragmented point of view that mimics the perspective of the men when they are forced to view the torture of other POWs from below, through the floor of the bamboo hut beneath which they are caged.[34]

The ideological ambiguity of *The Deer Hunter*, which results in part from the film's unconventional formal strategies, has vexed critics since its release. Initial reactions to the film in 1978 were split between those who admired it as an aesthetic achievement and others who criticized its perceived positions on the war and race. Those who defended the film tended understand it as a broad critique of the violence of war, whereas more critical responses viewed the depiction of Vietnamese cruelty and Americans as victims as evidence of a xenophobic politics at the heart of the film that inverted the actual power dynamics of the war in Vietnam.[35] A sympathetic reading of *The Deer Hunter* on ideological grounds depends on viewing Cimino's depiction of these power dynamics as part of an auteurial statement critiquing clear-cut notions American hegemony, a position that is difficult to reconcile with the one-dimensional representation of the Vietnamese in the film.

The portrayal of American masculine sufficiency in crisis pervades the film even before the narrative's violent middle section, remaining unresolved at the conclusion. The final minutes of Nick Chevotarevich's life hinge on an ambiguous moment of (mis)recognition that plays out between Nick and Michael just before Chevotarevich takes his own life. In her astute reading of what is perhaps the most well-known sequence from *The Deer Hunter*, Chong argues that "what is stable in this scene are not the specific roles the actors are playing but the syntactical relationship between them," interpreting *The Deer Hunter*'s Russian roulette sequences using Freud's "A Child Is Being Beaten" formulation as a way of understanding Nick Chevotarevich's essentially irrational act of self-inflicted violence in the final third of the film.[36] Chong reads this scene, and the earlier sequence in which Michael and Nick are forced to play Russian roulette by their captors, as restaging the infamous "Saigon Execution" photograph: Associated Press photographer Eddie Adams's Pulitzer Prize–winning image depicting the killing of Nguyen Van Lem, a Viet Cong squad captain, by Brigadier General Nguyen Ngoc Loan, who was, at the time, head of the Vietnamese national police, in downtown Saigon on February 1, 1968.

In the final section of Cimino's film, Vronsky goes back to Vietnam after returning to the States and discovering that Nick is still alive and has been anonymously sending money to Steven in the VA hospital from somewhere in Saigon. Eventually, Michael discovers that Nick has fallen under the influence of an unnamed Frenchman connected with illegal gambling and has been playing Russian roulette for money. With the man's help, Michael tracks down his friend at an underground game happening as the city is evacuated. In the final Russian roulette scene of *The Deer Hunter*, Michael attempts to reason with his friend by appealing to a shared bond based on identity categories that, for Nick, have largely collapsed. Though Nick responds to Michael's injunction to "Tell me it's Mike" by saying Vronsky's name, it quickly becomes clear that he is not identifying his friend in a gesture of recognition: Nick, dazed and seemingly drugged, simply repeats back what he has been told to say by an apparent stranger. Nick's willingness to repeat Vronsky's name and his inability to recognize his friend are characteristic of the repetition compulsion governing Chevotarevich's character in this scene. His rote repetition of actions on cue initially appears as a symptom of his loss of self; importantly, this loss of identity plays out intersubjectively in the character's inability to identify himself via his position in a relationship that once helped define him in a positive sense. Vronsky's most direct statements appealing to the bond they share ("Nicky, I love you. You're my friend. What are you doing?") are met not with confusion but with overt rejection as Nick responds to Michael's statement of fraternal love by spitting in his face, and Nick's eventual acknowledgment of Michael's identity only comes just before he fires the revolver held to his own temple.[37]

In this moment, acknowledgment and negation become hopelessly fused, yet it is ultimately not the danger of mutual precarity that undoes Chevotarevich's sense of self. As Michael and Nick face each other again across a table, each holding the gun to his own head in turn as demanded by the game, Michael's philosophy of "one shot" takes on a meaning that is different for each character than it was at the start of the film. For Vronsky, self-directed violence has strangely become a gesture of compassion, a willingness to risk his life in order potentially to preserve another. For Nick, each instance of "one shot" is merely another in a series performed by rote, the continuation of a repetition compulsion that leads inexorably to loss of self and eventually death. Though Michael may, by the end of the film, seem to represent a rejection of nihilism through his selfless devotion to his friend, that Nick can only be reached through violence undercuts such a reading of *The Deer Hunter.* Michael willingly revisits the site of his trauma in his effort to save Nick, but all that can be communicated between them is a reciprocal violence that cannot be transmogrified into a positive outcome.[38] Michael thus returns to America with his friend's body, only ironically fulfilling his promise from the start of the film.

The Deer Hunter ends with a funeral rather than a wedding ceremony, yet the rituals seem interchangeable. The film's opening scenes of friends drinking are restaged when the principals gather again to mourn Nicolas, rendering the film cyclical and melancholic and undercutting any patriotic resonance to the final shot, in which the bar patrons sing "God Bless America" after toasting to Nick's memory. John (George Dzundza), who owns the bar and has avoided the war due to bad knees, accidentally sets out "too many cups" for the mourners, a gesture of habit referencing Nick's absence and evoking the scene near the end of *The Sun Also Rises* in which Jake Barnes compares a postwar gathering of his friends to similar dinners during World War I: "The three of us sat at the table, and it seemed as though about six people were missing."[39] Loss and absence pervade the film's final scene as small eruptions of emotion (such as John's brief outburst of crying) punctuate an otherwise rather affectless sequence.[40] Jeffords reads the meaning of the singing in the final scene literally, as Cimino's final gesture reinscribing hegemonic masculine values in his film's conclusion, calling the work, on the whole, "an embarrassingly straightforward film."[41] Kathleen Brady, John Briggs, and Edward A. Hagen, in contrast, view Cimino's use of the patriotic song as a part of the film's intentional deconstruction of "the illusion of . . . an autonomous male self."[42] Both of these interpretations rest on assumptions about Cimino's intentionality and the stability of the film's resulting presentation of directorial intentions in a transparent, clearcut, and unmediated manner. Chong, in comparison, argues that "*The Deer Hunter* posits a violent, self-dissolving fantasy in which visual fascination ends at the radical point of non-being." Chong writes:

> If *The Deer Hunter* imagines suffering Vietnamese bodies, it also shows the American subject incorporating that suffering. When the self and the incorporated other become indistinguishable, that suffering emerges as

self-inflicted violence. . . . Nick's suicide complicates the critique that *The Deer Hunter* is a mirror that narcissistically reflects American identity and values and that ignores Vietnamese subjectivity. If a crude form of racist dehumanization allows killings like those in My Lai to take place—I can kill the other because the other is merely an object to me—then that objecthood is brought uncomfortably close to one's own subjecthood through participation in violence—if the other can kill me, I am thus potentially an object myself. In a structure that destabilizes human subjectivity so radically, what would it mean to "humanize" the victims of the Vietnam War? Even if we were to "rectify" the representational politics of *The Deer Hunter* by restoring Americans to the role of aggressor and the Vietnamese to that of victim (as it "really" was), we cannot escape the permutational logic that flows from the primal scene of violence. . . . After the Americans lose their innocence in the game of Russian roulette, there is no "coming home" for the hunters, no healing of wounds caused by the war. In this marriage of violence, both the deer and the hunter are sacrificed.[43]

In revising this argument for her 2012 book-length project, Chong backs away from language foregrounding intersubjectivity and the collapse of identity positions that results in annihilation of the self. She argues instead that the Vietnam-era films she discusses are marked by "the substitution of killed and maimed American bodies for the wounded and dead Vietnamese found in the iconic images," which results in an "orientalization of the American soldier [that] no longer carrie[s] an antiwar message [but] instead reflect[s] the dispersion of identification from the individual soldier to the American nation, which now mourns the loss of the war through the internalization of Vietnamese suffering."[44] The shift in discourse here, though subtle, marks a departure from the author's discussion of *The Deer Hunter* in her earlier article, putting her account more in line with tendencies present in other accounts of the Vietnam War and its representation in American cultural texts.

THE DISABLED MALE BODY AND THE VALANCES OF DISABILITY IN POST-VIETNAM AMERICA

Chong's psychoanalytic framework allows her to skillfully move between discussing indexical bodies inscribed on film and the presence of these bodies in images that, for the critic, become part of the deep structures of the American psyche post-Vietnam.[45] Her discussion of the Vietnam era—both historically and culturally—has much to recommend it, and I am in general agreement with a good deal of her points, particularly her reformulation of Said's concept of Orientalism in a specifically American context, yet her analysis of disability in the Vietnam-era context is a bit less nuanced.[46] The specificity of her argument thus limits its applicability beyond the distinct formation on which her book focuses: the repressed racial unconscious of the United States in the Vietnam War era, through which the American masculine subject internalizes images of the radicalized other to account for a loss of military hegemony and "embraces defeat as the very condition for American subjectivity, after Vietnam."[47] Chong's analysis of the tropes she sees informing the presentation of the Oriental obscene—the repressed site of violence covered over but not erased by depictions of bodies in peril in the context of the Vietnam War—does important work to shift focus onto populations often underconsidered in accounts of the violence of Vietnam and its aftermath, but a disability studies perspective can provide additional nuance to the author's argument. Chong's discussion of disabled bodies focuses, for the most part, on moments of excess in which individual bodies fail to contain themselves, reading these specific instances as representationally paradigmatic for the significance of disability in texts depicting the Vietnam War and its aftermath. Chong writes:

> Together these films outline the vicissitudes of what I call "the body incontinent," a messy, leaky, and permeable physical body that also serves as a metaphor for the loss of control that the Vietnam War imposed on the American soldier on multiple levels. Certainly we see instances of the body incontinent throughout the Vietnam War genre as well: Steven in *The Deer Hunter*, who returns to the U.S. paralyzed; Colonel Kurtz, whose indolent, corpulent body is sacrificed at the end of *Apocalypse Now*; and the vomiting and shitting Americans in *Go Tell the Spartans*. Hyperrealist violence in these films, with its visual attention to bodily ejecta, is itself an important vehicle for the representation of incontinence, as it transforms the human body from a volitional subject to a fleshy object subject to control of external, physical forces.[48]

Because these types of images tend to be foregrounded in texts that—as narratives of homecoming, rehabilitation, and social reintegration for injured veterans—"trace the effects of incontinence beyond the site of injury," Chong argues that the images of disability she describes "link the physical violence of Vietnam to other societal upheavals of the late 1970s, in particular second-wave feminism and its reconfiguration of national desire and the continuing racialization of 'law and order' through the specter of illegal drugs."[49] Though the author takes care not to conflate the specific representational patterns she identifies in textual formulations of bodily impairment with qualities seen as inherent in disabled bodies themselves, her formulation of "the body incontinent" nevertheless presents tendencies that result when disability is approached as a trope rather than an identity category or a subject position. The critic's discussion overprivileges textual examples of disability that present themselves as abject and focus on viscera and fluids associated with bodily injury (or with bodily processes that can elicit shame) at the expense of a more general category of experiences that might be described as "disabling" but would not read as examples of "incontinence." Moreover, in Chong's analysis, a loss of bodily control becomes synonymous with a disordered body politic even in contexts not explicitly related to disability or the body, reducing disability to a trope that signifies independently of actual disabled people.[50] Though her analysis makes insightful points regarding linkages between the body and the nation in the Vietnam era, Chong's indexical analysis of visual texts unintentionally fetishizes the disabled body, essentializing it as an object of pain and suffering and a site of shame instead of understanding disability as a nexus of socially constructed meanings experienced intersubjectively and produced citationally.

As noted in the introduction to *The Illegible Man*, disability provides the central metaphor for America after the Vietnam War in Ron Kovic's autobiography, *Born on the Fourth of July*. Kovic's book might seem to be an ideal text in which to find examples of the body incontinent: much of the author's distress in the work cannot be separated from his horror at his abject bodily state as he understands it, and both his injury and the arduous recovery process detailed in the book often put him in newly close contact with messy bodily processes due to his reduced control over them following his injury. The opening pages of the memoir teem with images of bodies that can no longer contain themselves, from the reference to blood "rolling off of [Kovic's] flak jacket from the hole in [his] shoulder" in the book's first sentence to the "young boy cupping his own intestines with his hands," whose screams echo through the text's opening pages.[51] Kovic's narrative obsesses over fragmented bodies and fragmentary experiences in its first chapter as the author recounts the initial moments of his injury and corresponding episodes of disassociation similar to those experienced by the protagonist of *Johnny Got His Gun*. The dominant images of the novel, particularly in the first chapter, however, tend to be both abstracted and disassociated from one another. We see hands, feet, faces, et cetera as denaturalized objects presented out of context as often as we see the "messy, leaky, and permeable body" Chong foregrounds in her analysis. Yet even as Kovic recounts an experience of disorientation and trauma, he emphasizes individualism and self-reliance, as in this passage: "I am in a hospital where they will operate on me and find out why I cannot feel anything from my chest down anymore. I know I am going to make it now. I am going to make it not because of any god, or any religion, but because *I* want to make it, *I* want to live. And I leave the screaming man without any legs and I am brought to a room that is very bright."[52] Haunted by the screams of a disemboweled young man from whom he willfully disavows any connection, Kovic's emphasis of the first person in this passage betrays a need to claim agency by isolating himself from those around him, even at the expense of potential solace through connection to others or solidarity expressed with those undergoing experiences like his own. Though Kovic is not deprived of the ability to communicate like the protagonist of Trumbo's novel, the first chapter of *Born on the Fourth of July* emphasizes feelings of isolation and separation in a manner very similar to that earlier text: Kovic's initial shift from first to third person in the book marks the beginning of the narrative's second chapter, the protagonist's release from the trauma unit in Vietnam, and the beginning of his rehabilitation in the United States. The familiarity of an American urban space comforts Kovic as his bus moves through the Queens neighborhood of New York. "For the first time on the trip everyone was laughing and joking," Kovic recalls. "He felt himself to begin to wake up out of a nightmare. The whole area was home to him—the streets, the parkway, he knew them like the back of his hand. The air was fresh and cold as the bus rocked back and forth." The use of past tense and third person introduce a semblance of order pointedly absent in the novel's opening chapter.[53]

Kovic's bodily experience in the second chapter, however, is ultimately one of reduction, an ongoing loss of self-identity, manifested corporeally: "He would sit in the shower like that every morning watching his legs become smaller and smaller, until after a month the muscle tone had all disappeared. With despair and frustration he watched his once strong twenty-one-year old body become crippled and disfigured. He was just beginning to understand the nature of his wound. It was the worst he could have received without dying or becoming a vegetable." A shift back to first person midchapter following this passage serves ironically to reemphasize Kovic's feelings of helplessness as he undergoes rehabilitation and remains continuously haunted by knowledge of his lost sexual potency. Early in the book, Kovic recounts a sexual dream about an imaginary woman, which is interrupted when a male orderly shows up to ready him for one of the regular enemas he receives now that he is paralyzed. Awakened from a stereotypical vision of masculine potency, Kovic waits for treatment in "a long line of men shoved up against the green hospital wall . . . tied down to their frames with their rear ends sticking out." The homophobic conflation of disability and sexual passivity strongly implied here reveals that perhaps the true horror of disability presented in *Born on the Fourth of July* is not only to have a body defamiliarized by violence but, ultimately, to experience a resulting loss of masculine status and, in this instance, a newly perceived vulnerability to the threat of sexual violence. Here, the narrator's helplessness is once again reinforced through his use of "I" statements: "I am angry and I want to kill everyone—all the volunteers and the priests and the pretty girls with the tight short skirts. I am twenty-one and the whole thing is shot, done forever."[54] The disabled body becomes a signifier of potential queerness and elicits inwardly directed violence redirected outward at others.[55]

In *Masculine Domination*, Pierre Bourdieu writes that "the body has its front, the *site of sexual difference*, and its back, sexually undifferentiated and potentially female, in other words passive, submissive."[56] This sort of essentialism, which Bourdieu's analysis of the body does not entirely reject, is at the heart of Kovic's deepest feelings about his gender and sexuality vis-à-vis his disability. Bourdieu's insight that "the dominated apply categories constructed from the point of view of the dominant to the relations of domination, thus making them appear natural" nevertheless remains useful in unpacking the dynamics of Kovic's feelings about disability and masculinity. The narrator's fantasies about women, detailed frequently in the text, present a naturalization of gendered dominance that becomes denaturalized when the same dynamic is mapped onto nightmarish fantasies of his own subjection, which come to the fore when the author, in his mind, loses his ability to inhabit the dominant position he perhaps unconsciously conflates with masculinity. In Bourdieu's analysis, norms of both femininity and masculinity are

> imposed for the most part through an unremitting discipline that concerns every part of the body and is continuously recalled through the constraints of clothing and hairstyle. The antagonistic principles of male and female identity are thus laid down in the form of permanent stances, gaits and postures which are the realization, or rather, the naturalization of an ethic. Just as the ethic of male honour can be summed up in a word, endlessly repeated by informants, *qabel*, to face up, face up to, and in the upright posture (our military 'attention'), the visible sign of rectitude, which it designates, so female submissiveness seems to find a natural translation in bending, stooping, lowering oneself, 'submitting'—curved and supple postures and the associated docility being seen as appropriate to women.[57]

For Bourdieu, the presentation of gender norms loads with meaning and value distinctions that are, at their root, naturally occurring and socially necessary.[58] In his view, the hierarchical value assigned to gender differences is arbitrary, but bodily difference as a function of sex and gender is ultimately a self-evident biological fact. *Masculine Domination* presents Bourdieu's departure from Butler and Foucault specifically in this manner. In his argument, though it is the socialization of "early upbringing" that "tends to inculcate ways of bearing in the body [that] initiates these differences that come to influence how we hold our bodies," ultimately this process merely "*records* and symbolically *ratifies* certain indisputable natural properties." Bourdieu argues that the dualisms that structure human understanding of the world are socially invested with value in a manner that perpetuates masculine domination through institutions such as "the family, the church, and the education system." In his analysis, however, "these dualisms are deeply rooted in things (structures) and in bodies, [and] do not spring from the simple effect of verbal naming and cannot be abolished by an act of performative magic, since genders, far from being simple 'roles' that can be played (in the manner of 'drag queens'), are inscribed in bodies and in a universe from which they derive their strength."[59]

Such a focus on conscious performativity, of course, is the very misunderstanding of Butler's theories of gender performativity that underlies many of the initial criticisms works like *Gender Trouble* and *Bodies That Matter* elicited. In their most well-known work, Butler builds on Foucault's disciplinary theories, extending them to their natural conclusion. Kovic's paralysis, as understood by his work, literalizes an exaggeration of the Foucauldian docile body even as his impairment frustrates his efforts to reshape himself into a masculine subject he can recognize due to his inability to relinquish the essentialist understanding of gendered embodiment that a Foucauldian perspective should preclude. In this view, disability impairs the subject's ability to control a body that has been rendered increasingly malleable through a violation of its essential (able-bodied) nature. Paralysis becomes docility *par excellence*, leaving the body malleable to external forces while reducing the subject's own ability to control it through loss of motor coordination. The docile body in Foucauldian thought represents a form that, though at times subjected to conscious manipulation, ultimately represents for Butler a "materiality" largely "rethought as an effect of power" that materializes as the product of a matrix of forces that exceed the subject's conscious control.[60] Kovic's disability causes confrontation with the nature of embodiment as a materialization of power relations, making him conscious of forces and their effects that tend to go unnoticed in daily life for subjects whose bodies do not, in their experience, depart from hegemonic norms. Kovic's body now defies his conscious efforts to influence its shape and presentation, which renders him able to perceive in a limited fashion the way in which his embodiment and its significance both ultimately remain socially contingent. Discussing the weight equipment used for his physical therapy, Kovic writes, "These are machines that make you stand again and fix your hands again, but the only thing is that when it's all over, when the guys are pulled down from the machines, unstrapped from them, it's the same body, the same shattered broken man that went up on the rack moments before, and this is what we are all beginning to live with, this is what the kid standing in the hallway is saying with his eyes." The author narrates his inability to reconcile a new awareness of his body as a social location with the deeply essentialist notion of embodiment on which his language insists. Kovic is disturbed in equal measure by the conscription of the body he experiences following his injury and the rupturing of its boundaries that disability, for him, necessarily represents. *Born on the Fourth of July* features many episodes such as the one described in the above passage, which play out intersubjectively and dramatize a fragmented subject position produced by an understanding of self that holds ability and disability as absolutely distinct terms and, as such, cannot allow for the possibility of wholeness subsequent to a disabling injury. Ultimately, the author's narrative of his body fails cohere into the stable account to which he clearly aspires. Kovic describes the writing of his autobiography as "a painful but beautiful birth" and revels his ability, through narrative, to make others see him again as he feels he once was; nevertheless, he remains so disturbed by his postinjury consciousness of the body-for-others that he is unable to conceive of his disability, or disability more generally, as anything but tragic.[61]

In their recent work on the relationship between self-narration and the subject, Butler argues that a fiction of narrative authority operates as an organizing force in novels of the nineteenth century and is, in the famous opening pages of *David Copperfield*, "clearly meant to counter and displace the infant's passivity and the lack of motor control." Yet the ultimate gap between literary accounts of subject formation and experiences of subject formation for beings in the world, Butler's primary interest in their recent theoretical discussions of the subject and self-narration, is an important part of understanding the specificity of disability as a subject position. Similarly, theorizations of disability offer key insights into understanding the nature of subject formation itself. A gap between narratives of the body and embodied experience will always be present, but instances of disability can make this gap more palpable for the subject: moments in which disability (an experience constituted in the world as a function of discourse "never simply formed" and yet never "fully self-forming") force a renegotiation of one's sense of self but might also enable a reconsideration of discourses that essentialize the body, whether for the purposes of understanding dis/ability, gender, biological sex, or other identity categories.[62] Here, Butler and Bourdieu are ultimately in agreement, despite the latter's objection to the former's constructivism. Bourdieu writes:

> Symbolic power cannot be exercised without the contribution of those who undergo it and who only undergo it because they *construct* it as such. But instead of stopping at this statement (as constructivism in its idealist, ethnomethodological or other forms does) one has also to take note of and explain the social construction of the cognitive structures which organize acts of construction of the world and its powers. It then becomes clear that, far from being the conscious, free, deliberate act of an isolated "subject," this practical construction is itself the effect of a power, durably embedded in the bodies of the dominated in the forms of perception and dispositions (to admire, respect, love, etc.) which *sensitize* them to certain symbolic manifestations of power.

Comparing late Bourdieu to post-1990s Butler in particular, we see a similar focus on intersubjectivity and rejection of the isolated, solipsistic subject in favor of an understanding of the individual as always embedded in a set of symbolic relations that are socially constructed and located. Bourdieu's focus on cognitive structures in addition to symbolic networks represents an effort to account for what he sees as the real-world effects of ideology on the subject. Yet as this chapter has hopefully shown, understanding the body in even partially essentialist terms can work to enable a rhetorical impaction of disability, homosexuality, and passivity in a manner that perpetuates the very symbolic violence Bourdieu decries. Even for Bourdieu, who explicitly positions *Masculine Domination* as a critical response to Butler's poststructuralist theorizations of gendered embodiment, his statement that in order to understand the effect of symbolic violence on the dominated, one must acknowledge "the opacity and inertia that stem from the embedding of social structures in bodies" is directed more at formulations presented by Marx and Lukacs, which, in Bourdieu's view, assume that the "false consciousness" of a dominated class of individuals would spontaneously fall away immediately as an effect of a raised consciousness. The true point of departure between Bourdieu and Butler is perhaps more semantic than real.

Bourdieu's statement that "the dominant principle of vision is not a simple mental representation, a fantasy, ('ideas in people's heads'), an ideology, but a system of structures durably embedded in bodies" is less incongruent with Butler if one avoids the ways in which their work has generally been misunderstood.[63] The language of materiality present here is meant by Bourdieu to critique what he sees as the ineffectuality of feminist critiques focused on heightening the social consciousness of oppression as a means to effect social change, but it is difficult to see how this distinction changes the way in which such a social change would ultimately need to play out in the world.

Perhaps disability studies scholars ought to see Butler and Bourdieu as representing two mutually constitutive positions that might be uneasily synthesized in a single, dynamic account of the disabled subject. Disability theory has postulated a formulation of complex embodiment, wherein disability is a unique state that can only be properly understood simultaneously as embodied and constructed, but it is insufficient in its account of the specific ways in which "disability" materializes as such. The goal of this book, then, could be stated as an effort to more rigorously account for the processes that constitute disability as a human experience. A dynamic experience of disability occurring in time might stress different aspects of complex embodiment in each given moment, yielding an ever-shifting position of potential pain, loss, insight, and acceptance that—by necessity—always remains in process. A body existing in perpetual change cannot and should not be understood as a fixed entity, either rhetorically or physically.

The collapse of boundaries of self and nation depicted in *The Deer Hunter* and *First Blood* thus ultimately makes the most sense when linked to critique of the unity of the body exemplified in Butler's work. Rhetorics surrounding disability and the body politic tend to become impacted on one another when societies directly confront the violence of war: as this book has shown, this is more often the case than not in the twentieth century. Understanding disability as a subject position necessitates rethinking the role of disability in accounts of American national identity that reduce it to a signifier of lack or excess, in which disability becomes synonymous with anything that defies control or mastery. Reformulating disability as a subject position rather than conceiving of it primarily as a representational trope helps us better understand the cultural, political, and personal meanings of bodies understood as deviating from the able-bodied norm. Equating disability with a loss of control replicates one of the more problematic vicissitudes of disability in American culture that demonstrates the extent to which disability and masculinity become rhetorically impacted on one another as mutual sites of contested national identity, particularly in times of national crisis. Viewing these identities instead from the perspective of the disabled subject makes visible structures underpinning American masculine sufficiency that have been so naturalized as to generally go unnoticed and unquestioned.

NOTES

1. Kovic, "Introduction," xv, xx.
2. Jeffords, *The Remasculinization of America*, 43.
3. Ibid., 51.
4. Here, Jeffords quotes statements referring to a specifically American collective unconscious made by William Broyles Jr. in *Brothers in Arms*, his nonfiction account of his return to Vietnam in 1986. Jeffords's own argument is that the perspective exemplified by Broyles's narrative is explicitly male, but she substitutes the designation *point of view* for Broyles's Jungian terminology when discussing the exclusion of the feminine from Vietnam War narratives produced by men. Ibid., 59.
5. Ibid., 117–18.
6. Ibid., 119.
7. Bly, *Iron John*, xvi.
8. Ibid., 1–27.
9. Ibid., 2, 1.
10. Ibid., 2, ix.
11. Elshtain, quoted in Jeffords, *The Remasculinization of America*, 126.
12. Belew, *Bring the War Home*, 42.
13. Ibid., 56, 60.
14. Ibid., 163.
15. Lawrence, *Studies in Classic American Literature*, 17, 82.
16. Cooper, *The Last of the Mohicans*, 66.
17. Cooper, *The Prairie*, 76, 4.
18. See, for example, Michael J. Pikus's presentation at the thirteenth Cooper Seminar, "James Fenimore Cooper: His Country and His Art," at the State University of New York College at Oneonta, July 2001, available as part of the James Fenimore Cooper Society's online holdings, as representative of this view.
19. Jeffords argues that the Vietnam era texts she discusses in her book can be broadly characterized by four representational tendencies: "the shift from means to ends, the valorization of performance, the aesthetic of spectacle through the male body as technology, and the (con)fusion of fact and fiction." Jeffords, *The Remasculinization of America*, 41.
20. Cimino, *The Deer Hunter*.
21. Jeffords, *The Remasculinization of America*, 96, 100.
22. Ibid., 77, 116.
23. Lawrence, *Studies in Classic American Literature*, 93.
24. Cimino, *The Deer Hunter*.
25. Jeffords, *The Remasculinization of America*, 99.
26. Deleuze, *Cinema 1*, 207. Chong similarly identifies the crisis of the action-image as understood by Deleuze as a central feature of Vietnam-era commercial cinema and media reportage depicting the war, arguing that it is images of often racialized suffering depicted in Vietnam-era visual texts that "provoke an American 'crisis of the action image.'" As this book's previous chapter makes clear, however, evidence of this formal crisis can be seen in American film at least a decade and a half before the texts on which this critic focuses. Chong, *The Oriental Obscene*, 79–92.

27. Morrell, *First Blood*, 70.

28. Caruth, *Trauma*, 9.

29. Butler, *Frames of War*, 43, 44, 44.

30. Disability studies scholars have likewise approached Foucault's work, which is foundational to Butler's understanding of the body, with varying degrees of acceptance. In *Enforcing Normalcy: Disability, Deafness, and the Body*, Lennard J. Davis explains that most work on the subject of disability "until quite recently, has been written . . . by professionals who work with, medically treat, or study the disabled. In that discourse, people with disabilities have been an object of study, and the resulting information produced has constituted a discourse as controlling as any described by Michel Foucault." Tobin Siebers alternately criticizes Foucault for using "natural metaphors to describe the health and vigor of the premodern soldier, while deliberately representing the modern one as malleable, weak and machinelike." Siebers is correct to note that "docility begins to resemble disability" in Foucault's analysis. Yet his argument that Foucault privileges the able body and believes that "hidden underneath the docile body—the body invented by the modern age and now recognized as the only body—is the able body" mischaracterizes Foucault's theory, in which the "disabled body" *and* the "able body" would both be forms produced as functions of the power structures characteristic of a given episteme. Davis, *Enforcing Normalcy*, 2; Siebers, *Disability Theory*, 58.

31. Butler, *Frames of War*, 54.

32. Chong, "Restaging the War," 94–95.

33. Chong, *The Oriental Obscene*, 135, 137.

34. Chong, "Restaging the War," 97.

35. Ibid., 91, 92.

36. Ibid., 98.

37. Cimino, *The Deer Hunter*.

38. Caruth's discussion of PTSD from the standpoint of trauma theory further illuminates the seemingly contradictory nature of this scene. "A very peculiar fact" characterizing posttraumatic stress, Caruth notes, is that "the pathology cannot be defined either by the event itself—which may or may not be catastrophic, and may or may not traumatize everyone equally—nor can it be defined as a *distortion* of the event. . . . The pathology consists, rather, solely in the *structure of its experience* or reception: the event is not assimilated or experienced fully at the time, but only belatedly, in its repeated *possession* of the one who experiences it." Caruth, *Trauma*, 4.

39. Hemingway, *The Sun Also Rises*, 228.

40. Cimino, *The Deer Hunter*.

41. Jeffords, *The Remasculinization of America*, 96.

42. Brady, Briggs, and Hagen, "The Enemy Is Us," 259.

43. Chong, "Restaging the War," 100.

44. Chong, *The Oriental Obscene*, 129.

45. Ibid., 130.

46. Ibid., 63.

47. Ibid., 281, 132.

48. Ibid., 141.

49. Ibid.

50. Ibid., 167, 170, 258.

51. Kovic, *Born on the Fourth of July*, 29, 31.

52. Ibid., 33.

53. Ibid., 41.

54. Ibid., 43, 46–47, 50.

55. Martin F. Norden notes that, like *Coming Home* and *Cutter's Way*, Stone's version of *Born on the Fourth of July* (created in collaboration with Kovic) "bestow[s] the privileged

status of white heterosexuality" on its protagonist. Norden, *Born on the Fourth of July*: Production and Assessment of a Turbulent Text," 226. The racial aspect of this privilege in particular is demonstrated in the section of Stone's film where Kovic's character, played by Tom Cruise, visits a brothel in Mexico frequented by paraplegic Vietnam veterans. Of note in this sequence is the extent to which the brothel serves as a site of failed remasculinization for the veterans. In this foreign setting, the disabled male figures attempt to exercise dominance over a racialized other in the form of Mexican sex workers. While Kovic's character romanticizes his sexual encounters depicted in this section of the film, Charlie (Willem Dafoe), a fellow quadriplegic Kovic befriends who accompanies him to Mexico, responds with a racist and misogynist diatribe when mocked by a sex worker for his injury-related impotence.

56. Bourdieu, *Masculine Domination*, 17.

57. Ibid., 27.

58. Ibid., 2.

59. Ibid., 27, 13, 85, 103.

60. In his chapter "Docile Bodies," Foucault describes how "recruits become accustomed to 'holding their heads high and erect; to standing upright, without bending the back. . . . to help them acquire the habit, they are given this position while standing against a wall such that the heels, the thighs, the waist and shoulders touch it . . .'" Foucault, "Docile Bodies," 135. Butler, *Bodies That Matter*, 63.

61. Kovic, *Born on the Fourth of July*, 55, 18.

62. Butler, *Senses of the Subject*, 4.

63. Bourdieu, *Masculine Domination*, 40, 41.

CODA

Disability, Resilience, and the Cost of American Hegemony under Neoliberalism

THE ILLEGIBLE MAN HAS FOCUSED its critique of postwar American masculinity on representations of the American male—both disabled and able bodied—drawn from texts produced between the mid-1920s and early 1980s, tracing sociopolitical developments in the real and imagined landscapes of the United States from the end of World War I to the end of the Vietnam War era. It has demonstrated how disability and masculinity became increasingly intertwined sites of contested identity as the country moved from the apparent normalcy of the post–World War II period into the growing uncertainty that characterized the Cold War. This coda explores the relevance of this book's themes to more recent cultural texts that depict disability and masculinity in a twenty-first-century context. The two texts discussed in this coda—Ben Fountain's 2012 novel *Billy Lynn's Long Halftime Walk* and the antiwar documentary *Body of War* made by Ellen Spiro and Phil Donahue in 2007—grapple with neoliberalism's effect on the male body and masculinity as normatively constructed and understood in the United States in the early twenty-first century in the context of America's foreign wars that began in the decade following September 11, 2001.

The Illegible Man began by considering the traditionally melancholic structure of Hemingway's *The Sun Also Rises* as a quintessential modernist response to disability following World War I, discussing how its regressive understanding of disability cannot be understood apart from the novel's broader stigmatization of otherness represented by any identity category excluded from white/cisgender/able-bodied heterosexuality. This final section wraps up this discussion of disability and masculinity by bringing the insights of the project to bear on more recent texts that address melancholic disability in a more recent, neoliberal context. This coda does not seek to resolve the concerns posed by this neoliberal moment but rather offers suggestions as to how neoliberalism reconfigures American notions of masculinity and self-reliance that exist in relation to the normatively constructed able body.

Drawing on work by Mark Neocleous that examines discourses privileging resilience as a coping strategy for individual actors in an increasingly chaotic economic landscape characterized by the withering of social safety nets developed by the state during the Depression era and in the years following World War II, Robin James reformulates conventional understandings of resilience and melancholia as strategies that alternately feed and subvert the logic of neoliberalism.[1] James writes:

> Resilience is neoliberalism's upgrade on modernist notions of coherence and deconstruction—the underlying value or ideal that determines how we organize artworks, political and social institutions, the economy, concepts of selfhood, and so on. Resilience is the hegemonic or "common sense" ideology that everything is to be measured, not by its overall systematicity (coherence) or its critical, revolutionary potential (deconstruction), but by its *health*. This "health" is maintained by bouncing back from injury and crisis in a way that capitalizes on deficits so that you end up ahead of where you initially started (one step back, two steps forward) (Neocleous). If resilience is the new means of production, this means that crisis and trauma are actually necessary, desirable phenomena—you can't bounce back without first falling.[2]

Notably, resilience discourse of this sort seems largely incompatible with the cultural understandings of disability discussed in this work. Ron Kovic, for example, links disability and post-Vietnam America because both represent for him the absolute, irredeemable loss of an idealized prior state: a norm his mind has naturalized and takes for granted as such. As James notes, however, "resilience discourse often treats crisis and injury as the only ways of getting ahead."[3] Disability narratives that compel disabled individuals to perform an overcoming of the physical and social effects of their impairment have long been criticized by disability studies scholars and activists within the disability community, but the texts discussed in this coda both examine and exhibit the neoliberal compulsion to render bodily and psychic damage productive in a way not generally allowed by the texts examined earlier in this book. What differentiates the neoliberal disability narratives discussed here from the disability narratives discussed previously is that the disabled masculine subject under neoliberalism is called on to embody and perform feminized bodily damage so that his narrative of emasculating disability (and subsequent overcoming of this damage) can ultimately be leveraged for the purposes of his remasculinization in hegemonic terms.

In *Billy Lynn's Long Halftime Walk*, members of Bravo Squad, a fighting unit of eight men hailed as heroes after their battle with Iraqi insurgents is caught on video and broadcast worldwide, return to the United States to be honored during the halftime show of a Dallas Cowboys home game and must reckon with a newfound celebrity status that includes negotiations over the rights to their story for a major movie deal. The award-winning novel was generally well received as a critical take on the patriotic fervor of the Bush/Cheney years and has been praised for capturing the point of view of the American soldier through use of contemporary vernacular authentic to America's military. Fountain renders the all-male world of Bravo Squad through a third person narrator who, though not a character in the novel, clearly presents the ideological and emotional perspective of the various squad members, synthesized into a disembodied but culturally specific masculine voice and point of view usually—but not always—limited to the perspective of the eponymous title character. The novel presents Billy Lynn as a somewhat naive nineteen-year-old whose war experience nevertheless gives him a knowledge of the reality of the Iraq conflict his more blindly patriotic admirers lack. The novel includes frequent short sections in which the otherwise straightforward prose is broken up on the page using visual devices borrowed from concrete poetry to defamiliarize the jingoistic phrases and ideas the soldiers hear in conversations with ordinary Americans during a short furlough celebrating their victory. Fountain's critique of elements of American culture in the first decade of the twenty-first century focuses on the commodification of an elite American fighting squad's narrative within neoliberal economic structures, presenting a narrative of masculine sufficiency reshaped by market forces that were only starting to emerge during the latter part of the period covered in the chapters of this book.

In Fountain's novel, the prospect of Bravo Squad's story becoming a major motion picture offers Billy Lynn and his fellow soldiers an opportunity to turn individual experiences of trauma into a commoditized narrative that promises to render their damage productive and optimize them as ideal, resilient neoliberal subjects. Yet Fountain underscores the limitations of Bravo Squad's newfound social capital (derived from status as heroes) as the men are repeatedly shown to lack control over their lives and personal narratives despite the promise of financial gain offered by selling their story. Albert Ratner, a Hollywood producer who accompanies the men of Bravo Squad to Dallas, where they will appear beside Destiny's Child at halftime of the Thanksgiving Day Dallas Cowboys home game, presents the men with a lucrative but illusively defined offer to make their story into a major motion picture. According to the novel's narrator, "Albert's target is a hundred thousand for each Bravo's life story, plus all manner of arcane fees, points, percentages, and other unintelligible stuff they will just have to trust him on."[4] Here, the novel's narrative voice paraphrases the producer's language as heard by Billy, demonstrating the protagonist's limited understanding of the financial specifics of the deal Bravo has yet to sign. As Wendy Brown notes, "neoliberalism transmogrifies every human domain and endeavor, along with humans themselves, according to a specific image of the economic. All conduct is economic conduct; all spheres of existence are framed and measured by economic terms and metrics, even when those spheres are not monetized."[5] Though Billy and the rest of Bravo occupy a privileged position in a sense, they "know their fame is not their own" and remain disenfranchised within an economic system that promises financial remuneration in exchange for giving over control of their narrative to the apparatus of the culture industry.[6] The language of capital permeates Fountain's text in a way that is framed as a critique, but the novel's ideological point of view is at times difficult to parse, particularly in relation to the book's stance on its vision of masculinity. The Bush administration, Hollywood elites, and well-meaning but ignorant patriotic Americans are all at various times objects of the novel's critique and even disdain. While Billy Lynn's perspective is often framed as naive, the novel does uphold him as a kind of masculine ideal very much in line with the formations of masculinity examined and critiqued in The Illegible Man.

Spiro and Donahue's protest documentary Body of War presents a more straightforward ideological perspective than Fountain's text, aligning itself explicitly with the American antiwar movement of the early to mid-2000s. The film's narrative details the struggles of disabled Iraq War veteran Tomas Young and his participation in the antiwar effort subsequent to his injury, alternating his story with a parallel narrative that details the efforts of a small number of mostly Senate Democrats who oppose the vote to authorize the use of military force in Iraq, represented in the film primarily by Senator Robert Byrd of West Virginia. The sections of the film focusing on Young hit familiar beats established by government-sponsored documentaries from the World War II era depicting narratives of postwar rehabilitation and focus in particular on the details of Young's disabling injury, its treatment, and his physical and emotional struggles to adapt to the changed circumstances of his life that result from his impairment. *Body of War*'s presentation of Young's disability is blunt and at times graphic, and the film deserves praise for scenes that present Young and his condition in a generally empathetic manner. Young's injury impairs his sexual performance and alters his relationships in much the same manner depicted in the works by Hemingway, Wyler, and Kovic this book has discussed in its earlier chapters. Young and his first wife, Brie (Townsend) Young, both speak openly about the effects of Young's disability on their physical and emotional relationship, discussing intimate details of their diminished sex life early in the film before we witness their separation near the conclusion of the narrative. The film also includes a sequence in which Young's mother learns to catheterize her son during a road trip they take while participating in antiwar demonstrations and rallies. Simultaneously clinical and tender, the scene displays intimate details of the protagonist's injury and its effect on his life as the application of a catheter is shown on-screen, only partially obstructed. The scene has echoes of the sequences in *The Best Years of Our Lives* that detail Homer Parrish's dependence on first his father and later his fiancée for assistance with his prosthetics as he prepares for bed and (in a manner of speaking) shows directly the type of disabling injury Hemingway's novel is so intent on hiding. In *Body of War*, the tension of this potentially emasculating scene is cut by a moment of humor when both mother and son acknowledge their mutual discomfort as Young's mother fumbles with her son's catheter, spilling some of his urine as she helps him empty his bladder.

The foregrounding of intimate details of Young's injury and the display of Young's disabled body on-screen functions as a key feature of *Body of War*'s rhetorical strategy. Where Hemingway's withholding of the specifics of Jake Barnes's injury is central to both the novel's regressive message and its representational practices, the straightforward presentation of private details of Young's life and his postinjury embodiment lend the documentary political force and moral authority by asking viewers to directly contemplate the human consequences of the vote to authorize the invasion of Iraq in 2003. Jake Barnes and Tomas Young are alike in that both become bodies of war standing in for and individualizing larger authorial statements about the harsh realities of modern warfare and its aftermath; however, unlike Barnes, whose embodiment is rendered obliquely to further its narrative function as an abstract symbol, Tomas Young functions as the documentary's concrete example of the Bush administration's betrayal of

America's soldiers and their families and the lasting consequences of that betrayal.

Body of War thus participates in the same type of social documentary practice discussed by Rabinowitz and Kahana (and perhaps attempted by John Huston in his War Department films of the 1940s): the film is a "report that seeks to account for—but, more importantly, to change—reality." A tribute to the movement that opposed the Iraq War and to those who voted against it, *Body of War* is also a cinematic work produced to help foster that resistance and force a change in a presidential administration's misguided foreign policy. In her work on social documentary, Rabinowitz breaks from traditional schools of film theory by conceiving of the documentary film audience as both collective and corporeal—a specific assemblage of potential actors with the capacity for historical agency rather than the disembodied hypothetical spectator of psychoanalytic apparatus theory or the subjective experiencer of film's tactility postulated more recently by phenomenological accounts of the film viewing experience. Like earlier works of social documentary, *Body of War*'s goal is thus to "remand, if not actively remake, the subject into a historical agent."[7]

When the film contrasts Tomas Young's rehabilitative experience with that of a paraplegic Vietnam veteran who suffered the same type of injury as Young, *Body of War* incorporates a criticism of the quality of health care for disabled veterans into its larger antiwar message. The exchange between Young and the older veteran is also one of several explicitly masculinist moments in the film. Introduced as a potential mentor figure, the unnamed Vietnam veteran who meets with Young at the film's midpoint is visibly more fit than the younger man, and he expresses surprise and dismay at the much shorter inpatient and outpatient treatment Young received from the VA following his injury while implicitly chastising *Body of War*'s protagonist for neglecting certain aspects of his physical recovery. When the men discuss the impact of their injuries on their sex lives, the older man alludes to potential advantages of diminished genital sensation following a spinal cord injury, stating that, if Young manages to regain his sexual potency, he will not be "one of those hop and pop guys."[8] The older man's explicit framing of Young's disability as something he could learn to leverage for sexual prowess clearly makes the younger man uncomfortable, but the elder veteran's statement to his protégé instructs Young on a way he can turn his disability to his advantage in a libidinal rather than material economy. If the economy of documentary cinema is one of persuasion, then Young's body could be said to function as capital in this exchange. Just as Tomas Young has lost and can work to regain his sexual potency—even perhaps becoming more potent than prior to his injury—he can also, by affecting social change though participation in an activist work of social documentary, reclaim the agency denied him by the Bush administration, the medical establishment, and even, as he understands it, his own body.

A primary concern of political theorists who write about neoliberalism is the way in which contemporary globalized power structures have adapted to resist and even subsume strategies of resistance developed prior to the late twentieth century by progressive movements for social change. Brown's analyses of neoliberalism's subversion of democratic institutions foreground her significant concern regarding our seemingly diminished capacity to steer the course of our individual lives and the broader course of history due to bureaucratic structures and market forces that emerged and have become increasingly globalized in the late twentieth and early twenty-first centuries.[9] James's *Resilience & Melancholy* details ways the responsibilization of individual subjects under neoliberalism reconfigures traditional modes of opposition to sexism and racism into acts that ultimately serve to shore up and even extend the very structures and institutions of oppression these strategies were developed to resist.[10]

Body of War and *Billy Lynn's Long Halftime Walk* both struggle against and exemplify this double bind, albeit in different ways. Spiro's and Donahue's film seems aware of the burden placed on its protagonist by his position in the narrative, a role Young willingly (if at times ambivalently) embraces; the film's narrative concludes with the development of a potential friendship between its two principal figures (the disabled antiwar activist and the aging Democratic senator presented as a lead figure in the opposition to the invasion of Iraq) rather than in a resolution of the conflicts related to the film's political concerns. These conflicts, ultimately located in the political landscape of the United States, are left to the film's audience—the American body politic—to resolve, and the documentary thus ends on a resolute rather than a triumphant note.

Young's 2014 obituary in the *New York Times* following his suicide is ambivalent in its discussion of the legacy of the film, noting both its award-winning status and the mixed reviews it received. It cites the "hard hitting" nature of *Body of War* and the film's "polemic tone" as factors that prevented its finding a distributor for theatrical release, perhaps limiting its cultural impact. In the same obituary, Phil Donahue himself notes, "It's not a take-your-girl-to-the-movies-movie."[11] These statements seem to make the case that the very strategy from which the film derives its power also limits its ability to achieve its political goals. The text's foregrounding of Young's disabled body, displayed in service of an antiwar message, proved unpalatable for mainstream American film outlets and many filmgoers, Douglas Martin (the author of the obituary) implies. Donahue's own comments, cited above, reinforce this implicit critique. The film's story, however, also fails to fully conform to accepted narrative tropes regarding trauma and adversity in neoliberal American culture due to its inability to resolve tensions regarding Young's disability and its larger implications for his life postinjury, even at the film's conclusion. James notes that resilience narratives require the subject to overcome their trauma (or, as James puts it, damage) in a manner that is legible within a neoliberal framework. She writes, "Resilience discourse thus follows a very specific logic: first, damage is incited and made manifest; second, that damage is spectacularly overcome, and that overcoming is broadcast and/or shared so that; third, the person who has overcome is rewarded with increased human capital, status, and other forms of recognition and recompense, because: finally, and most importantly, this individual's own resilience boosts society's resilience."[12] Neoliberalism takes the interior landscapes of mourning and melancholia formulated in Freudian thought that reside within our psyches—and remain, for the most part, private—and maps them onto socially located exchanges that play out in public, between people, for the benefit of the status quo produced under neoliberal rationality. The meaning of the term *trauma* has itself shifted over time from a term used by surgeons in the seventeenth century to designate a purely physical state (wounds of the flesh) to a designation also naming a psychological experience following World Wars I and II (*shell shock* and *nervous trauma*) and finally to a psychiatric category that not only references a person's response to individual experiences but also names ongoing collective responses to large-scale events like war, genocide, or ecological disaster. This shift in how trauma is understood has led to the corresponding development of strategies of social management that privilege the value of resilience as an individual and collective mode of dealing with adversity.[13] Individual instances of resilience performed "correctly" serve a social function, and resilience is thus subject to social regulation. The functioning of individual acts of resilience as such, however, depends on their legibility within the framework of neoliberal social structures that value, valorize, and compel the production of narratives that ultimately reproduce oppression or at the very least fail to critique it. *Body of War*'s presentation of Tomas Young's disability narrative as part of a political critique and its failure to produce a vision of Young as "properly" resilient by overcoming his disability in a way that would allow him to reclaim a heteronormatively masculine status is, in the neoliberal context, a failure of legibility.

Both *Body of War* and *Billy Lynn's Long Halftime Walk* include figures who present a declension from "neoliberalism's unit of analysis, the generic individual who becomes responsiblized human capital [and] is, unsurprisingly, socially male and masculinist in a persistently gendered economic ontology and division of labor."[14] Although neither text frames its central character explicitly as such, the everyman nature of these figures at least in part derives from how they conform to norms of cisgender and heteronormative white masculinity: Billy Lynn presents an idealization of able-bodied status Tomas Young has lost. Yet Billy Lynn only represents a neoliberal idealization via his hypermasculinity. He and the other members of Bravo Squad are pointedly unable to integrate into the economic power structures they remain at the mercy of for the entirety of the book, and the failure of a display of violence by the Bravos at the novel's conclusion to improve their situation only serves to emphasize the extent of their disenfranchisement.

In the novel, Billy's physically disabled father presents a contrast to his son and stands in as a synecdoche representing the working-class Bush supporters rendered more abstractly in the rest of the book. Readers of Fountain's novel meet Ray Lynn halfway through the narrative. The character spends the majority of the flashback section at the narrative's midpoint in his wheelchair: "a dark purple motorized job with fat whitewalls and an American flag decal stuck on the back" that Billy's younger sister Kathryn has christened "The Beast." The wheelchair becomes synonymous with Billy's father. Introduced as "a proactive asshole" who is not merely detestable but actively "works at it," Ray is never seen apart from his motorized chair and its omnipresent whir, a grating sound the narrator states "captures . . . the essence of his personality."[15] A misanthrope who lost his job due to downsizing before suffering a stroke in middle age, Ray's sense of victimhood derives from his disability and influences his politics; he and his son are alike in that both experience economic disenfranchisement as white men with limited education.

In the neoliberal context, resilience is characterized by a logic of overcoming in which the individual's struggles, setbacks, and traumas become material for the building of social and economic capital. The problem with this type of resilience is that it is a self-defeating coping mechanism rather than a strategy of broader resistance to systemic oppressions. In her work, James discusses how women's experiences with patriarchy tend in this context to be framed as individual narratives of overcoming sexism such that the material conditions giving rise to oppression remain uncritiqued.[16] The neoliberal subject thus bears sole responsibility for overcoming unexpected physical and/or economic setbacks or experiences of discrimination. By this logic, it is individual women who fail to overcome isolated experiences with sexism and individual people of color who fail to overcome isolated instances of racism, leaving obscured a system of interlocking oppressions that continues to operate in the United States and globally despite the prevalence of hegemonic narratives to the contrary.[17]

James uses her examples, drawn primarily from contemporary pop music performed and sometimes produced by female artists, to demonstrate the prevalence of contemporary postfeminist narratives displaying a surface-level critique that ultimately acts to shore up the social structures that enable the oppression of women excluded by the narrow purview of white feminism. In this framework, "women's gender performance is a two-step process: femininity is performed first as damage, second as resilience." James's analysis draws on the work of Iris Mason Young, who discusses the felt effect of patriarchal discourse on experiences of female embodiment, arguing that patriarchal knowledge structures so deeply link femininity and fragility as to blur any meaningful distinction between these terms as hegemonically understood. James writes that "for a body to feel and be felt as feminine, it must be fragile." James's description of the "fragile body" as a feminized object produced through patriarchal discourse has clear implications for the relationships structuring interconnected notions of gender and ability/disability. In James's words, "A fragile body is both unable to support one's intentions and desires and in need of support and therapeutic control/discipline. Fragile, feminine bodies can't do what you want them to, so they need constant attention to 'make sure they'—both women and feminine bodies— 'are doing what we wish them to do.' Feminine bodies—and the people who have them—need therapeutic monitoring and control to keep their fragility in check."[18] This formulation of the fragile body reinterprets Foucault's docile body in an explicitly feminizing context. In Foucault's analysis, the body of the soldier-male that first emerges in the eighteenth century is subject to a constant, ongoing process of conscious and unconscious monitoring and corporal modification that results in a militarized masculine subject produced as a new norm for all males in emerging industrial and then postindustrial society. *The Illegible Man* has examined how masculine bodies are policed for physical excesses and surplus meanings outside of the bounds of masculinity as normatively constructed in this manner. That this very same process can, in a different context, be culturally understood both as a necessary response to a feminine body and as a process that is itself feminizing demonstrates the inherent contradictions structuring hegemonic understandings of gendered embodiment and points to the extent to which the discourses that produce our notions of disability, gender, and sexuality are interrelated and mutually constitutive.

I would like to suggest that the emergence of *homo oeconomicus*, the subject produced by neoliberalism's impulse to render all conduct as economic conduct, entails a transition from the logic of the docile body to that of the fragile body. While docile bodies are remade in the ongoing, iterative disciplinary process described by Foucault and Butler, fragile bodies subjected to neoliberal disciplinary structures are displayed as examples of lack and then leveraged such that they can be optimized as capital. Though the neoliberal logic that emerged over the course of the twentieth century can be seen as an effort to bring coherence to the incoherencies this book has tracked, neoliberal logic itself is "illegible in its own terms."[19]

The argument of *The Illegible Man* has not necessarily been that the rhetoric that emerged surrounding disability in the mid- to late twentieth century feminized disabled male bodies. This book's project has instead been to make the case that increased concern with disability, which emerged over the course of the twentieth century, failed to produce a coherent discourse surrounding disability. Efforts to account for disability by state and medical establishments often participated in a broader culture of scrutiny that continued to stigmatize otherness as deviance and ultimately helped to produce disability, gender, and sexuality as a central nexus for demarcating the American masculine subject. This trajectory is a continuation of long-standing, deeply held cultural notions about the relationship between heteronormative masculine sufficiency and self-reliance that nevertheless results in a newly incoherent definition of the American masculine subject historically specific to the period focused on in this book.

While the neoliberal resilience narratives of disability that emerged subsequent to the twentieth century can be seen as a further development of the type of rehabilitation narrative examined in this book's previous chapters, neoliberalism's imperative that disability be overcome in a manner legible within the strictures of neoliberal rationality ultimately reconfigures the nature of the disabled masculine body as constructed and understood in American culture. In a sense, one might say that, under neoliberalism, resilience itself becomes melancholic, compelling a continual return to a site of loss for the subject on the promise that this loss will be overcome if it is made legible in hegemonic terms.

Notes

1. Neocleous, "Don't Be Scared, Be Prepared," 188; James, *Resilience & Melancholy*, 18–21.
2. James, *Resilience & Melancholy*, 4.
3. Ibid., 5.
4. Fountain, *Billy Lynn's Long Halftime Walk*, 16.
5. Brown, *Undoing the Demos*, 10.
6. Fountain, *Billy Lynn's Long Halftime Walk*, 28.
7. Rabinowitz, *They Must Be Represented*, 5, 8.
8. Spiro and Donahue, *Body of War*.
9. Brown, *Undoing the Demos*, 220.
10. James, *Resilience & Melancholy*, 7.
11. Donahue, quoted in Martin, "Tomas Young, Army Veteran, Dies at 34," n.p.
12. James, *Resilience & Melancholy*, 7.
13. Neocleous, "Don't Be Scared, Be Prepared," 188.
14. Brown, *Undoing the Demos*, 107.
15. Fountain, *Billy Lynn's Long Halftime Walk*, 74, 75.
16. James, *Resilience & Melancholy*, 82.
17. Ibid., 83.
18. Ibid., 82, 80.
19. Brown, *Undoing the Demos*, 106.

BIBLIOGRAPHY

"ableism." *OED Online*, March 22, 2014.

Armengol, Josep M. "In the Dark Room: Homosexuality and/as Blackness in James Baldwin's *Giovanni's Room*." *Signs: Journal of Women in Culture and Society* 37, no. 3 (2012): 671–93.

Baldwin, James. *Another Country*. New York: Vintage Books, 1990.

———. *Giovanni's Room*. New York: Delta, 2000.

Barnouw, Erik. *Documentary: A History of the Non-fiction Form*. 2nd ed. New York: Oxford University Press, 1993.

Barthes, Roland. "Myth Today." In *Mythologies*, translated by Annette Lavers, 109–59. New York: Hill and Wang, 1972.

Baynton, Douglas C. "Disability and the Justification of Inequality in American History." In *The New Disability History: American Perspectives*, edited by Paul K. Longmore and Lori Umansky, 53–57. New York: New York University Press, 2001.

Bazin, André. "The Western: Or the American Film Par Excellence." In *What Is Cinema?* Vol. 2, translated by Hugh Gray, 140–48 Berkeley: University of California Press, 2005.

Belew, Kathleen. *Bring the War Home: The White Power Movement and Paramilitary America*. Cambridge, MA: Harvard University Press, 2018.

Benjamin, Walter. "The Author as Producer." In *Reflections*, edited by Peter Demetz, translated by Edmund Jephcott, 220–38. New York: Shocken Books, 1986.

———. "Theses on the Philosophy of History." In *Illuminations*, edited by Hannah Arendt, translated by Harry Zohn, 253–64. New York: Shocken Books, 1968.

Bertelsen, Lance. "San Pietro and the 'Art' of War." *Southwest Review* 74, no. 2 (Spring 1989): 230–56.

Bly, Robert. *Iron John: A Book about Men*. New York: Addison-Wesley, 1990.

Bombaci, Nancy. *Freaks in Late Modernist American Culture*. New York: Peter Lang, 2006.

Bourdieu, Pierre. *Masculine Domination.* Translated by Richard Nice. Stanford: Stanford University Press, 2001.

Bradford, William. "Chapter IX: Of Their Voyage, and How They Passed at Sea; and of Their Safe Arrival at Cape Cod." In *Of Plymouth Plantation. The Norton Anthology of American Literature*, Vol. A., 8th ed., edited by Julia Reidhead, 122–56. New York: Norton, 2012.

Brady, Kathleen, John Briggs, and Edward A. Hagen. "The Enemy Is Us: Misconstruing the Real War in *The Deer Hunter* and Other Post-Vietnam War Narratives." In *Dressing up for War: Transformations of Gender and Genre in the Discourse and Literature of War*, edited by Aránzazu Usandizaga and Andrew Monnickendam, 257–70. Amsterdam: Rodopi, 2001.

Breslin, Howard. "Bad Time at Honda." In *No, but I Saw the Movie: The Best Short Stories Ever Made into Film*, edited by David Wheeler, 16–30. New York: Penguin, 1989.

Brill, Lesley. *John Huston's Filmmaking.* Cambridge Studies in Film. Cambridge: Cambridge University Press, 1997.

Brooks, Richard. *The Brick Foxhole.* New York: Sun Dial Press, 1946.

Brown, Wendy. *Undoing the Demos: Neoliberalism's Stealth Revolution.* Brooklyn: Zone Books, 2015.

Butler, Judith. *Bodies That Matter: On the Discursive Limits of "Sex."* New York: Routledge, 1993.

———. *Frames of War: When Is Life Grieveable?* London: Verso, 2010.

———. *Gender Trouble: Feminism and the Subversion of Identity.* New York: Routledge Classics, 2008.

———. *Senses of the Subject.* New York: Fordham University Press, 2015.

Caruth, Cathy. *Trauma: Explorations in Memory.* Baltimore: John Hopkins University Press, 1995.

Chong, Syvia Shin Huey. *The Oriental Obscene: Violence and Racial Fantasies in the Vietnam Era.* Durham, NC: Duke University Press, 2011.

———. "Restaging the War: *The Deer Hunter* and the Primal Scene of Violence." *Cinema Journal* 44, no. 2 (Winter 2005): 89–106.

Chopra-Gant, Mike. "Reinvigorating the Nation." In *Hollywood Genres and Postwar America: Masculinity, Family and Nation in Popular Movies and Film Noir*, 26–64. London: I. B. Taurus, 2006.

Cimino, Michael. *The Deer Hunter.* EMI, 1978. Universal Studios Home Entertainment, 2006. DVD.

Coen, Joel. *The Man Who Wasn't There.* USA Films, 2001. DVD.

Combat Exhaustion. National Archives and Records Administration, 1945. Createspace, 2007. DVD.

Comley, Nancy R., and Robert Scholes. *Hemingway's Genders: Rereading the Hemingway Text.* New Haven, CT: Yale University Press, 1994.

Conrad, Joseph. "Heart of Darkness." In *The Norton Anthology of English Literature*, Vol. 2, 9th ed., edited by Greenblatt et al., 1951–2011. New York: Norton, 2012.

Cooper, James Fennimore. *The Last of the Mohicans.* New York: Barnes and Noble Classics, 2003.

———. *The Prairie.* New York: Penguin, 1987.

Craig, Siobhan S. "The Ghost in the Rubble." In *Cinema after Fascism: The Shattered Screen*, 69–90. New York: Palgrave Macmillan, 2010.

Cronon, William. *Changes in the Land: Indians, Colonists, and the Ecology of New England*. New York: Hill and Wang, 2003.

Davis, Lennard J. *Enforcing Normalcy: Disability, Deafness, and the Body*. London: Verso, 1995.

Debord, Guy. *The Society of the Spectacle*. New York: Zone Books, 1995.

Deleuze, Gilles. *Cinema 1: The Movement Image*. Minneapolis: University of Minnesota Press, 2007.

———. *Cinema 2: The Time Image*. Minneapolis: University of Minnesota Press, 2007.

Deleuze, Gilles, and Felix Guattari. *Anti-Oedipus: Capitalism and Schizophrenia*. Translated by Robert Hurley, Mark Seem, and Helen R. Lane. New York: Penguin, 2009.

Derrida, Jacques. ". . . That Dangerous Supplement. . . ." In *Of Grammatology*, translated by Gayatri Spivak, 141–64. Baltimore: John Hopkins University Press, 1997.

Dickey, James. *To the White Sea*. New York: Delta, 1994.

Doane, Mary Ann. *The Emergence of Cinematic Time: Modernity, Contingency, the Archive*. Cambridge, MA: Harvard University Press, 2002.

———. "The Moving Image: Pathos and the Maternal." In *Imitations on Life: A Reader of Film and Television Melodrama*, edited by Marcia Landy, 283–306. Detroit: Wayne State University Press, 1991.

Doherty, Thomas. *Projections of War: Hollywood, American Culture, and World War II*. New York: Columbia University Press, 1993.

Eberwine, Robert. "As a Mother Cuddles a Child: Sexuality and Masculinity in World War II Combat Films." In *Masculinity: Bodies, Movies, Culture*, edited by Peter Lehman, 149–66. New York: Routledge, 2001.

Edgerton, Gary. "Revisiting the Recordings of Wars Past: Remembering the Documentary Trilogy of John Huston." *Journal of Popular Film and Television* 15, no. 1 (Spring 1987): 27–41.

Ellis, Jack C., and Betsy A. McLane. *A New History of Documentary Film*. New York: Continuum, 2007.

Elsaesser, Thomas, and Malte Hagener. *Film Theory: An Introduction through the Senses*. New York: Routledge, 2010.

Forter, Greg. *Gender, Race, and Mourning in American Modernism*. Cambridge: Cambridge University Press, 2011.

———. "Melancholy Modernism: Gender and the Politics of Mourning in *The Sun Also Rises*." In *Hemingway: Eight Decades of Criticism*, edited by Linda Wagner-Martin, 55–74. East Lansing: Michigan State University Press, 2009.

Foucault, Michel. "Docile Bodies." In *Discipline & Punish: The Birth of the Prison*, translated by Alan Sheridan, 135–69. New York: Vintage Books, 1995.

———. *The History of Sexuality: An Introduction*. Vol. 1. New York: Vintage Books, 1990.

———. "Of Other Spaces." *Diacritics* 16, no. 1 (1986): 22–27.

Fountain, Ben. *Billy Lynn's Long Halftime Walk*. New York: Harper Collins, 2012.

Freud, Sigmund. "Mourning and Melancholia." In *The Freud Reader*, edited by Peter Gay, 584–89. New York: Norton, 1989.

Garland-Thomson, Rosmarie. *Extraordinary Bodies: Figuring Physical Disability in American Literature and Culture*. New York: Columbia University Press, 1997.

Garrett, Greg. "John Huston's *The Battle of San Pietro*." *War, Literature, and the Arts* 5, no. 1 (Spring–Summer 1993): 1–12.

———. "*Let There Be Light* and Huston's Film Noir." *Proteus: A Journal of Ideas* 7, no. 2 (1990): 30–33.

Gates, Henry Louis, Jr. *The Signifying Monkey: A Theory of Afro-American Literary Criticism*. New York: Oxford University Press, 1988.

Gerber, David. "Heroes and Misfits: The Troubled Social Reintegration of Disabled Veterans in *The Best Years of Our Lives*." *American Quarterly* 46, no. 4 (1994): 545–74.

Gledhill, Christine. "The Melodramatic Field: An Investigation." In *Home Is Where the Heart Is: Studies in Melodrama and the Woman's Film*, edited by Christine Gledhill, 5–42. London: BFI, 1987.

Hawthorne, Nathaniel. "Young Goodman Brown." In *Nathaniel Hawthorne's Tales*, edited by James McIntosh, 84–96. New York: Norton, 2013.

Hayward, Susan. "Melodrama." In *Key Concepts in Cinema Studies*, 203–15. London: Routledge, 1996.

Hemingway, Ernest. *The Sun Also Rises*. New York: Scribner, 2006.

Hickel, K. Walter. "Medicine, Bureaucracy, and Social Welfare: The Politics of Disability Compensation for American Veterans of World War I." In *The New Disability History: American Perspectives*, edited by Paul K. Longmore and Lori Umansky. 236–67. New York: New York University Press, 2001.

Himes, Chester. *If He Hollers Let Him Go*. Cambridge: Da Capo Press, 2002.

Hughes, Dorothy B. *In a Lonely Place*. New York: New York Review Books, 2017.

Huston, John. *The Battle of San Pietro*. 1945. DVD.

———. *Capt. John Huston's Team Coverage*. Italy. December 1943. Moving Images Related to Military Activities, 1947–1964. Record Group 111: Records of the Chief Signal Officer, 1860–1985. National Archives Identifier: 14395. Local Identifier: 111-ADC-588. National Archives, College Park Maryland. August 8, 2011. Film.

———. Italy. January 20, 1944. Moving Images Related to Military Activities, 1947–1964. Record Group 111: Records of the Chief Signal Officer, 1860–1985. National Archives Identifier: 14371. Local Identifier: 111-ADC-564. National Archives, College Park Maryland. August 8, 2011. Film.

———. Italy. January 23, 1944. Moving Images Related to Military Activities, 1947–1964. Record Group 111: Records of the Chief Signal Officer, 1860–1985. National Archives Identifier: 14369. Local Identifier: 111-ADC-562. National Archives, College Park Maryland. August 8, 2011. Film.

———. Italy. February 22, 1944. Moving Images Related to Military Activities, 1947–1964. Record Group 111: Records of the Chief Signal Officer, 1860–1985. National Archives Identifier: 14700. Local Identifier: 111-ADC-839. National Archives, College Park Maryland. August 8, 2011. Film.

———. Italy. February 1944. Moving Images Related to Military Activities, 1947–1964. Record Group 111: Records of the Chief Signal Officer, 1860–1985. National Archives Identifier: 14713. Local Identifier: 111-ADC-906. National Archives, College Park Maryland. August 8, 2011. Film.

———. *John Huston: An Open Book*. New York: Alfred A. Knopf, 1980.

———. *Let There Be Light*. 1946. Nobility Studios, 2007. DVD.

———. *Report from the Aleutians*. 1943. Synergy Entertainment, 2006. DVD.

James, Henry. "The Beast in the Jungle." In *The Portable Henry James*, edited by John Auchard, 236–82. New York: Penguin, 2004.

James, Pearl. *The New Death*. Charlottesville: University of Virginia Press, 2013.

James, Robin. *Resilience & Melancholy: Pop Music, Feminism, Neoliberalism*. Winchester: Zero Books, 2015.

Jeffords, Susan. *The Remasculinization of America: Gender and the Vietnam War*. Bloomington: Indiana University Press, 1989.

Johnson, Barbara. "Melville's Fist: The Execution of *Billy Budd*." *Studies in Romanticism* 18, no. 4, The Rhetoric of Romanticism (Winter 1978): 567–99.

———. "Translator's Introduction." In *Dissemination*, vii–xxxiii. Chicago: University of Chicago Press, 1981.

Judt, Tony. *Postwar: A History of Europe after 1945*. New York: Penguin, 2005.

Kafer, Alison. *Feminist, Queer, Crip*. Bloomington: Indiana University Press, 2013.

Kahana, Jonathan. *Intelligence Work: The Politics of American Documentary*. New York: Columbia University Press, 2008.

Kaufman, Millard. "A Vehicle for Tracy: The Road to Black Rock." *Hopkins Review* 1, no. 1 (Winter 2008): 70–88.

Kotcheff, Ted. *First Blood*. Orion Pictures, 1982. Lions Gate Home Entertainment, 2000. DVD.

Kovic, Ron. *Born on the Fourth of July*. Brooklyn: Akashic Books, 2005.

———. "Introduction (1990)." In *Johnny Got His Gun*, written by Dalton Trumbo, xiv–xxiv. Brooklyn: Citadel Books, 1991.

Kristeva, Julia. *Powers of Horror*. New York: Columbia University Press, 1982.

Langdon, Jennifer E. *Caught in the Crossfire: Adrian Scott and the Politics of Americanism in 1940s Hollywood*. New York: Columbia University Press, 2007.

Laplanche, J., and J. B. Pontalis. *The Language of Psychoanalysis*. Translated by Donald Nicholson-Smith. London: Hogarth Press and Institute of Psycho-Analysis, 1973.

Lawrence, D. H. *Studies in Classic American Literature*. Exeter: Shearsman Books, 2011.

Linett, Maren Tova. *Bodies of Modernism: Physical Disability in Transatlantic Modernist Literature*. Ann Arbor: University of Michigan Press, 2017.

"lurch." *OED Online*, June 17, 2012.

Macor, Alison. *Making "The Best Years of Our Lives": The Hollywood Classic That Inspired a Nation*. Austin: University of Texas Press, 2022.

Marshall, George. *The Blue Dahlia*. Paramount Pictures, 1946. DVD.

Martin, Douglas. "Tomas Young, Army Veteran, Dies at 34; Critic of Iraq War in Film." *The New York Times*, November 16, 2014.

McRuer, Robert. *Crip Theory: Cultural Signs of Queerness and Disability*. New York: New York University Press, 2006.

Menninger, William C. *Psychiatry in a Troubled World: Yesterday's War and Today's Challenge*. New York: Macmillan, 1948.

Mitchell, David T. "Narrative Prosthesis and the Materiality of Metaphor." In *Disability Studies: Enabling the Humanities*, edited by Sharon L. Snyder, Brenda Jo

Brueggemann, and Rosemarie Garland-Thomson, 15–30. New York: Modern Language Association of America, 2002.

Mitchell, David T., and Sharon L. Snyder. *Narrative Prosthesis: Disability and the Dependencies of Discourse.* Ann Arbor: University of Michigan Press, 2000.

Morrell, David. *First Blood.* New York: Grand Central, 2000.

Mulvey, Laura. "Visual Pleasure and Narrative Cinema." In *Visual and Other Pleasures*, 2nd ed., 14–27. London: Palgrave Macmillan, 2009.

Neale, Steve. "Masculinity as Spectacle: Reflections on Men in Mainstream Cinema." *Screen* 24, no. 6 (1983): 2–17.

Neocleous, Mark. "Commentary: Resisting Resilience." *Radical Philosophy* 178 (March–April 2013): 2–7.

———. "Don't Be Scared, Be Prepared: Trauma-Anxiety-Resilience." *Alternatives: Global, Local, Political* 37, no. 3 (August 2012): 188–98.

Newman, Joseph M. (uncredited). *Diary of a Sergeant.* 1945. DVD.

Nielsen, Kim E. *A Disability History of the United States.* Boston: Beacon Press, 2012.

Norden, Martin F. "*Born on the Fourth of July*: Production and Assessment of a Turbulent Text." In *Different Bodies: Essays on Disability in Film and Television*, edited by Marja Evelyn Mogk, 219–29. Jefferson, NC: McFarland, 2013.

———. *The Cinema of Isolation: A History of Physical Disability in the Movies.* New Brunswick: Rutgers University, 1994.

Okubo, Miné. *Citizen 13660.* Seattle: University of Washington Press, 1983.

Outka, Elizabeth. *Viral Modernism: The Influenza Pandemic and Interwar Literature.* New York: Columbia University Press, 2020.

Parker, Joshua. "Hemingway's Lost Presence in Baldwin's Parisian Room." In *Hemingway and the Black Renaissance*, edited by Gary Edward Holcomb and Charles Scruggs, 38–54. Columbus: Ohio State University Press, 2012.

Peckinpah, Sam. *Straw Dogs.* MGM, 2004. DVD.

Petry, Ann. *Country Place.* New York: Signet Books, 1947.

Pikus, Michael J. "Chopping Away at the New World." In *James Fenimore Cooper: His Country and His Art, Papers from the 2001 Cooper Seminar*, no. 13, edited by Hugh C. MacDougall. Oneonta: State University of New York College at Oneonta, 2001.

Plant, Rebecca Jo. "William Menninger and American Psychoanalysis, 1946–48." *History of Psychiatry* 16, no. 2 (2005): 181–202.

Pryor, Thomas M. "William Wyler and His Screen Philosophy." *New York Times*, November 17, 1946.

Rabinowitz, Paula. *American Pulp: How Paperbacks Brought Modernism to Main Street.* Princeton,: Princeton University Press, 2014.

———. *Black & White & Noir: America's Pulp Modernism.* New York: Columbia University Press, 2002.

———. "Pulping Ann Petry: The Case of *Country Place*." In *Revising the Blueprint: Ann Petry and the Literary Left*, edited by Alex Lubin, 49–71. Jackson: University of Mississippi Press, 2007.

———. *They Must Be Represented: The Politics of Documentary.* London: Verso, 1994.

Reid-Pharr, Robert. *Once You Go Black: Choice, Desire, and the Black American Intellectual.* New York: New York University Press, 2007.

———. "Tearing the Goat's Flesh." In *Black Gay Man: Essays*, 99–134. New York: New York University Press, 2001.

Riefenstahl, Leni. *Triumph of the Will*. 1935. Synapse Films, 2006. DVD.

Roberts, Mary Louise. *What Soldiers Do: Sex and the American GI in World War II France*. Chicago: University of Chicago Press, 2013.

Roosevelt, Theodore. "From *American Ideals:* From *Chapter II: True Americanism.*" In *The Norton Anthology of American Literature*, Vol. C., 8th ed., edited by Julia Reidhead. New York: Norton, 2012.

Rossellini, Roberto. *Germany Year Zero*. Janus Films, 2009. DVD.

Rudat, Wolfgang E. H. "Hemingway on Sexual Otherness: What's Really Funny in *The Sun Also Rises*." In *Hemmingway Repossessed*, edited by Kenneth Rosen, 169–79. Westport: Praeger, 1994.

Sartre, Jean-Paul. "The Body." In *Being and Nothingness: A Phenomenological Essay on Ontology*, 401–70. New York: Washington Square Press, 1984.

Schalk, Sami. *Black Disability Politics*. Durham,: Duke University Press, 2022.

Sedgwick, Eve Kosofsky. *The Epistemology of the Closet*. Berkeley: University of California Press, 1990.

Serlin, David. "Disability, Masculinity, and the Prosthetics of War, 1945–2005." In *The Prosthetic Impulse: From a Posthuman Present to a Biocultural Future*, edited by Marquard Smith and Joanne Morra, 155–83. Cambridge,: MIT Press, 2006.

Shildrick, Margrit. *Dangerous Discourses of Disability, Subjectivity, and Sexuality*. New York: Palgrave Macmillan, 2009.

Siebers, Tobin. *Disability Theory*. Ann Arbor: University of Michigan Press, 2008.

Silverman, Kaja. "From Sign to Subject, A Short History." In *The Subject of Semiotics*, 3–53. New York: Oxford University Press, 1983.

———. *Male Subjectivity at the Margins*. New York: Routledge, 1992.

———. "Suture." In *The Subject of Semiotics*, 194–236. New York: Oxford University Press, 1983.

Sobchack, Vivian. "What My Fingers Knew: The Cinesthetic Subject, or Vision in the Flesh." In *Carnal Thoughts: Embodiment and Moving Image Culture*, 53–84. Berkeley: University of California Press, 2004.

Sontag, Susan. *Illness as Metaphor and AIDS and Its Metaphors*. New York: Picador, 1990.

Spiro, Ellen, and Phil Donahue. *Body of War*. 2007. DVD.

Stiker, Henri-Jacques. "The Birth of Rehabilitation." In *A History of Disability*, translated by William Sayers, 121–90. Ann Arbor: University of Michigan Press, 1999.

Streamas, John. "Patriotic Drunk: To Be Yellow, Brave, and Disappeared at *Black Rock*." *American Studies* 44, no. 1–2 (Spring/Summer 2003): 99–119.

Sturges, John. *Bad Day at Black Rock*. MGM, 1955. Turner Entertainment Corporation, 2005. DVD.

Sturken, Marita. "Absent Images of Memory: Remembering and Reenacting the Japanese Internment." In *Perilous Memories: The Asia-Pacific War(s)*, edited by T. Fujitani, Geoffrey M. White, and Lisa Yoneyama, 33–49. Durham,: Duke University Press, 2001.

Terkel, Studs. "Reflections on Machismo: Ted Allenby." In *The Good War: An Oral History of World War Two*, 178–85. New York: Random House, 1985.

Theweleit, Klaus. *Male Fantasies, Volume I: Women, Floods, Bodies, History*. Minneapolis: University of Minnesota Press, 1987.

Thompson, John. "Introduction." In *Studies in Classic American Literature*, 7–36. Exeter: Shearsman Books, 2011.

Traber, Daniel S. "Whiteness and the Rejected Other in *The Sun Also Rises*." *Studies in American Fiction* 28, no. 2 (Autumn 2000): 235–53.

Trumbo, Dalton. *Johnny Got His Gun*. New York: Citadel Press Books, 1991.

Vidor, King. *The Big Parade*. 1925. MGM, 2020. Blu-ray.

Washington, Bryan R. *The Politics of Exile: Ideology in Henry James, F. Scott Fitzgerald, and James Baldwin*. Boston: Northeastern University Press, 1995.

Wilder, Billy. *Death Mills*. 1946. National Archives and Records Administration, 2008. DVD.

———. *A Foreign Affair*. 1948. Universal Studios, 1998. DVD.

Williams, Raymond. *Keywords: A Vocabulary of Culture and Society*. Revised ed. New York: Oxford University Press, 1983.

———. "Preface to Film." In *Film Manifestos and Global Cinema Cultures: A Critical Anthology*, edited by Scott MacKenzie, 607–13. Oakland: University of California Press, 2021.

Wright, Richard. *Native Son*. New York: Harper Perennial, 1991.

Wyler, William. *The Best Years of Our Lives*. 1946. MGM, 2006. DVD.

Zinneman, Fred. *High Noon*. Republic Entertainment, 1952. Artisan Home Entertainment, 2002. DVD.

Žižek, Slavoj. "Why Is Woman a Symptom of Man?" In *Enjoy Your Symptom: Jacques Lacan in Hollywood and Out*, 35–70. New York: Routledge, 1992.

INDEX

employment: in disability history, 8–10, 21n17; and gender, in interwar labor markets, 25–26; on the home front, in homosexual panic, 134–141; and integration, in *The Best Years of Our Lives,* 101; in the postwar culture of scrutiny, 64–66; and the veteran problem, in *Let There Be Light,* 82–83, 84–85

Enlightenment / Enlightenment rationalism, 7–8

epistemology: of the closet, 27–30, 49–52, 134–141; of masculinity, in *Bad Day at Black Rock,* 130–131; of masculinity, in postwar cinematic landscapes, 101–102, 104–107; and sexuality, in postwar fiction, 41–45

eroticism, 36–38, 45–46, 102–103, 107–109, 127–128, 138–140, 141–144

essentialism, 136–137, 181–185

eugenics, 9–11

expatriate status, 16–17, 24–25, 30–31, 38, 45–46, 54n3

families / family structure: in disability history, 7–8; in postwar cinema, 96, 109–110; in postwar fiction, 24–25, 38–39, 46–47, 53, 101–102; in War Department documentaries, 61–63, 64–66, 72–73, 82–83, 87, 88–89, 99

fascism, 107–111

femininity / the feminine: in defining masculinity, 25–26; effeminacy, 5, 60, 133, 163–164; in fascism, 107–109; under neoliberalism, 198–199; in *The Sun Also Rises,* 31–33, 35, 41–42, 43–45; in Vietnam-era narratives of remasculinization, 160–161, 163–164, 165–166, 181–182

feminism / feminist theory, 14–15, 19–20, 96, 118–119, 163–166, 178–179, 198–199

feminization: in disability history, 11–12; of landscape by wartime trauma, 103–107; in narratives of masculine victimization, 163–164; and neoliberalism, 190–191, 198–199; in postwar fiction, 31–32, 41–42; in Vietnam-era narratives of remasculinization, 160–161, 163–164; in War Department documentary rhetoric, 82–83

fetishization of the disabled body, 178–179

filmmakers: collaboration with US government of, 62–63, 67–68, 69, 70; Depression-era rhetorical strategies of, 71–72

First Blood, 18–19, 161–163, 166–168, 170–171, 185–186

Forter, Greg, 25, 30–33, 34, 41–42

Foucault, Michel, 49–50, 107–109, 126–127, 182–183, 186n30

Fountain, Ben: *Billy Lynn's Long Halftime Walk,* 19–20, 189, 191–192, 197

fragility, 97–98, 198–199

freak shows, 21n21

frontier narratives, 161–162, 164–166

Garland-Thomson, Rosemarie, 4–5, 98–99, 118–120

Garrett, Greg, 63–64

Gates, Henry Louis, Jr., 47

Genet, Jean: *Our Lady of the Flowers,* 47

genre: gendering of melodrama, 99–104; Western, 141–153

Gledhill, Christine, 101–102

Great Depression, 60–63, 64–69, 71–72

grievability, 162–163

Guattari, Felix, 89

Hawthorne, Nathaniel: "Young Goodman Brown," 3

Hayward, Susan, 101–102, 103–104

head of household status, 8, 61–62, 101. *See also* families/family structure

hegemony, American: in construction of the masculine subject, 6–7, 14–15, 25; and narratives of violence on the home front, 131; neoliberal, 19–20, 189–199; in postwar cinema, 96–97; in Vietnam-era narratives of remasculinization, 174, 176, 177–178

Hemingway, Ernest: *In Our Time,* 3; *The Sun Also Rises,* 16–17, 23–25, 26–27, 30–45, 51–52, 53–54, 189–190

heroism, masculine, 8–9, 70–71, 73–74, 102–103, 130, 145–146, 191–192

heterosexuality: in disability history, 11–12; in narratives of violence on the home front, 141; under neoliberalism, 189–190; in postwar cinema, 119–120; in postwar fiction, 16–17, 26–28, 30–32, 41–42, 52; in theorizing disability as subject position, 14–16; in Vietnam-era narratives of remasculinization, 167–168

heterotopias, 126–127

High Noon, 143, 152–153

Himes, Chester: *If He Hollers Let Him Go,* 153–155

History and Memory: For Akiko and Takashige, 144

history of disability in the US, 7–12

homecomings / home front: myth and masculinity in, 141–155; in postwar cinema, 99–100, 111–118; in Vietnam-era narratives of remasculinization, 162–163, 167–168; violence and anxiety in narratives of, 127, 129–130, 131–141; in War Department documentaries, 11–12, 63–64 homoeroticism, 138–140, 141–144

homophobia, 48–50, 102–103, 130, 134–140, 180–181

homosexuality / homosexual identity: in disability history, 10–11; in *Giovanni's Room,* 16–17, 26–30, 45–54, 54–55n7, 135–136; homoeroticism, in *Bad Day at Black Rock,* 141–144; homosexual panic, in postwar violence on the home front, 133–141; in theorizing disability as subject position, 14–15; in *The Sun Also Rises,* 34–35, 36–37, 41–42; in Vietnam-era narratives of remasculinization, 167–168, 184–185; War Department scrutiny of, 60

Hughes, Dorothy B.: *In a Lonely Place,* 127–128

Huston, John: *Battle of San Pietro,* 17, 62–63, 70–82, 93n31; *Let There Be Light,* 17, 62–64, 82–91; *Report from the Aleutians,* 62–63, 69–70

hypermasculinity, 144, 164, 197

ideology: in documentary filmmaking, 66–67, 71–72, 78, 80–81; as dominant fiction, 101–102, 123n14; military, in disability history, 11–12; neoliberal, 189–199; in postwar cinema, 101–102, 107–111, 117; in subject formation, in *Giovanni's Room,* 52–53; in theorizing disability as subject position, 13; in Vietnam-era narratives of remasculinization, 160–161, 165–166, 174, 184–185; in War Department documentaries, 61–62, 66–67, 71–72, 78, 80–82, 91–92

illness: definitions of, 9–10, 14; as deviance, 26–27; and exclusion from family life, 25–26; homosexuality as, 26–27, 34–36, 46, 48–50, 124n39, 137–139; as metaphor for post-fascist German men, 107–109; and nonnormative masculinity, in postwar fiction, 16–17, 34–35, 48–49, 55n28; in othering disabled men, 17–18, 30; in War Department documentaries, 63, 82–83, 85–87, 89

immediacy in documentaries, 64–66, 71–72, 81–82

immigration, 5–6, 9, 20n11, 21n24, 57n57

impotence, 5, 26–27, 30–39, 180–181

incontinence, 177–180. *See also* control, bodily

individuation in War Department documentaries, 70–72, 87–88, 89–91

insularity, cultural and political, 16–17, 143–144, 155

interpellation, 52–53

intersubjectivity: in the epistemology of the closet, 27–29, 136–137; in identity formation, 171–172; in postwar cinema, 116, 118–119, 122; in

Vietnam-era narratives of remasculinization, 175, 176–177, 178–179, 182–185

Iraq War veterans, 191–197

James, Henry: "The Beast in the Jungle," 28–30, 52

James, Pearl, 24

James, Robin, 19–20, 195–199

Japanese American internment, 143–145, 153–154, 156–157n35

Jeffords, Susan, 160–161, 167–168, 170–171

Judt, Tony, 103–104, 106–107

Kafer, Alison, 14–15

Kahana, Jonathan, 62–63, 66–69, 71–72, 78, 80–81

Kaufman, Millard, 145–146

Klein, Melanie, 171–172

Kotcheff, Ted: *First Blood,* 18–19, 161–163, 166–168, 170–171, 185–186

Kovic, Ron: *Born on the Fourth of July,* 1–3, 18–19, 158–159, 161–162, 179–181, 187–188n55

Kristeva, Julia, 120–121

landscapes, American: in cultural narratives of American masculine identity, 2–4; in narratives of postwar violence on the home front, 127, 143–144, 148–151, 153–154, 155; in postwar cinema, 103–104, 111–112, 113–114; in Vietnam-era narratives of remasculinization, 162–163, 165–167, 170–171

landscapes: European, 103–111, 112–114; Vietnamese, 18–19, 170–171

Langdon, Jennifer E., 133–134

Lange, Dorothea, 68

language: of capital, under neoliberalism, 191–192; cinematic, in War Department documentaries, 64–66; of gender, in postwar fiction, 26, 41–42; photographic, of physical pain, 68; in postwar cinema, 106–107, 118; in sexualization of French women, 128; in *The Sun Also Rises,* 36–42, 43; and valances of disability in post-Vietnam America, 182–183, 184–185

Lawrence, D. H., 4–5, 89, 165–166, 167–168

Let There Be Light, 17, 62–64, 82–91

Linett, Maren Tova, 9–10, 15–16

Lorentz, Pare, 92–93n19

Lost Generation, 30–32, 34

Love, Albert G., 10–11

marriage, 7–8, 43–45, 50–51, 100–102, 122, 132–133, 168–169

Marshal, George, 60–61, 82–83

"weakness of character," PTSD as, 87–89

West, American, 143–144, 148–149, 164–165

Western film genre, 141–153

whiteness / white masculine identity, 15–16, 26, 45–46, 144–145, 164–166

white power movement, 163–166

Wilder, Billy: *A Foreign Affair,* 104–106

wilderness, American, 3–4, 162–163, 170–171. *See also* landscapes, American

Williams, Raymond, 52–53

work. *See* employment

World War I, 9–10, 24, 30–32, 36–39

World War II: in disability history, 10–12; in emergence of modern understandings of disability, 6–7; mobilization for, in documentary filmmaking, 67–68; in modern understandings of disability, 13–14; violence of, in understandings of masculinity as identity, 101–104. *See also* documentary films; War Department, American

Wright, Richard: *Native Son,* 47

Wyler, William: *The Best Years of Our Lives,* 17–18, 95–97, 99–104, 111–118, 147–148, 192

Young, Iris Mason, 198–199

Young, Tomas, 19–20, 192–197

Žižek, Slavoj, 109–111

Will Kanyusik is Associate Professor of English at Loras College.

www.ingramcontent.com/pod-product-compliance
Lightning Source LLC
Chambersburg PA
CBHW031129270326
41929CB00011B/1555